Principles of Economics
MICRO

IRWIN PUBLICATIONS IN ECONOMICS
Advisory Editor   Martin S. Feldstein, *Harvard University*

Principles of Economics
MICRO

Willis L. Peterson
University of Minnesota

Seventh Edition   1989

Homewood, Illinois 60430

Acquisitions editor: *Gary L. Nelson*
Project editor: *Mary Lou Murphy*
Production manager: *Irene H. Sotiroff*
Artist: *Jill Smith*
Compositor: *TCSystems, Inc.*
Typeface: *10/12 Times Roman*
Printer: *Arcata Graphics/Kingsport*

Library of Congress Cataloging-in-Publication Data

Peterson, Willis L.
    Principles of economics : micro / Willis L. Peterson. – 7th ed.
        p.   cm.
    Includes bibliographies and index.
    ISBN 0-256-06796-1 (pbk.)
    1. Microeconomics.   I. Title.
HB172.P48 1989
338.5–dc19   88-1695

Printed in the United States of America
1 2 3 4 5 6 7 8 9 0 K 5 4 3 2 1 0 9 8

Preface

The general philosophy of this book probably is best expressed by Alfred North Whitehead in *The Aims of Education and Other Essays:* "Whatever be the detail with which you cram your student, the chances of his meeting in afterlife exactly that detail is almost infinitesimal; and if he does meet it, he will probably have forgotten what you taught him about it. The really useful training yields a comprehension of a few general principles with a thorough grounding in the way they apply to a variety of concrete details. In subsequent practice the men will have forgotten your particular details; but they will remember by an unconscious common sense how to apply principles to immediate circumstances."

In line with this philosophy, the book strives for three main objectives. The first is to help students improve their understanding of how a market economy operates. How are prices and wages determined and why are they continually changing? Who determines what will be produced and how much? The second objective is to help students acquire an understanding of the major tools or principles that have proved useful in making economic decisions or solving economic problems. The third and most important objective, but also the most difficult to attain, is to help students acquire a skill in using these tools or principles to conduct economic analysis.

Hopefully, the student will not be so unfortunate as the economist who decided to build his own house. After acquiring the necessary tools—hammer, saw, level, etc.—he proceeded to go about his task. After finishing the house, it didn't look quite right to him so he asked a carpenter friend to take a look at his accomplishment. A quick glance at the structure prompted the carpenter to reply, "Of course it doesn't look right, you've built it upside down"; to which the economist replied, "Oh, I thought something was wrong, I kept falling off of the porch." Unfortunately, "upside down" answers to economic questions are much less recognizable than upside down houses. To avoid such answers, it is necessary to be able to use the tools of economic analysis as well as just to learn of their existence.

This seventh edition represents the greatest change in organization of any of the preceding editions. First, the most difficult and technical material has been removed or simplified. Second, the chapter length has been reduced while the number of chapters has been increased. The book is a bit leaner than the past several editions, and more closely resembles the early editions in brevity.

Each chapter now contains about enough material for a class session, and is designed to be read and assimilated in forty-five minutes to an hour. The smaller bites should be easier for the reader to digest.

Special thanks for helpful comments and suggestions go to the reviewers of the sixth edition, the editorial staff at Irwin, and my students.

Willis L. Peterson

Contents

PART IV   PRODUCT MARKETS   127

PART V   MARKET STRUCTURE   159

PART ONE

Micro Foundations

CHAPTER 1

Introduction

OVERVIEW

This is a get-acquainted chapter. After a brief introduction of what economics is and why it exists, there is a short discussion on the nature of economic decisions and the usefulness of theory. The second half of the chapter provides an overview of how resources are allocated in a market economy and in a centrally planned (Communist) society.

WHAT IS ECONOMICS?

Economics has been defined as "what economists do." While this is not a very helpful definition, it does show that economics encompasses an array of human activities, and it is not possible to adequately define the field with a single sentence.

In general terms, economics is a social science that deals with the behavior of people. The aim of economics is to help people obtain the greatest possible satisfaction or utility out of the resources at their disposal—to do the best they can with what they have. Economics also is concerned with increasing the amount of resources available to people—economic growth—and with how income is distributed.

As economics developed into a discipline, two major areas of study emerged: micro and macro. Microeconomics is concerned mainly with the economic activities of individual consumers and producers or groups of consumers and producers known as markets. In the area of consumer behavior, major emphasis is given to the question of how consumers can maximize their utility or satisfaction given their tastes and income levels. Consumer behavior also is related to the concept of demand for goods and services. Producers or business firms represent the supply side of the economy. Here we will see how producers can minimize costs for a given level of output and how they decide the level of output that will maximize their profits. Producer behavior is then translated into the supply of goods and services. Markets consist of buyers and sellers. The interaction of buyers and sellers in markets establishes the prices of goods and services as well as productive resources such as labor and capital. In microeconomics, considerable emphasis is given to price determination in both the product and resource markets—how prices are established and why they change.

Macroeconomics, on the other hand, is concerned with economic aggregates or the economy as a whole. The two major problem areas of macroeconomics are unemployment and inflation. These areas are of great concern to individuals, but they are also problems over which the individual has relatively little control. Both the causes and the solutions to these problems tend to lie in the realm of government action, which affects the entire economy.

It would be a mistake, however, to conclude that the micro and macro areas are distinct or unrelated fields of study; there is a certain amount of overlap. For example, we will see in later chapters that much of what the government does in enacting laws or levying taxes directly affects individuals and markets, and these effects can be analyzed with the tools of microeconomics. However, the actions of large groups of individuals, such as the increased desire to save on the part of many people, are analyzed with macroeconomic tools.

Because it is impossible to completely separate the micro from the macro, some economists argue that more appropriate labels would be price theory instead of microeconomics and monetary and income and employment theory rather than macroeconomics. In more advanced courses, particularly at the graduate level, microeconomic principles are generally referred to as *price theory,* mainly because the material deals with the determination of prices and their effect on the output and input mix in the economy.

THE PROBLEM OF SCARCITY

In studying economics, as in any other activity, we like to have some reason for exerting effort. We attend the theater or go to a ball game because it is enjoyable. We attend school to learn or to make it possible to have a job and earn a living. But why study economics?

There may be a few people who would be willing to study economics purely for the enjoyment it brings. For most, however, learning economics is not 100 percent entertainment. Mastering a subject provides a certain amount of intellectual satisfaction, but it is hard to justify economics on only this basis. Crossword puzzles or chess might do as well or better on this score. The social science of economics must rest on a different foundation. I have posed this question to my students and so far all have been too kind (or too smart) to say that we study economics because it is a required subject. Why is it required?

The answer can be simplified to a single word—*scarcity*. Human wants are greater than the resources available to satisfy them. In fact, economists traditionally have argued that human wants are unlimited or insatiable. At first you may find this hard to believe. Surely there is some level of income or standard of living where one would be completely satiated. But if you spend a few minutes making a list of the goods and services that you wouldn't mind having, chances are that their purchase would put a millionaire in a financial bind. Of course, you need not limit your list to the familiar private–sector goods and services, such as housing, cars, or vacation trips. You might want to include cleaner air and water, or a comfortable and convenient public transportation system.

Suppose by some stroke of magic that all the items on your list were supplied. Would you be completely satisfied or satiated? Probably not—especially if everyone else also were granted their fondest wishes. Human nature being what it is, we always seems to be just a little dissatisfied with what we have. A new compact car may satisfy for a time, but eventually we give admiring glances to a Mercedes or a BMW. In addition, we must remember that entirely new goods and services, many of which do not even exist in our imagination, will be developed and come on the market in the future. A dream list prepared by your great-grandparents would not have contained many of the items on your list because they were not imagined at that time.

It is less difficult to envision the scarcity of resources at our disposal. In recent years, attention has been drawn to the day when our nonrenewable natural resources, especially fossil fuels, will be exhausted. Although less newsworthy, it is important to realize that most resources, including land area, labor, and man–made capital such as buildings and machines, are in limited supply. Being finite, these resources can produce only a finite amount of goods and services. Since human wants appear much greater than the resources to satisfy these wants, people must decide what they will produce and what they will forego. In other words, we are forced to make economic decisions.

ECONOMIC DECISIONS

We must make these decisions (or, if you wish, economize) from the time we are aware of the world around us. This harsh reality becomes apparent the first time a child stands in front of a candy counter clutching a quarter. The coin might buy a candy bar, a package of gum, or a roll of Life-savers, but not all three. An economic decision must be made.

It would be misleading, though, to conclude that economic decisions all involve money. Probably the best example of a nonmonetary economic decision is how we allocate our time—a scarce resource that seems to become scarcer as we become older. The student must decide if he or she will spend the evening studying mathematics or history, or even more fundamentally, whether to devote time to study or leisure. Allocating time to its best use is one of the most important economic decisions we make. It is one of the most important experiences gained in college.

More traditional types of economic decisions involve the operations of households and firms. For the household, a continuing array of economic decisions must be made on how to allocate the weekly or semimonthly paycheck. How much money goes to housing, food, clothing, transportation, entertainment, and so forth? Managing a modest income for a fmaily requires thousands of economic decisions each year.

Considering the complexity of a household's economic decisions, we can appreciate the decisions that must be made in managing a business. What items should the firm produce? Should it specialize or diversify? Should it produce a large volume and sell at a low price or produce less and charge more? How do the decisions of rival firms affect each business? Should the firm employ more labor and save on machines, or should it substitute machines for labor? These are some examples of economic decisions each manager must make. How well these decisions are made largely determines the success or failure of the firm.

The need to make economic decisions does not stop at the level of the household or the firm. Economic decisions must be made at all government levels, ranging from local governments, such as townships and municipalities, to the states and federal government. Perhaps the most basic of these economic decisions concerns how much of the total production of society is provided through the public sector and how much is provided through the private sector. In a democracy, government decisions tend to reflect the broad wishes of society, but they cannot please everyone. People of a more conservative philosophy tend to desire a greater share of production in the private sector, while persons of a more liberal bent stress the need for more public goods and services.

Once society settles on a mix between public and private goods, it must decide what kinds of public goods and services should be produced. For example, what is the appropriate mix between military and nonmilitary public goods? Should we have fewer weapons and greater public expenditures for slum clearance, public parks, pollution control, and so forth? Economic decisions involving governments or nations have this in common with the decision made by the child at the candy counter: Both require making a choice among alternatives involving as little as a quarter or as much as billions of dollars.

THE USEFULNESS OF THEORY

Economic theory has suffered from a bad press for many years, and not entirely without justification. Students tend to be turned off by theory because they visualize dry, abstract material that has little relevance to their world. But theory does not have to be dry or irrelevant. In fact, little is to be gained by theory if it cannot help in making day-to-day economic decisions or resolving economic problems.

A theory is an abstraction or simplification of the real world. It encompasses only the important information bearing on a decision, question, or problem. The main value of theory is that it provides a framework for thinking. We need such a framework because the world is too complex to account for every bit of information that affects a decision or problem, and we have to sort out important from unimportant knowledge. But information neither comes in neat categories labeled "important" and "unimportant," nor is it always obvious which is which. For example, some goods and services increase in price during their peak seasons, such as Christmas cards and hotel rooms on Miami Beach. Other products decrease in price during the time of year they are most actively bought and sold—such as fresh fruits and vegetables in the northern states. For some commodities, price rises when the quantity exchanged increases; for others, it declines when the quantity increases. To the person untrained in economics, there may appear to be little order in markets. But, after gaining an understanding of the theories of demand and supply (by the end of Chapter 11), you will be able to explain such phenomena and even predict future changes in price and the quantity of goods and services. In the latter sense, theory serves as a sort of crystal ball.

Theory has come to be known by a number of names. One synonym is *principle*, as in the title of this book. A theory is also sometimes referred to as a *model*, probably because theory represents and predicts reality without necessarily duplicating it exactly or in detail.

In the use of economic theory, it is common to see the phrases *other things equal* or *other things constant*. To simplify reality, it is useful to consider the effect of one factor at a time—holding everything else constant. This practice allows us to focus our attention on a specific point, pushing into the background other factors or bits of information, even though they may also be an important part of the theory. In the real world there may be a number of important factors operating simultaneously. But if we tried to incorporate all of them at once into the analysis, it soon would become too complex to be useful. Thus, the *other things equal* phrase is not an attempt to distort the real world but an attempt to better understand and predict the world's events by making the theory more manageable and more powerful.

Three Economic Questions

Regardless of its economic organization—capitalism or Communism, rich or poor, large or small—every society must answer three important economic questions:

1. What and how much of each good should be produced?
2. How should each good be produced?
3. For whom?

A major share of this book deals with these three economic questions. In the rest of this chapter, we will introduce how these three questions are answered in three different economic settings: (1) the private sector of a market economy, (2) the public sector of a market economy, and (3) a Communist society.

THE PRIVATE SECTOR OF A MARKET ECONOMY

Let us look first at the question of what and how much of each good is produced in the private sector of a market economy. At any time, there are thousands of goods and services available to consumers in various quantities.

With the passage of time, some of these goods and services disappear or are no longer produced, while other new goods and services appear. Who decides what is to be produced and in what quantities? In the private sector, there are two groups of decision makers: producers and consumers. This is not to say that people are either one or the other. Everyone has to be a consumer to stay alive. Also, just about everyone is a producer, that is, one who contributes to the production of goods and services. (In Chapter 7, we will see that production occurs in both homes and businesses.) The producers we are concerned with in this section include those who make decisions regarding what and how much to produce; they are largely the entrepreneurs and managers of businesses.

In making decisions about what to produce, producers are constrained by the resources and technology at their disposal. For example, before the discovery of petroleum and the development of the internal-combustion engine, transportation producers were limited to vehicles drawn by animals or powered by steam. Most resources result from some production process as opposed to being a free gift of nature. The same is true of technology. As we will see at the end of the book, knowledge and technology also result from production activities such as education and research. For our purposes, we will consider resources and the state of the art as given to the individual producer, recognizing that these do change over time.

Given the resources and technology available, the most important factor that producers must take into account is whether or not they can sell the product and make a reasonable profit. In making a decision on whether to introduce a new product, producers must try to anticipate the reaction of consumers. In making such a decision, producers must rely on their judgment of consumer behavior as well as information obtained from consumer surveys and test marketings.

Although producers must take the initiative in developing and introducing new products, consumers have the last word in determining whether a product stays on the market. If consumers receive a large amount of satisfaction from a product in relation to its price, it will tend to stay on the market, providing that producers can make a profit at the price consumers are willing to pay. On the other hand, products that do not provide a good measure of satisfaction to consumers in relation to what they cost will not be purchased and will eventually go off the market.

For products that stay on the market, this question remains: How much of each should be produced? Products that enjoy a large demand because they yield a good measure of satisfaction tend to bring an attractive price (to producers) in the market. A favorable price is an incentive for producers to increase the output of the good or service. As the output increases, the price eventually declines. As the price declines, producers know that the market is becoming saturated and that they should stop increasing the output of that good.

In addition, productive efficiency and resource prices influence what and how much is produced. Goods that can be produced efficiently and sold cheaply will enjoy a relatively large share of the total output of the economy. Of course, changes in resource prices will change production costs and also change the level of consumption. For example, if a resource becomes more expensive, the cost of producing products that utilize this resource also is likely to increase. As a result, producers must ask a higher price for these products to cover increased production costs. Some consumers will likely decide that these particular products are no longer a good buy and will quit buying or reduce their purchase rate of the items in question. In response, producers will have to reduce their output or face an inventory buildup of goods they cannot sell for a price that covers their costs.

The answer to the question of what and how much of each good is produced continually changes as economic, social, and political conditions change. As a nation develops and per capita incomes increase, people may desire a different mix of goods and services than when the majority of people were poor. As incomes increase, there tends to be an increase in demand for services relative to the demand for goods. For example, much of our food now comes with many services embodied, such as cake mixes, frozen dinners, baked bread, meat that is already cut into servings, and so forth. Even more service is embodied in food when it is consumed in restaurants. Higher-income people can afford and purchase more luxury items, such as air conditioners for home and car, winter vacations in tropical settings, accessory-laden automobiles, and air travel, to name a few. Other goods, such as starchy foods, old-fashioned washboards, and bus travel, which people buy less of when incomes grow, gradually decline in sales and can disappear in a growing economy.

Market prices of goods and services perform a key role in transmitting information in a market economy and provide both producers and consumers with the incentives to act upon this information. For example, when incomes increase and with them the demand for luxury goods such as stereo components, the prices of such items will increase relative to other goods. The higher price increases the profitability of producing such items, which provides the incentive for producers to increase output. Thus, the higher price provides the signal to producers that consumers want more of these items, and the resulting profit increase provides the incentive to change the kind and quantity of output. Conversely, a decrease in demand and price causes the opposite change.

Not all changes in the what and how much question are precipitated by economic conditions. Social and psychological factors also play a role. In recent years, designer jeans have become popular, especially with young people. Again, the higher prices resulting from the increased demand stimulated production of this product. The concern of people over the effect of diet on health has led to decreased consumption of fatty meat and butter. Here, lower prices and/or surpluses in the market dampened production.

Thus far we have described changes in the kinds, qualities, and quantities of goods that have initiated with consumers or the demand side of the market.

Changes from the supply side are equally important. Two factors precipitate most of these changes: (1) technology and (2) input or resource prices. Producers can supply only the goods and services they know how to make. Advances in technology create new items and improve the quality or lower the price of existing goods. New drugs that come on the market because of advances in genetic engineering, and popular new electronic calculators and personal computers made possible by advances in electronic circuit technology are examples of new products that widen the choices available to consumers. If they give consumers good value for their money, their sales will increase and the companies producing these items will prosper.

New technology also can lower the cost of producing existing products. The result is an increase in supply of these items and a decrease in their price. The new lower price provides an incentive for consumers to increase their consumption of these products. An example of such a good is poultry. A half-century ago, poultry was considered a delicacy and consumed mainly on Sundays and holidays. Now, because of advances in breeding, nutrition, and disease control, the relative cost of producing poultry has declined; consumers have responded by increasing the amount of poultry purchased. Growth in income has caused consumers to add more protein to their diets. The same is true for fresh fruit and vegetables; advances in production and transportation technology of these products also have contributed to their affordability.

Resource prices also play an important role in determining production costs and the resulting price of goods and services. Perhaps the best example is the relative decrease in the cost of energy that occurred between 1930 and the early 1970s. As shown in Table 1–1, the real price of regular gasoline (current-year price adjusted for changes in the general price level) declined by more than one third between 1930 and 1970. There is little doubt that cheap gas contributed to the increasing size of the typical American automobile during the 1950s, 1960s, and early 1970s. In Europe, where taxes on gasoline made the price three to four times higher than in the United States, consumers demanded

TABLE 1–1   U.S. Retail Prices of Regular Gasoline at the Pump, Selected Years 1930–1986 (constant 1984 price level)

Year	Price	Year	Price
1930	$1.00	1965	$0.68
1940	0.91	1970	0.66
1950	0.87	1975	0.88
1955	0.83	1980	1.54
1960	0.73	1986	.81

SOURCE: Survey of Current Business, corresponding years.

smaller, more fuel-efficient cars, and car manufacturers responded by producing that product.

The turnabout in the downward trend of energy prices that occurred during the mid-1970s caused large changes in the size and fuel efficiency of cars demanded by U.S. consumers and in turn changed the products produced by U.S. car makers. The higher cost of operating large cars led to an increase in demand for smaller, fuel-efficient cars. It also led to advances in technology for building small cars; the Japanese had a lead in this area. Notice, however, that the real (inflation-adjusted) price of gasoline declined by nearly one half between 1980 and 1986. Whether consumers will increase their purchases of large cars again in response to lower gasoline prices is an open question. They probably will if the price decline persists. However, at this writing, people are not yet convinced that the price of energy will continue to decline. Hence, there is some reluctance to shift away from down-sized cars, at least for the time being.

Government policies and laws also influence the kinds and amounts of goods and services produced and consumed. Laws that forbid the production and/or consumption of a good or service should reduce the quantity of the item exchanged in the market.[1] The effect of such a law on the item's price depends on whether suppliers or demanders face the greatest penalty. If supply is restricted because of a harsh penalty on suppliers, the price will rise. On the other hand, price will fall if demand decreases due to a penalty on consumers. The topic of illegal goods and services will be discussed more thoroughly in Chapter 12.

Other policies that affect market prices and quantities include sales and excise taxes, environmental legislation, price and rent controls, price supports, tariffs and quotas on goods imported or exported, laws affecting labor unions, antitrust and other laws affecting businesses, and minimum wage legislation for labor. Many economists argue that one of the main reasons for studying microeconomics is to better understand how government policies influence the behavior of consumers and producers.

Let us turn next to the second of the three economic questions—how goods are produced. Resource or input prices along with the available technology play leading roles. Perhaps the most basic question is the relative amounts of labor and capital utilized in the production process. In virtually all production, there is some flexibility in using these two basic resources. Consider the production of automobiles. At one extreme are handcrafted products where much labor and little capital is employed. In this case, the metal might be bent and formed by hand rather than by giant presses. At the

---

[1] This assumption can be questioned. It is reported that alcoholic beverage consumption actually increased during prohibition.

other extreme are the highly automated factories pioneered by Japan where robots do much of the welding of a car body.

While technology sets the physical limits on the degree of automation, the relative prices of labor and capital determine its economic feasibility. In countries where wages are high relative to capital, it pays producers to substitute capital for labor to minimize production costs. Producers who substitute enjoy higher profits while those who do not experience higher costs. They may be forced out of business because of losses. The substitution of capital for labor has been common in the United States and the other developed countries where wages have been increasing relative to the prices of capital services. In these countries, production is capital intensive. In other places, namely the less-developed countries (LDCs) where wages are low relative to the price of capital, more labor-intensive production techniques are utilized. Chapter 8 contains a more detailed discussion of the impact of relative input prices on production techniques and how producers choose the cost-minimizing input mix.

Although it is common to take technology as a given, relative input prices also influence the direction of technological advances. For example, if wages are rising relative to the cost of capital, scientists and engineers employed by private firms as well as universities and government will attempt to develop new forms of capital that will do jobs previously done by labor. The development of factory robots is a good example. Further discussion on the role of science and technology in the economy is contained in Chapter 24.

The third economic question, the "for whom?," is answered in broad terms in that all production is carried out to satisfy the desires of consumers. Unless each good and service contributes in some way to the satisfaction of consumers, there is no demand for the item and therefore no reason to produce it. A somewhat more difficult question is "which consumers?" Consumer tastes have some bearing on who buys what. The production of olives, for example, is not carried out for people who dislike this product.

Given the tastes of individuals, the "for whom?" question depends largely on incomes and wealth. People who enjoy high incomes are able to claim a larger share of the total output of the private sector than their low-income counterparts. Incomes differ because of differences in wages and salaries and because of differences in the amount of capital owned. People who possess scarce and highly valued skills and are willing to work hard are remunerated by relatively high incomes. Similarly, people who own a large amount of capital are remunerated for their contribution to production. Hence, the more resources a person provides, the more output he or she will enjoy. This means that people who lack skills, ambition, or the ownership of capital will not be able to lay claim on as many goods and services produced in the private sector as their higher-income counterparts.

Most societies, including the United States, have attempted to increase the amount of goods and services going to low-income people. This can be done in two ways: (1) by increasing the capacity of low-income people to produce, primarily through more and better education, and (2) by taking away income and wealth from high-income people through taxes and transferring them to low-income people through welfare payments and goods and services provided by the government. More in-depth coverage of income redistribution policies is contained in the companion macro text.

To summarize, producers generally take the initiative in developing new products, but consumers ultimately determine the products that stay on the market. The amount of each good and service that is produced depends in part on the demand of consumers for the item. Goods that are highly demanded tend to bring a relatively high price in the market, which provides an incentive for producers to step up the production of such items. Productive efficiency and resource prices influence production costs, which influence the prices that must be obtained to at least cover these costs. Resource prices also influence the method of production. The amount of goods and services that each person can claim from the private sector is determined in large part by the resources that the person contributes to the overall production process. This contribution is reflected by the person's income and wealth.

Consumer decisions regarding what and how much of each good to purchase as well as who will purchase it are reflected by the demand for goods and services. Producer decisions regarding what and how much to produce and by what method are reflected by the supply of goods and services. Much of the discussion throughout the remaining chapters centers on consumer and producer decisions, how these decisions affect demand and supply, and how demand and supply influence prices and quantities exchanged in the market.

The Public Sector of a Market Economy

In the United States, about one third of the total output is purchased and distributed by various agencies of the federal, state, and local governments. Thus, it is important to consider each of our three economic questions from the standpoint of the so-called public sector. The goods and services purchased and distributed by the public sector tend to be those that do not lend themselves to individual purchase and use. They are frequently known as *public goods*. The major public goods include the military, police and fire protection, streets and highways, waste and water treatment, the postal service, and public parks. The government also provides regulatory services such as law enforcement, labeling, keeping harmful products off the market, and reducing pollution, with the aim of improving the working of the market economy. In addition, the government plays an important role in subsidizing the purchase of certain goods and services such as education and in transferring income to certain people through the various welfare programs and Social Security.

In a democracy, the short-run decisions of what and how much of each public good is to be produced are made by elected officeholders and their appointed officials. Of course, over the long run the general public has the final say because elected officeholders serve at the discretion of the electorate. Different people have different ideas regarding the proper kinds and amounts of public goods. People with a conservative political philosophy tend to prefer fewer public goods (with the possible exception of the military) and less government influence over private decisions than their more liberal counterparts. Thus, the actual kinds and amounts of public goods produced tend to be a compromise between different wants.

The preference for public goods also is likely to be influenced by the incidence of benefits and costs. People who perceive the benefits of public goods to be small relative to the taxes they pay will likely favor a reduction in the production of such goods, or at least a slowing down of their growth. On the other hand, people who benefit from government spending more than in proportion to the taxes they pay are more likely to favor increased government spending, or at least no reduction in such spending.

In the United States and most other market economies, the actual production of most public goods is carried out by private firms under contract to the government. For example, aircraft companies produce the nation's military aircraft and construction companies build the highways and dams. However, in the case of services, most people providing services such as military personnel, teachers, postal workers, and regulatory personnel are employed by government agencies.

There is a class of goods and services that falls somewhere between the public and private goods categories. These are called *public utilities;* examples include local power and light or telephone companies. Goods and services provided by these companies generally are purchased by individuals in the marketplace, so in this sense they resemble private goods. But for reasons that will become clear in a moment, society has decided that the normal production of these goods by many firms in each area would not be desirable. Thus, the government regulates their production, and in this sense public utilities resemble public goods.

The main reason for having public utilities is to avoid a costly duplication of facilities and services. Suppose, for example, there were 10 electric power companies serving a given locality. If each company owned its own power lines, the duplication would increase costs over what would exist if just one set of lines served each street. The same is true for each local telephone company. Natural gas also is commonly supplied by privately owned public utilities. For other goods and services, such as the postal service and city water and sewers, ownership is vested in governmental agencies.

In recent years, there has been increasing pressure to inject more competition among private firms and for public utilities and publicly owned enterprises. The breakup of AT&T reflects this trend. The U.S. Postal Service is under increasing pressure to allow private firms to compete for the first-class mail business. Private firms are delivering an increasing share of packages and third-class mail. The emergence of electronic mail computers will add an additional element of competition for the postal service.

By giving a business exclusive rights to operate, the government makes a public utility a virtual monopoly, free from the competitive forces in the market. To guard against excessive prices or inferior service to the public, the government also regulates these firms by setting the prices they charge and establishing standards of performance.

The Centrally Planned Economy

Communist countries such as the Soviet Union, The People's Republic of China, and their satellites are frequently described as centrally planned economies because the basic economic decisions regarding: (1) what and how much to produce, (2) how each good shall be produced, and (3) for whom, are made by political leaders in the central government. Under a Communist system, the nation's resources are owned and controlled by the government, and the government decides where and how the nation's available resources are used. These allocative decisions reflect what the authorities have decided is best for the country, at least at the macro level. For example, the Soviet planners have traditionally devoted a larger share of their resources to investment goods compared to the U.S. economy. Although Soviet consumers have at times voiced a desire for more consumer goods, the authorities have largely followed their long-run plans. At the micro level, however, the wishes of consumers carry a bit more weight. For example, if the people desire less bread and more meat, there is a tendency for some bread to go unsold and for the meat shelves to empty quickly. As a result, the authorities may attempt to increase meat production and decrease bread production.

In recent years, the Soviet Union has utilized prices a bit more in attempts to modify consumer behavior. If the authorities think the people should continue to eat large amounts of bread and little meat, they will lower the price of bread and raise the price of meat. Even though prices are set by the government, people in these countries respond to price changes just as people do everywhere—buying less of the item that is increased in price and buying more of the less expensive item.

The ability to set price is a powerful force in the hands of government. By manipulating price, the authorities can often get people to do things voluntarily that they might otherwise not do, even under direct orders. For example, to reduce the consumption of cocoa, Soviet authorities increased the price of chocolate candy bars. Similarly, the price of vodka was increased a few years ago to reduce consumption.

Price manipulation does not solve all problems. If the price set for an item does not correspond to the price people wish to pay for the quantity produced, there will tend to be either a shortage or a surplus of the item. If the price is set lower than what would exist in a free market, there will be a shortage; long lines of prospective buyers will form, and black-market activities or bribing will emerge. If the price is higher than what people would be willing to pay to buy all that is produced, unsold stocks will amass.

The question of *how* goods and services will be produced also is answered by the central planning committee. By setting quotas for the production of capital, planners implicitly determine the capital-labor ratios in various industries. However, the actual use of capital tends to fall short of its potential use due to the problem of providing spare parts. Some machines are cannibalized for parts to keep others running while other machines may remain idle for long periods waiting to be repaired. The production of spare parts has not ranked high on the agenda of central planners. Perhaps spare parts are less visible than new machines. Also, once the machines are produced they become the problem of somebody else, and these people have little control over the production plans.

The "for whom" question has always received high priority in the centrally planned economies and, in fact, provides much of the motivation for adopting such an economic system in the first place. The main argument in favor of the Communist system is that it provides for a more equal distribution of income than a capitalist or free-market system. Because individuals cannot own capital such as machines, buildings, and land, the income from property does not give rise to differences in personal income. Also, the government sets all wages and salaries, and as a result there is not as large a difference between the lowest and highest salaries as in a free-market setting. In addition, the government subsidizes some of the basic necessities of life—mainly housing, medical care, and education. This is intended to reduce the disparity in the standard of living between the lowest- and highest-income people. The government obtains the income or resources to provide free or subsidized necessities from income received through the ownership of capital and by paying workers less than they produce. The latter setup is similar to the system used in capitalist economies. Here, workers receive less than their contribution to output after paying taxes.

The costs of achieving a more egalitarian distribution of income are divided into two categories: economic and noneconomic. The economic cost is due in part to the loss of economic efficiency inherent in the centralized planning process. A small group of central planners, no matter how intelligent and well-informed, cannot know the billions of bits of information that bear on the billions of economic decisions that are made each year, particularly in large countries such as the Soviet Union and the People's Republic of China (PRC). Consequently, many errors are made in deciding what and how much to produce, and how to produce it. The end result is a slower rate of economic growth than these economies are capable of attaining. Granted, decision makers in capitalist economies also make errors, but being closer to the point where the decisions have their impact, both physically and intellectually, increases the available information and reduces the possibility of colossal errors. In recent years, the PRC has moved to decentralize decision making.

Incentives in centrally planned economies constitute another major economic problem. While there have been increased efforts to provide more material incentives for workers in these economies, the potential rewards for the use of valuable skills and for hard work are small. Few persons, outside of the government, harbor any illusions of becoming wealthy. Perhaps more importantly, there is little room in such economies for entrepreneurship. As a result, these societies do not receive the maximum benefit from their citizens who have the talent for creating new products and/or coming up with innovative and less costly ways of doing things.

Another major economic problem in centrally planned economies is the significant drain on their resources caused by large military establishments. Without exception, Communist governments have come into being through military action and retain their control through military power as demonstrated in Hungary in the 1950s, Czechoslovakia in the 1960s, Vietnam, Cambodia, and Laos in the 1970s, and Poland in the 1980s. Moreover, the billions of dollars spent on the military each year by the United States and other nonCommunist countries to counteract the military threat of the Soviet Union and its satellites is an added cost for the world as a whole—to say nothing of the lives lost in Korea, Vietnam, and in other terrorist activites around the world since World War II. Should the confrontation between Communist and nonCommunist countries end in nuclear war, the economic and human costs would be incalculable.

In the area of noneconomic costs, the loss of virtually all personal freedoms would rank at the top, at least by people who value freedom. It is not clear why Communist governments exercised such extreme repression over their people.[2] Perhaps it is the necessity for the government to have monopoly in all areas of political and economic life to make the system work. But this takes us out of the realm of economics into political science.

GLOSSARY

microeconomics Deals primarily with the economic decisions of households and businesses and with the pricing of goods and services as well as resources.

macroeconomics Concerned mainly with the problems of unemployment and inflation, and what can be done to avoid or alleviate these problems.

price theory A name given to microeconomics in more advanced courses.

theory Simplification or abstraction of the real world. Contains the important information bearing on a decision or problem.

other things equal Allows the impact of events to be considered one at a time.

scarcity Exists because resources are limited in supply and human wants exceed our ability to produce goods and services.

economic decisions Choosing among alternatives. Must be made at every level of society because of scarcity.

---

[2] See, for example, Aleksandr Solzhenitsyn, *The Gulag Archipelago, 1918–1956*, trans. Thomas P. Whitney (New York: Harper & Row, 1974).

the three economic questions (1) What and how much of each good to produce, (2) How to produce each good, and (3) For whom?

market economy Decentralized economic decision making by consumers and producers. Market price plays a key role in answering the three economic questions.

public sector Comprised of federal, state, and local governments.

public goods Produced and/or distributed by governments for society's use.

public utilities Firms given exclusive right to supply a good or service to avoid duplication of facilities. They are regulated by government rather than by competition.

centrally planned economy Another name of a Communist or Socialist society whose resources are owned and controlled by the central government. The resources are allocated by a central planning committee.

QUESTIONS

1. What is economics?

2. What is an economic decision and why is it necessary for everyone to make economic decisions?

3. Of what use is economic theory in making economic decisions?

4. What are the three economic questions that must be answered by every society?

5. Suppose there is a sudden cutoff of oil from the Middle East as occurred in the early 1970s. Trace the effects of this disruption in a market economy.

6. a. What is the main argument used in favor of a centrally planned economy?
b. What are the main problems of this economy?

7. Suppose your instructor announces during the first class that everyone, regardless of performance on exams, will receive a C in the course. How would you react? Now compare the analogy to the entire economy.

CHAPTER 2

How to Read Graphs

OVERVIEW

Both micro- and macroeconomics make extensive use of graphs. A two-dimensional graph is a relationship between two variables. Two possible relationships exist—positive and negative. Two variables are positively related when both move in the same direction: up or down. A negative relationship exists when the two variables move in opposite directions: one moves up, the other moves down, or vice versa.

In studying economics, graphs are frequently used to convey concepts or ideas. In a way, a graph is a picture of an idea. While the cliché "a picture is worth a thousand words" may exaggerate a bit, a graph provides a precise means of expressing an idea.

All graphs presented in this book are of two dimensions; they express a relationship between two variables. Therefore, each graph has two axes—vertical and horizontal. When drawing or viewing a graph, it is important to specify or ascertain what each axis represents.

A graph can convey either a positive or a negative relationship between the two variables. A positive relationship exists when both variables move in the same direction. Both either increase or decrease as illustrated by panels A–C of Figure 2–1. Positive relationships are graphed with upward-sloping lines. There is a negative relationship when the two variables move in opposite directions—one increases and the other decreases as illustrated by panels A–C of Figure 2–2. These graphs have downward-sloping lines.

LINEAR POSITIVE RELATIONSHIP

Figure 2–1A illustrates a *linear positive relationship* between the two variables—nickels and dimes. The line represents the number of nickels and dimes that have equal value: one dime equals two nickels, and so on. In this graph, the upward-sloping line comes out of the origin. It is possible for such lines to begin at a point on either the vertical or horizontal axis.

CURVILINEAR POSITIVE RELATIONSHIP

Panels B and C of Figure 2–1 represent a *curvilinear positive relationship* between the two variables—points obtained on an examination and the number of study hours used to prepare for the exam. In panel B, hours are on the

FIGURE 2–1 Positive Relationships

(A) Linear

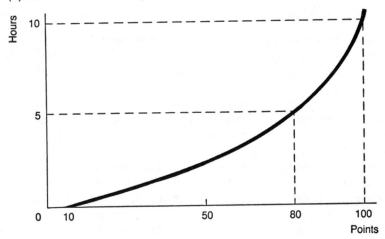

(B) Increases at an increasing rate

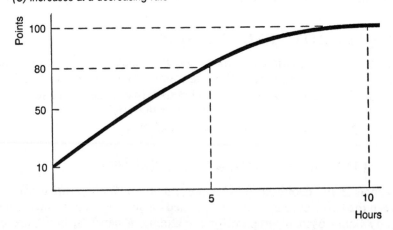

(C) Increases at a decreasing rate

FIGURE 2–2 Negative Relationships

(A) Linear

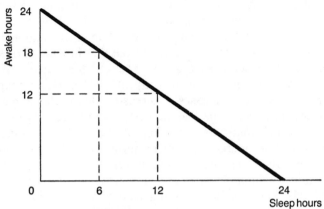

(B) Decrease at an increasing rate — concave to the origin

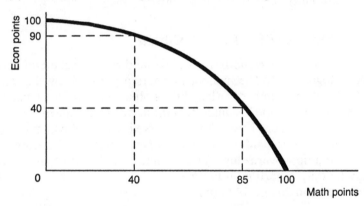

(C) Decrease at a decreasing rate — convex to the origin

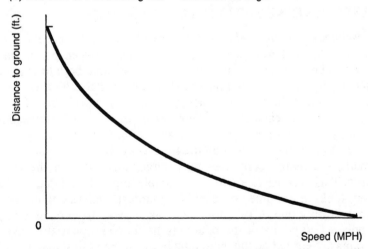

vertical axis and points are on the horizontal axis. The graph shows that 10 points out of a maximum 100 are obtained with zero study; 5 hours yields 80 points, and a perfect score (100 points) is obtained with 10 hours of study. Also note that it takes more and more time to obtain each additional point the closer the student gets to a perfect score. In the first few hours of study, the easy material is learned but a perfect score requires the mastery of the more difficult material that takes more time to grasp. While a graph cannot prove that this relationship holds true in all cases, it is reasonable to believe that it usually exists. Notice that in panel B the line increases at an increasing rate. When it reaches 100 on the horizontal axis, it becomes vertical. After 10 hours of study, more study time will not increase points because 100 is the maximum.

Panel C graphs the same two variables except the variable represented on each axis is switched—hours of study now are on the horizontal axis and points on the vertical axis. This line increases at a decreasing rate. After 10 hours and 100 points, the line becomes horizontal. Notice also that the same two variables can yield differently shaped graphs simply by changing the label on each axis.

LINEAR NEGATIVE RELATIONSHIP

A *linear negative relationship* is illustrated between the two variables in panel A of Figure 2–2. The number of hours a person is awake each day is graphed against the number of sleep hours obtained. The two must add up to 24. At the point where the line intersects the vertical axis, the person is sleeping 24 hours and awake zero hours. The converse is true at the intersection of the horizontal axis. It is hard to imagine either extreme. Therefore, it is not necessary for a downward-sloping line to intersect the two axes. The relevant area may be only a portion in the middle of the line—say between 4 and 10 hours of sleep and 20 and 14 hours of awake time.

CURVILINEAR NEGATIVE RELATIONSHIP

Curvilinear negative relationships are illustrated by panels B and C of Figure 2–2. Panel B represents the relationship between points on an economics exam and points on a math exam. Let's say that both tests are given on the same day and that only 10 hours of study are available for the two. To have the graph intersect the two axes, assume that with zero hours of study, zero points are earned on each exam. Therefore, at the point of intersection on the vertical axis, 100 points are earned on the econ. test and zero points on the math quiz. As the student takes a little time away from economics and devotes it to math, the math score rises by a larger amount than the econ. score decreases. This is consistent with the example in panels B and C of Figure 2–1 where it took more time to learn the hardest material than the easiest. Therefore, if only one or two hours are taken away from econ. and given to math, only a few points of the relatively hard econ. material is given up but more points are earned on the math quiz because the easiest material is learned first. At the other extreme, the last few hours taken from econ. causes a large loss of points compared to what is gained in math. A graph that bends out and away from the origin is called *concave to the origin*. Such a line decreases at an increasing rate.

Panel C of Figure 2–2 decreases at a decreasing rate. Such a line, which bends in toward the origin, is called *convex to the origin*. This line might represent a ski jumper coming off a ski jump. At the point where the line intersects the vertical axis, the ski jumper is ready to push off. Distance to the ground is at a maximum and speed is zero. Coming down the slide, distance to the ground decreases rapidly at first, and then decreases at a decreasing rate. At the point where the skier first touches the ground, speed is at a maximum. It is not necessary for the graph of a line convex to the origin to intersect either or both axes, although in this example, it does.

Graphs may or may not imply a cause and effect relationship between the two variables. In panels B and C of Figure 2–1, and panel B of Figure 2–2, it was implied that the amount of study time influences the grades on examinations. In other words, study is a cause and grades are an effect. The other panels show a relationship between two variables. Most of the graphs used in economics imply some kind of cause and effect relationship.

SLOPE OF A LINE

The slope of a line is obtained by dividing a given change along the vertical axis by the corresponding change along the horizontal axis as shown in Figure 2–3. Change along the vertical axis is ΔV and change along the horizontal axis is denoted by ΔH. An easy way to remember the numerator and denominator is

FIGURE 2–3   Slope of a Line

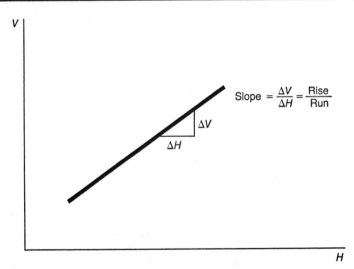

$$\text{Slope} = \frac{\Delta V}{\Delta H} = \frac{\text{Rise}}{\text{Run}}$$

to think of ΔV as the rise of the line and ΔH as the run. Thus, slope is rise over run. Upward-sloping lines have a positive slope and downward-sloping lines have a negative slope.

GLOSSARY

positive relationship Both variables change in the same direction; both either increase or decrease.

negative relationship The variables change in opposite directions; when one increases the other decreases.

linear positive relationship A straight, upward-sloping line.

curvilinear positive relationship A curved, upward-sloping line that increases at either an increasing or decreasing rate.

linear negative relationship A straight, downward-sloping line.

curvilinear negative relationship A downward-sloping line that decreases at either an increasing or a decreasing rate.

concave to the origin A line that bends out from the origin and decreases at an increasing rate.

convex to the origin A line that bends in toward the origin and decreases at a decreasing rate.

slope of a line Change in the vertical axis divided by change in the horizontal axis, or rise over run.

QUESTIONS

1. *On a graph, show the likely relationship between hours of study and points on an exam. Show points on the vertical axis and hours of study on the horizontal. Would the line be different for an average student than for a brilliant student? Explain.*

2. *a. Graph the relationship between earnings per week from part-time employment and average scores on exams during the term using the numbers in the following table:*

Earnings	Points
$300	0
200	50
100	75
0	80

Graph points on the vertical axis and earnings on the horizontal.

b. *Connect the points. What are the three ways of describing the shape of the line?*

c. *What is the meaning of the line?*

3. a. *Draw an upward-sloping line that first increases at an increasing rate and then increases at a decreasing rate.*

b. *Draw a downward-sloping line that first decreases at an increasing rate and then decreases at a decreasing rate.*

4. *Which of the two graphs in question 3 most accurately describes the relationship between hours of study per week on economics and average points on the examinations? Let points be on the vertical axis and hours of study on the horizontal.*

5. a. *What is the meaning of a vertical line that intersects the horizontal axis?*

b. *What is the meaning of a horizontal line that intersects the vertical axis?*

6. a. *What is the slope of the line in panel A of Figure 2–1? What would be its slope if dimes were graphed along the vertical axis and nickels on the horizontal?*

b. *Does the slope of an upward-sloping, straight line change at different points along the line? Explain. What about a downward-sloping, straight line?*

c. *How does the slope of a line that is concave to the origin change as you move from points high on the curve to lower points?*

d. *What are the slopes of the lines referred to in questions 5A and 5B?*

CHAPTER 3

Opportunity Cost

OVERVIEW

If one were to send a questionnaire to economists asking them to rank the 10 most important concepts in economics, opportunity cost would probably rank high on the list. After defining opportunity cost, this chapter presents the related ideas of the production possibilities schedule and the production possibilities curve, and it illustrates how they are useful for making economic decisions at all levels.

OPPORTUNITY COST DEFINED

Opportunity cost is defined as what has to be given up to obtain more of something else. Opportunity cost exists because resources are scarce. We cannot produce everything we want or would like. Thus, if we want more of something, we must be willing to settle for less of something else.

The idea of opportunity cost was already introduced in Chapter 2, Figure 2–2 panel B, without calling it such. Recall that ten hours were available to study for two exams—economics and mathematics. In this case, time was the scarce resource. Twenty hours of study could have yielded a perfect score in both. But only 10 hours could be spared from other courses or activities. Thus, to obtain more points in one exam, a lower score must be accepted on the other.

PRODUCTION POSSIBILITIES SCHEDULE

The exact relationship between the two exam scores can be more easily seen with a *production possibilities schedule*. This is a table showing alternative combinations of two goods (exam scores) that can be produced from a given amount of resources (ten hours of study time).

Possibility	Economics points	Mathematics points
I	100 (A)	0 (f)
II	90 (A)	40 (C)
III	40 (C)	85 (B)
IV	0 (f)	100 (A)

From this table, it is possible to compute how much of one good must be given up to obtain an additional unit of the other good. Let us begin with possibility I and move to II. A useful formula to calculate the cost of each additional math point obtained is:

$$\text{Give up/Get} = 10/40 = 1/4$$

Moving from I to II, each additional math point obtained costs one quarter of an econ. point. The opportunity costs of moving down the table among the other combinations are given below:

Possibility	Econ. points given up for each math point obtained
I - II	.25
II - III	1.1
III - IV	2.7

One could begin with possibility IV and move up the table. In this case, more econ. points are obtained by giving up math points.

Possibility	Math points given up for each math point obtained
IV - III	.38
III - II	.90
II - I	4.0

Notice the increase in the size of the above numbers moving from one extreme to the other. At first, just a fraction of an econ. point must be given up to obtain one more math point. This figure becomes successively larger in the next two steps. The same is true moving to higher econ. scores. This example represents *increasing opportunity cost*. The cost of each additional unit of whatever is being increased becomes larger and larger as one approaches the maximum output of that item. Increasing opportunity cost occurred in this case because it became more time-consuming to add points the closer one came to the maximum 100; the hard material took longer to learn than the easy material.

FIGURE 3–1   Production Possibilities Curve Showing Increasing Opportunity Cost

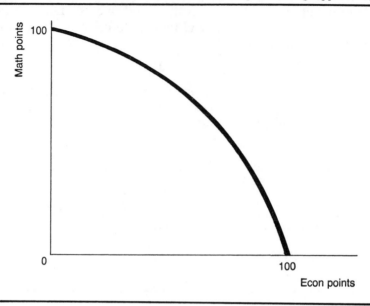

PRODUCTION POSSIBILITIES CURVE

Plotting the numbers from a production possibilities schedule yields a *production possibilities curve,* as illustrated in Figure 3–1. This is a line showing various combinations of two goods that can be produced from a given amount of resources. Increasing opportunity cost always yields production possibility curves that are concave to the origin—they bend out. You can prove this by plotting the econ.–math point combinations from the production possibilities schedule.

Before leaving this example, you might ask, which combination of econ. and math points (or grades in parentheses) would the student choose? The two extremes where an *F* is obtained on one or the other exam most likely would be avoided. Aside from that, it is hard to tell. If the student wished to maximize grade points, possibility II is the best—a grade of *A* in econ. and a *C* in math. However, if the student were a math major and wished to avoid a *C* in math, possibility III might be chosen—*C* in econ. and a *B* in math. It is important to remember that when moving from one possibility to another, move only if what you get is worth more than what you give up.

It is virtually impossible to come up with realistic examples of *constant opportunity cost* where the cost of adding a unit of one good in terms of another good given up does not change over the entire range of observations. If such an example did exist, it would be characterized by a straight, downward-sloping production possibilities curve such as in Figure 3–2.

FIGURE 3–2   Production Possibilities Curve Showing Constant Opportunity Cost

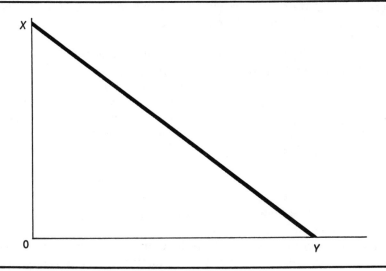

Social Choices

The production possibility curve is a useful device for illustrating choices that must be made by every society. Three important choices are: (1) the share of resources devoted to military goods versus nonmilitary production, often called guns and butter, (2) public versus private goods, and (3) consumption versus investment.

War and Peace.   A nation that needed to maintain a large military establishment or went to war with another nation would be located at point *B* on its production possibilities curve, as opposed to point *A* in Figure 3–3. The

FIGURE 3–3   War and Peace

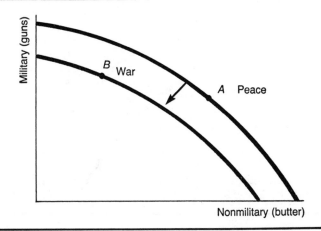

opportunity cost of the military is the nonmilitary goods and services given up. Of course, war also destroys resources—people and property. This is illustrated by a shift to the left of the curve as shown in Figure 3–3.

Public versus Private Goods.   Public goods are goods produced and/or distributed by government. In contrast to private goods, which are consumed by the individuals or families that purchase them, public goods are consumed by the society-at-large. Examples include public parks, streets and highways, the military, and police and fire protection. Governments also may subsidize certain kinds of private goods such as education, housing, food, and medical care, with the objective of helping low-income people attain the basic necessities of life.

The amount of public goods available to a society depends on its willingness to levy taxes to pay for these goods, and the wealth or total resources owned by a nation. Figure 3–4 illustrates the case where people living in a rich nation enjoy more of both public and private goods than the inhabitants of a poor nation. But given the wealth of a nation, the decision to produce more public goods must cause a reduction in private goods, and vice versa.

Consumption versus Investment.   A third way to divide up the output of a society is between consumption and investment. Investment goods are capital such as buildings and machines that increase the total resources of a society. In turn, these resources increase society's output in the future. The greater the share of a nation's resources devoted to the production of investment goods, the smaller the share devoted to consumer goods production. The absolute amount of consumer goods will increase over time due to the increase in the

FIGURE 3–4   Public versus Private Goods

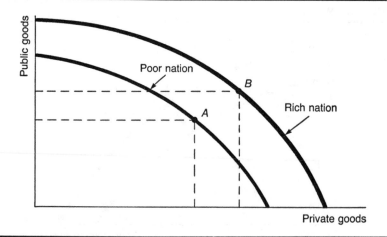

FIGURE 3–5   Production Possibilities on Transformation Curve

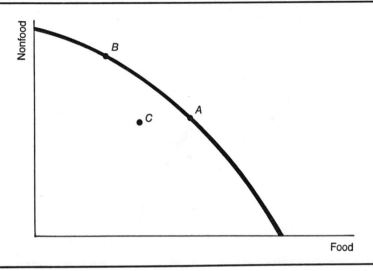

nation's capital resources. The investment versus consumer goods trade-off can be illustrated with a diagram similar to Figure 3–4.

Transferability of Resources

Virtually all production possibilities curves drawn to illustrate social choices are concave to the origin. Recall that this implies increasing opportunity cost. This phenomenon is thought to exist for every society because resources are not equally productive in all uses. As a nation moves toward the extremes—the intersection of the curve with either axis—resources must be pressed into tasks for which they are not well-suited. Or, perhaps they cannot be used at all. For example, as a nation moved up and to the left past point *B* in Figure 3–5, farmland and machinery would become redundant. Thus, a small increase in nonfood output causes a large reduction in food production.

The production possibilities curve is also known as the *transformation curve*. As a nation moves along the curve, it transforms one kind of output into another. Moving from point *A* to point *B* in Figure 3–5 transforms food into other goods.

Also, when a nation moves in small increments somewhere in the middle of the curve, *increasing* opportunity cost is not so evident. In this region, the resources that are suited to just one kind of production can be utilized in that area. The smaller incidence of increasing opportunity cost is especially true when time is allowed for resources to adjust to their new uses. For example, time allows farm people to acquire skills that are necessary for other occupations.

FIGURE 3–6 Production Possibilities Curve Illustrating Economic Growth

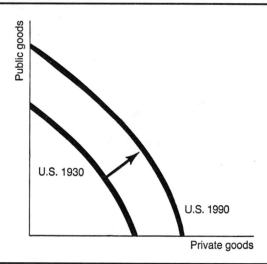

Efficiency and Full Employment

When drawing a production possibilities or transformation curve, two implicit assumptions must be made: (1) resources are used efficiently, and (2) resources are fully employed. Much of the material in microeconomics deals with the attainment of maximum efficiency in resource use, and reducing unemployment is an important issue in macroeconomics. If these assumptions are not met, the nation will be at a point below the surface of the curve—such as point C in Figure 3–5. By reducing unemployment or increasing efficiency, the nation can increase the output of both goods and improve its standard of living.

Economic Growth

An increase in the output of goods and services over time is known as *economic growth*. Sustained economic growth is attained only by an increase in a nation's resources. In recent history, nations have increased their resources mainly by producing more capital—both nonhuman and human. *Nonhuman capital* includes machines, tools, computers, buildings, roads, communications facilities, and so on. *Human capital* is the increase in knowledge made possible by research and education. Both forms of capital enhance the productivity of labor—thereby increasing society's per capita output.

Economic growth is illustrated by an outward shift of a nation's production possibilities curve, as in Figure 3–6. The increase in total resources increases the nation's ability to produce. The curve drawn in Figure 3–6 refers to *total* output of society. While an increase in total output is an acceptable definition of economic growth, the standard of living will increase only if total output increases at a faster rate than population.

GLOSSARY

opportunity cost That which is given up to obtain more of something else.

increasing opportunity cost The amount of one good that is given up to obtain an additional unit of another good becomes larger and larger as the maximum output of the good being increased is approached.

production possibilities schedule A table showing various possible combinations of two goods that can be produced from a given amount of resources.

constant opportunity cost The amount of one good that is given up to obtain an additional unit of another good remains the same as the maximum output of the good being increased is approached.

production possibilities curve A line showing various combinations of two goods that can be produced with a given amount of resources.

transformation curve Another name for a production possibilities curve.

economic growth Sustained increase in the real output of society.

nonhuman capital Resources such as machines, tools, computers, and buildings.

human capital New knowledge mainly from research and education.

QUESTIONS

1. Consider the following production possibilities schedule for a college student:

Possibility	Earnings from a part-time job	Grade points
I	$ 0	250
II	500	225
III	750	175
IV	1000	100

· *a. Calculate the opportunity cost of increasing earnings moving from possibility I to IV one step at a time.*
  b. Do the same calculation for increasing grade points moving from IV to I.
  c. What is the shape of the production possibilities curve drawn from these figures? What does it illustrate?

2. a. Would you expect increasing opportunity cost to be important in your allocation of time? Consider, for example, spending more of your time on economics and less on other subjects.
   b. In allocating an extra hour of study to a certain subject, what should be

true of the return to this activity in comparison to the return to all other activities that could be done at the same time?

3. *Suppose that later in the day you have an hour available for anything you wish to do. What factors should you consider in deciding how to spend that hour?*

4. *a. What is the opportunity cost to you of this economics course?*
   b. What can be inferred from your decision to take this course rather than doing something else with your time and money?

5. *Why is increasing opportunity cost a normally expected phenomenon in the economy?*

6. *Is it possible for a nation to increase the production of both goods represented on a transformation curve without adding to its stock of resources? Explain and illustrate.*

7. *Using a production possibilities curve, illustrate the following:*
   a. A nation goes to war.
   b. A drought reduces food production.
   c. Economic growth.
   d. Unemployment.

PART TWO
Consumer Choice

CHAPTER 4

Utility Maximization

OVERVIEW

The main objective of this chapter is to develop the utility maximizing rule. By following this rule, consumers obtain the greatest possible utility or satisfaction from a given expenditure. In conjunction with the utility maximizing rule, the law of diminishing marginal utility is presented. The law of diminishing marginal utility and utility maximization form the foundation of all economic theory relating to consumer behavior and demand.

CONSUMER SOVEREIGNTY

It is fitting to begin the study of microeconomics with the individual consumer, because without consumption there would be no justification for production. The ultimate aim of all production is to satisfy the wants of consumers. In some instances, the producer also is a consumer. The artist, musician, or craftsperson who receives satisfaction from a job well done is in effect "consuming" part of the product even though the product may be purchased by a second party. In cases where a person produces for home consumption, production and consumption are embodied in the same person or family.

In the U.S. economy and in all other free-market economies, the consumer is king (or queen). It is in the interest of producers to cater to the wishes of consumers because if they produce what is most highly demanded, they are rewarded by higher profits and a better standard of living for themselves and their families. Economists refer to an economic system where production is carried on to satisfy the wishes of consumers as one characterized by *consumer sovereignty*.

Society has found it necessary to restrict the sovereignty of the individual consumer somewhat, however. If consumption of a good is seen as harmful to either the consumer or to others, society may pass a law against it. The use of habit-forming drugs is one example. Drug addicts, as well as harming their health, may also harm others if they drive an automobile under the influence of drugs or turn to crime rather than employment to obtain money for their purchase. Laws regulating the consumption of alcoholic beverages are another example of restricting consumer sovereignty to a certain degree. Although society might prefer that consumers have cornflakes for breakfast rather than bourbon, in general, consumers are free to choose what they most desire, and producers respond to their wants.

In recent years, however, some people have begun to question whether the idea of consumer sovereignty accurately depicts our current economic system. They argue that today's giant corporations, with their multimillion-dollar annual advertising budgets, are able to persuade consumers to buy what the corporations want to produce, and this is not necessarily the same as what consumers would buy in the absence of such advertising. If the basic wants of consumers are altered or determined by the advertising campaigns of corporations, it might be more accurate to refer to "producer sovereignty" rather than consumer sovereignty.

Probably the most compelling argument in favor of consumer rather than producer sovereignty is that it would be unprofitable and, hence, irrational for corporations to spend millions of dollars to change the basic wants of consumers. Rather, it is much more profitable for producers to discover the basic consumer wants, cater to these wants, and then advertise to expand the sales of their particular product brand.

The increase in demand by consumers for smaller automobiles that gave better gas mileage during and after the Arab oil embargo, and the consequent scramble by the auto manufacturers to satisfy this demand, is a case in point. When the abrupt increase in the price of gasoline prompted consumers to switch to smaller cars, the auto manufacturers did not mount a large advertising campaign in an attempt to convince consumers to continue buying large cars, while continuing to produce them in the same numbers as before. Instead, the companies invested millions of dollars to retool some of their factories to increase their production of small cars. Then, each company began to advertise in an attempt to convince consumers to buy its small cars instead of the small cars produced by competitors.

TASTES

Since consumers are such an important part of our economic system, it will be useful to study them in some detail. No two consumers are exactly the same in likes and dislikes. One may like to spend leisure time watching baseball on television while drinking beer and eating pretzels; another may prefer to attend the opera or a symphony concert or travel to far-off places.

Even though it is generally recognized that tastes differ among people, we have a tendency to forget this when we criticize others for liking things that do not appeal to us or for spending their income on a different mix of goods and services than we do. One person may place an expensive home high on the list of priorities, while another prefers to spend more on travel or an expensive automobile. But who is to say which is the superior taste—the expensive home or the expensive auto? If a person were forced to sell the expensive auto and buy a higher-priced home, his or her total satisfaction might be decreased considerably. For this person, the superior taste is represented by the automobile. The main point to remember about taste is that there is no absolute standard—each person decides what he or she likes best and then tries to satisfy these wants.

UTILITY

Although tastes and satisfaction are familiar ideas, it is difficult to express them in concrete terms. Suppose you had just eaten an apple and a candy bar. Could you tell someone how much satisfaction you received from each of these items? Possibly you could tell which item you liked best, but could you tell how much better you liked one than the other? You might say "quite a bit" or "just a little" or some such vague descriptive term. But how much is "just a little" or "quite a bit"?

We need a more quantitative measure of satisfaction. For this reason, economists have developed the concept of utility. The word *utility* means the same thing as satisfaction. For illustrative purposes, however, economists have created the concept of a "util," which is a unit of utility. Although it is not possible to measure utils in a quantitative sense, for the purpose of instruction it is useful to assign numbers to levels of utility or satisfaction. This is not as unrealistic as one might think as long as it is agreed that a large number represents greater satisfaction than a small number. Suppose you agreed to arbitrarily assign 100 utils as the satisfaction or utility you received from the apple. If you liked the candy bar less, you would then assign it a number smaller than 100, or if you liked it more, you would give it a number greater than 100. If, for example, you assigned 50 to the candy bar, we could say that you liked the apple about twice as much as the candy bar.

If you wanted to take the time, you could assign utils to all the things you consume or might consume, using one of the items as a reference point. The important things in assigning utils to each item is not the absolute size of the util measure of each item but its size relative to the other items. Because tastes are an individual matter, utility is not something that can be compared from person to person. An individual might assign numbers to a partial list of the things consumed during one week in the following manner:

Items consumed per week	Number of utils
Two pounds of steak	100
One-fourth pound of coffee	30
Two quarts of milk	60
Shelter of house	300
Repair of auto	200

This example illustrates two important points. First, consumption is measured as an amount per unit of time. In this example, we used one week. It does not make sense to say two pounds of meat were consumed if you do not specify per day, per week, per year, or per lifetime. The time dimension is necessary to know how much is being consumed relatively. The second point is that we consume services as well as goods. In the example, the repair of the automobile is a service. We could list services purchased from a doctor, lawyer, dentist, barber, or beauty shop operator. In economics, a service is treated as if it were a good. For our purposes, they are essentially the same; both yield satisfaction or utility to the buyer.

THE MARGINAL UNIT

A concept that is often used in economics is the marginal unit. Perhaps the easiest way to grasp this idea is to think of marginal as the same as extra or additional. If you have 10 units of something, say 10 pencils, and you acquire one more, then the eleventh one is the marginal pencil. The marginal unit is the one that is added to or subtracted from the top of whatever you have.

The marginal unit is one of the most important and useful concepts employed in economics. This is because most economic decisions involve relatively small (or marginal) changes. For example, you do not decide whether to spend all your income on steak or none on steak. Rather, you decide whether you should buy a little more steak and a little less hamburger or vice versa. Thus, the decisions you make generally involve the extra or marginal unit. It is the unit where economic decisions are made. In understanding this idea, do not confuse the marginal with the average or the total, which may be more familiar measures.

MARGINAL UTILITY

Marginal utility is the extra or additional utility you obtain by consuming one more unit of a good or service per unit of time. It can also be the utility you lose by reducing your consumption by one unit. In a previous utility example, 100 utils were obtained by consuming two pounds of steak per week. Now suppose you increased your steak consumption to three pounds per week and received 140 utils from this amount. The utility received from the third, or marginal, pound of steak in this case would be 40 utils. We could take the same example and subtract one pound of steak from weekly consumption. If, for example, we received 55 utils from one pound, then the marginal utility of the second pound is 45 utils. The following table summarizes what total and marginal utility might be for zero, one, two, and three pounds of steak consumed per week.

You will note that the utility added by the marginal unit—the marginal utility—can be calculated by subtracting the total utility obtained *before* the marginal unit is added from the total utility obtained *including* that unit.

Pounds of steak consumed per week	Total utility (utils)	Marginal utility (utils)
0	0	—
1	55	55
2	100	45
3	140	40

Another method of calculating marginal utility is to divide the *change* in total utility by the *change* in the number of units consumed:

$$\text{Marginal utility} = \frac{\text{Change in total utility}}{\text{Change in units consumed}}$$

Also note that the total utility of a given quantity is the sum of all the marginal utilities up through and including that quantity.[1]

LAW OF DIMINISHING MARGINAL UTILITY

The preceding example also illustrates the *law of diminishing marginal utility*. This means that as you increase consumption of one good or service, say steak, holding constant the other things you consume, beyond some point the extra or marginal utility you obtain from the last unit will begin to decline. The intuitive appeal of diminishing marginal utility stems largely from our personal experience. If we consume more and more of something, even steak, we soon tire of it and desire more variety.

The idea of diminishing marginal utility also is supported by lack of evidence of "monomania" among people, even among heroin addicts. If diminishing marginal utility did not prevail, there is no reason why some people would not spend all their income on one thing. In that case, you could choose an item that gives you the most satisfaction for the first dollar spent and then devote your entire income to it.

MARGINAL UTILITY AND PRICE

The utility or satisfaction we receive from a good or service is a major reason we buy the things we do. Generally, if we do not like a product, we do not buy it. But it is not quite this simple. For one thing, likes or dislikes are not all-or-nothing concepts. We all have varying degrees of likes and dislikes, as indicated by the diminishing marginal utility concept. Also, there is another problem we all have to face: the problem of price.

---

[1] For students with a knowledge of the calculus, the marginal utility is the first derivative of the total utility function.

When faced with a choice between two or more items that we could buy, we often deliberately choose the item we like the least. Looking over a menu in a restaurant, for example, you may prefer the $15 T-bone steak to the $6 chopped beef, but you choose the latter. Or, when buying a car, you may like the $25,000 sports car better than any car in the showroom, but you buy the $8,000 sedan. Is your behavior irrational or inconsistent with the concept of utility? Not at all. In purchasing decisions, you must consider price and utility.

When you choose an item that is less desirable and less costly, you implicitly decide that the extra cost is not worth the extra satisfaction it brings. You decide, for example, that the additional satisfaction from the steak over the hamburger is not worth $9 to you. There are other things you can buy with that $9 that will give you more utility. In deciding what things to spend your money on, you really look at marginal utility per dollar rather than marginal utility alone. Using the steak example, suppose the marginal utility, price, and marginal utility per dollar (marginal utility divided by price) are as follows:

	Marginal utility (utils)	*Price*	*Marginal utility per dollar*
Chopped beef	60	$ 6	10
T-bone	90	$15	6

This example illustrates that choosing chopped beef over T-bone steak is a rational choice. The marginal utility per dollar of the cheaper cut exceeds the marginal utility per dollar obtained from the T-bone. This is only an example; we could have easily created an example in which T-bone would have been the best choice by raising its marginal utility or lowering its price. The point is that it is not always best to buy the cheaper item.

UTILITY–MAXIMIZING RULE

So far we have considered choosing between only two items. We know, however, that life is more complex than this. During a normal shopping trip to the supermarket, for example, we have thousands of items to choose from. How do we decide what to buy?

The first thing we must realize is that our budget is limited; we have just so much to spend. Given this constraint, our objective is to maximize our satisfaction or utility. The basic rule is to equalize, as much as possible, the marginal utility per dollar for all the goods and services we buy. Recall that marginal utility per dollar is obtained by dividing marginal utility by price. For example, if the marginal utility (MU) of good A is 30 and its price is $5, then its marginal utility per dollar is 6. The general rule to follow for all goods and services A through Z is:

$$\frac{\text{MU of } A}{\text{Price of } A} = \frac{\text{MU of } B}{\text{Price of } B} = \cdots = \frac{\text{MU of } Z}{\text{Price of } Z}$$

Thus, to maximize utility, we should try to make the marginal utility per dollar of good or service A equal to that of good or service B, and make these equal to all other things we consume.

Why does an equalization of the marginal utility per dollar for all goods we consume result in maximum satisfaction for us? This is perhaps easiest to see if we look at a situation where they are not equal. Suppose the marginal utility per dollar you spend on housing per month is 50 but the marginal utility per dollar spent on your automobile per month is only 30. Consider what would happen if you spent one dollar less on your automobile and one dollar more on housing. Your total utility from the auto would decline by 30 utils, but your total utility from housing would increase by 50 utils. You would give up 30 but gain 50, for a net gain of 20 utils. Thus, you could gain 20 utils per month simply by rearranging your purchases. This idea applies to everything you buy. If certain goods or services are not giving you as much marginal utility per dollar as other goods or services are providing, reduce your purchases of the low-return items and increase your spending on items that give you a higher marginal utility per dollar. By doing so, you can increase your total satisfaction without spending an extra cent.

If a person is not at the utility-maximizing equilibrium how does the adjustment process reestablish this equilibrium? A person will buy more of the high MU/P items and less of those with low MU/P ratios. Because of the law of diminishing marginal utility, an increase in the purchase of the high-ratio items lowers their marginal utilities which, in turn, lowers their MU/P ratios. Conversely, a decrease in the purchase of the low-ratio items increases their marginal utilities and increases their MU/P ratios. At some point, the high and low ratios will equalize, or come together. No one can tell you how many units of each good or service you should purchase per week or month when you reach equilibrium. This will depend on your tastes and income.

THEORY VERSUS REALITY

Although the preceding rule for maximizing utility cannot be questioned from the standpoint of pure logic, one might question its practical usefulness. Surely, you might argue, no one takes time to think of the utils obtained from consuming an item, much less writing them down and dividing by price. It might come as a surprise to learn that most people implicitly follow such a rule in their daily purchases. Many of us have felt at one time or another that an item was a good buy or that it wasn't worth it. In doing so, we have made an implicit calculation of the item's marginal utility per dollar. If we decide that an item is a good buy, it is an indication that its marginal utility per dollar is large relative to other things we could buy. If an item isn't worth it, its marginal utility per dollar for us is low. We have also purchased items that we could not be sure were good buys; these items provided a marginal utility per dollar that was about equal to that of the other things we buy.

If people do attempt to maximize utility, how can charity and gift-giving be explained? Here, people give without expecting anything in return. But givers do receive something in return—the good feeling that someone else's utility is increased by the charity or gifts. Thus, people who accept charity or gifts do a favor to people who give. We can only infer that people who give are better off by giving than by not giving, or else they wouldn't donate.

CHANGES IN THE OPTIMUM MIX

If a person reaches the utility-maximizing optimum, will that mix of goods and services be consumed for all time to come? No. The MU/P ratio of an item will change if either the MU or its price changes. MU can change for several reasons. First, we may grow tired of something that we have consumed for a long while; most of us like some variety in our lives. Thus, the marginal utility of what we consume today depends somewhat on what we consumed yesterday. Second, new products or services may appear on the market that make old ones less desirable. This phenomenon is most evident in products that change in fashion or style. How many times have we admired a certain model of automobile only to have a new model come out that made our former dream car seem ugly and old-fashioned? Third, our tastes or estimates of utility may be changed by advertising. If a popular movie star or athlete uses a product, for example, it might become more appealing to some people.

A second reason to change the mix of goods we consume is because prices are always changing. If the price of one item increases relative to other alternatives, its marginal utility per dollar will decrease relative to other things. We would then want to buy less of it.

INTERDEPENDENCE OF UTILITIES

The marginal utility of each good or service we consume may depend on the other things consumed along with it. Economists call this *interdependence of utilities*. Interdependence between goods can take the form of either a complementary or a substitute relationship. Two goods are *complements* to each other if consuming one enhances the marginal utility of the other. Bacon and eggs are a good example. Most people find eggs more appealing at breakfast when accompanied by a strip or two of bacon. Or, take the woman who has purchased a new dress; a new handbag, gloves, and shoes generally will make the dress more desirable, and the dress also complements the accessories. On the other hand, a *substitute* relationship between goods exist if consuming one good reduces the marginal utility of another. For instance, the marginal utility you obtain from consuming a glass of orange juice at breakfast probably would decline if you also had a glass of grapefruit juice at the same meal.

Because of the many complications that have the effect of changing the marginal utility of each good or service we buy or consider buying, the optimum bundle of goods and services that will maximize utility is constantly changing. Therefore, it is necessary to continually reevaluate purchase decisions if we hope to get the most for our money.

CONSUMPTION VERSUS SAVING

Although we must decide what mix of goods and services will give the most utility for a given expenditure, this does not imply that all income is spent. Most people attempt to save at least a small portion of their current income for various reasons. We may save "for a rainy day" to have something to fall back on in case we cannot work, or for retirement to supplement a pension. Most people save to make a large purchase such as a car or a down payment on a house. Others may wish to leave an estate for their heirs or some institution.

The decisions to save or not to save and what to save for are like the expenditure decisions we have just considered. The marginal utility of saving is the satisfaction we can expect to obtain when we eventually spend that extra dollar, or the satisfaction we now obtain from knowing that someone else will be able to spend it.

The marginal utility obtained from an extra dollar saved varies among individuals. Some people like to spend what they earn relatively quickly and do not place a high value on saving. Economists say that these people have a *high rate of time preference*. They prefer to consume now rather than later. The stereotyped soldier or sailor who epitomizes the eat, drink, and be merry attitude is a good example of someone with a high rate of time preference. The marginal utility of present consumption to this person is high relative to that of future consumption.

Other people, perhaps more patient, are willing to devote a relatively large share of their current income to saving, with the idea of adding to their consumption in the future. These people have a *low rate of time preference*. The miser represents the extreme case of a person with a low rate of time preference, although it is doubtful that most misers ever envision spending the entire amount of their savings at some future date. Even the miser has some degree of time preference. No one can postpone all consumption for the future; if a person tried, there would be no future!

Most of us fall somewhere between the spendthrift and the miser regarding time preference. Persons who have a low rate of time preference tend to obtain more utility from future consumption than their counterparts with a high time preference. Hence, they will be likely to save a larger fraction of their income.

In estimating the marginal utility of future consumption, it is also necessary to account for the interest or dividends received on savings. If the rate of interest received on savings is 10 percent, $1 saved today will be worth $1.10

TABLE 4–1   Price of Present Consumption and Marginal Utility

	Marginal utility of an extra dollar consumed at present	Interest rate	Price of present consumption	Marginal utility per dollar
Situation 1:				
Spendthrift	20	00.10	$1.10	18.18
Miser	10	00.10	1.10	9.09
Situation 2:				
Spendthrift	20	00.20	1.20	16.67
Miser	10	00.20	1.20	8.33

one year from now. Assuming no increase in prices,[2] the extra dollar saved will buy somewhat more in the future than it buys today. Hence, the interest return on savings compensates us for waiting to consume in the future. The higher the interest or dividend returns on our savings, the more each dollar saved at the present will buy in the future. In other words, a higher interest rate increases the price of present consumption compared with future consumption.

THE PRICE OF PRESENT CONSUMPTION

The basic idea that the combination of goods we presently consume depends on both marginal utility and price also applies to decisions to consume now or in the future. The price or opportunity cost of present consumption is what must be given up in the future. The higher the rate of interest, the more $1 saved will buy in the future, and consequently the higher the cost or price of present consumption.

We can therefore consider the price of $1 in present consumption as the dollar plus the interest return. If we specify the marginal utility that an extra dollar of present consumption will provide, we can divide this by price to obtain marginal utility per dollar. As an example, consider two individuals, one a spendthrift and the other a miser. In situation 1, both receive a 10 percent rate of interest on their savings; in situation 2, the rate is 20 percent. The two situations are shown in Table 4–1.

Because the spendthrift in this example enjoys spending money in the present more than the miser, whatever the rate of interest, the marginal utility

---

[2] A stable price level is assumed to simplify the example. But the rule still holds; the higher the interest rate, the higher the price of present consumption for any given rate of inflation. The effect of inflation on the interest rate is discussed in Chapter 20.

per dollar of present consumption is higher for the spendthrift. But, at higher rates of interest, the price of present consumption rises, which results in a reduction in marginal utility per dollar of present consumption for both individuals.

The decision to save or to consume at the present, therefore, is similar to the decision on what mix of goods to buy, depending on taste and price. Theoretically a low rate of time preference and a high price (high interest) are associated with a high rate of saving, and vice versa. Empirically, however, economists have found it difficult to measure the relative importance of each of these factors in people's decisions to save or to spend. For one thing, an independent, quantitative measure of time preference is lacking. Although there is general agreement that the rate of time preference affects the proportion of income saved, there is much less agreement on the importance of the rate of interest. The measurement of the impact of the interest rate on saving is complicated by other factors that also are expected to influence saving. These include the level of income, changes in the general price level (mainly inflation), and expectations of future economic conditions. The probable impact of these factors on saving is discussed more thoroughly in the companion macro text.

GLOSSARY

consumer sovereignty   Where the aim of production is to satisfy the wants of consumers.

utility   Another name for satisfaction.

util   A unit of satisfaction.

marginal unit   The unit added to or subtracted from the top of whatever is being considered.

marginal utility   The additional satisfaction received by consuming one more unit of a good or service.

law of diminishing marginal utility   Beyond some point the additional satisfaction received from consuming an additional unit of a good will become less and less—holding constant the amounts of all other items consumed.

utility maximizing rule   Equalized MU/P ratios (marginal utility per dollar) for all goods and services available for purchase.

complements   Increasing the consumption of one good increases the marginal utility of another good.

substitutes   Increasing the comsumption of one good decreases the marginal utility of another good.

high rate of time preference   A strong desire to consume now rather than later.

low rate of time preference   A willingness to postpone consumption—to save.

price of present consumption   The amount of future consumption given up to consume one more dollar today.

QUESTIONS

1. *Because of the large amount of advertising that currently takes place, some people have argued that consumer sovereignty no longer characterizes the United States and other market economies. Is there any evidence to suggest that consumer sovereignty still exists? Explain.*

2. *a. What is the marginal unit?*
   b. Why is it important in making consumer decisions?

3. *a. What is marginal utility?*
   b. What is the law of diminishing marginal utility?
   c. What evidence is there to suggest that diminishing marginal utility exists?
   d. Calculate the marginal utilities of additional glasses of orange juice from the following figures:

Number of glasses	Total utility
0	0
1	100
2	190
3	200
4	150

4. *Suppose you are in the market for a new bicycle. A sales person shows you a new 10-speed model for $249. You say the bicycle is nice but you cannot afford such an expensive model. What do you really mean when you say you cannot afford this item? Surely you could find $249 in either your savings or a small loan?*

5. *The marginal utility of a steak and a fish dinner for an individual is given below. Under the following prices, is the individual maximizing utility for a given expenditure? Why or why not?*

	MU	Price
Steak dinner	100	$10
Fish dinner	75	5

6. *Let's say that the combination of food that maximizes your satisfaction for lunch consists of one cheeseburger, one slice of apple pie, and one cup of coffee. According to the marginal utility over price approach to making consumer decisions, you should continue to consume this mix of foods for lunch the rest of your life. True or false? Explain.*

7. *It is a common practice in restaurants for customers to be given as much coffee as they desire free of charge when they purchase a meal. Under these circumstances, what is the marginal utility of the last cup of coffee; that is, what is the marginal utility of the last unit consumed of goods received "free."*

8. *a. What is the price of present consumption?*
   b. How does the rate of interest affect this price?

CHAPTER 5

Substitution among Goods

OVERVIEW

When product prices change relative to one another, consumers have an incentive to substitute the relatively cheaper items for more expensive items. The main objective of this chapter is to provide a framework for classifying substitution possibilities. This framework is known as indifference curves.

INDIFFERENCE CURVES

An *indifference curve* is a line showing various combinations of two goods that yield a constant level of satisfaction or utility. The best way to understand indifference curves is to construct one from a specific example. Since we are limited to a two-dimensional diagram, the example is restricted to considering two goods at a time. In this case, let us use the entertainment obtained from viewing football games and theater plays as the two goods.

As a starting point, suppose you are given 10 tickets to see your favorite football team and 10 tickets to the theater of your choice. We can represent this combination by point A in Figure 5–1. Ask yourself this question: If two football tickets were taken away from me, how many additional theater tickets would I have to be given to remain equally satisfied? Assume there is no chance to sell the tickets, so you cannot exchange the extra theater tickets for football tickets. Also, do not be concerned about the price of the tickets. Assume they are given to you or taken away without charge or compensation.

Your answer to this question will depend on how well you like football and the theater. Suppose you decide that two additional theater tickets would compensate you for the loss of the two football tickets. In other words, you are indifferent between the combination of 10 football and 10 theater tickets and the combination of 8 football and 12 theater tickets. Let this second combination be point B in Figure 5–1.

We might go through the same procedure again, this time taking away a total of eight football tickets. Now you only have two football tickets left. How many theater tickets would you have to be given to remain as satisfied as you were in the original combination of 10 of each kind of tickets?

According to the idea of diminishing marginal utility, additional nights at the theater will provide less and less satisfaction. Moreover, the closer you come to no football tickets, the loss of football tickets will mean increasingly

FIGURE 5–1   An Indifference Curve

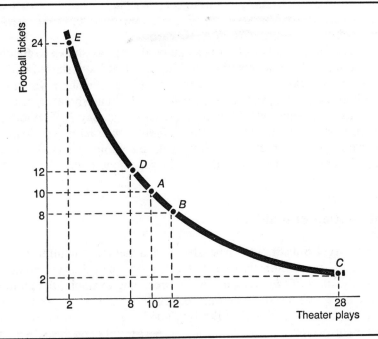

less satisfaction. It is reasonable, therefore, that you will require more than eight additional theater tickets to compensate for the loss of eight football tickets. Suppose you want 18 more theater tickets. We could say that you are indifferent to the following combinations:

Combination	Theater	Football
A	10	10
B	12	8
C	28	2

Thus, we are tracing alternative combinations that would make you equally well off. We could also trace out points on the upper part of the curve by taking away theater tickets in exchange for football tickets. For example, you might choose eight theater and 12 football tickets, or two theater and 24 football tickets as additional combinations, labeling these points *D* and *E*, respectively.

Assuming that the general relationship holds between the points as on them, we can connect points *A* through *E*. We have now constructed what economists call an *indifference curve*. From the standpoint of total satisfaction, you are indifferent at all points along this curve.

Of course, any number of curves can be drawn, as shown in Figure 5–2. We started out with 10 tickets of each, but we might have started with six. If you prefer more tickets to less, then the smaller combination would be on a lower indifference curve, such as I_0 in Figure 5–2. Similarly, a larger combination, such as 14 of each, would be on a higher curve, say I_2. Economists call many such curves on a single diagram an *indifference map*. The indifference map is a picture of your preferences, much like a contour map is a picture of the landscape. Curves farther from the origin represent higher levels of satisfaction.

Substitution Possibilities

1. Imperfect Substitutes. The shape of a person's indifference curves tells us the degree of substitution that exists between the two goods represented on the axes of the diagram. In the preceding example, the indifference curves are drawn with a slight curvature, convex to the origin. An indifference curve of this shape implies that the two goods represented on the axes are substitutes for one another but that they are imperfect substitutes. This means that as you move down along the curve, more and more units of the abundant

FIGURE 5–2   An Indifference Map

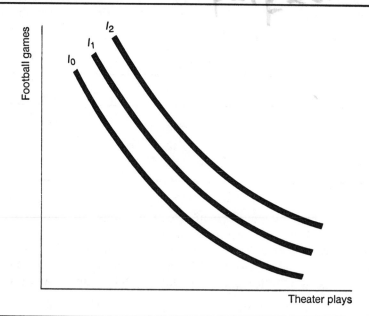

good must be obtained to make you willing to give up each successive unit of the relatively scarce good. This is illustrated by Figure 5–1. Moving from point *A* to point *B,* you are willing to give up two football tickets if you gain two theater tickets. In other words, one theater ticket is enough to compensate you for giving up one football ticket. Now move from point *B* to point *C*. By giving up these six football tickets, you insist on 16 additional theater tickets. In other words, you now require nearly three theater tickets to compensate you for the loss of one football ticket. Under these conditions, we say that the two goods are imperfect substitutes. It is possible to substitute between them but as one moves to the extremes, it takes more of the abundant good being added to substitute for each unit of the scarce item given up.

2. Perfect Substitutes. Two items are defined as perfect substitutes if the amount of one good that is necessary to compensate for giving up each unit of another good remains constant at all possible combinations. For example, under most conditions, a person should be willing to give up one dozen white-shell eggs for one dozen brown-shell eggs of comparable size and quality, regardless of the combination being consumed. Indifference curves depicting perfect substitutes are drawn as straight, downward-sloping lines as illustrated by Figure 5–3. Notice that one brown-shell egg compensates for one white-shell egg regardless of where one is on the curve.

FIGURE 5–3   Indifference Curves for Perfect Substitutes

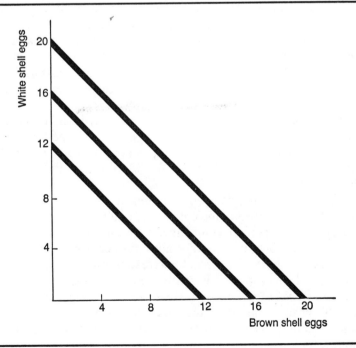

However, the ratio between the two items does not have to be one for one to have perfect substitutes. It may be that a person who had a preference for brown-shell eggs would have to be given two white-shell eggs to compensate for each brown egg given up. Or it could be that the size of the eggs are different. If the brown-shell eggs are large and white eggs are small, the ratio may have to be two white for one brown. The distinguishing characteristic of perfect substitutes is that the ratio remains constant at various combinations, not that the ratio is always one for one.

3. Perfect Complements.   The third possible kind of substitution relationship that may exist between two items is zero substitutability. These items often are called *perfect complements* because they always must be used in a certain ratio or proportion to yield any utility. The best examples are right and left shoes. Presumably a two-legged person would not be any better off with one left shoe and two right shoes than with one left shoe and one right shoe. The individual would be on the same indifference curve with the one left and one right shoe combination as with one left and two right shoes. The indifference curve reflecting this situation is rectangular in shape as illustrated by Figure 5–4.

Remember that a person is on the same level of utility or satisfaction at all points along an indifference curve. Thus, adding more right shoes to the one left shoe does not, in this example, give the person more satisfaction. Moreover, it is not possible to stay on the same level of satisfaction by taking away left shoes and adding right shoes. In other words, two right shoes are not as good as one left and one right. Thus, the indifference curve runs parallel to each axis after the exact combination that makes the two items useful is attained. More units of one or the other good are redundant and add nothing to satisfaction. These goods are perfect complements because they must be used in the fixed ratio to be useful. Again, the ratio does not necessarily have to be one for one, although most pairs of perfect complements seem to occur in this ratio. The main point is that the ratio cannot be altered.

Note in the case of perfect complements that the indifference curves are parallel (Figure 5–4). In the cases of imperfect and perfect substitutes, however, the curves do not have to run parallel to each other. The only restriction is that they do not cross, for if they did, they could not be indifference curves.

In the area of consumer behavior, economists have not been interested in perfect substitutes or perfect complements. For all practical purposes, pairs of perfect substitutes or perfect complements are seen as just one good. For example, white- and brown-shell eggs are considered eggs, or right and left shoes as pairs of shoes. The most interesting case is that of imperfect substitutes, in which various alternative combinations of two goods can provide the same level of satisfaction. Does this mean, therefore, that it doesn't make any difference to the individual which combination is selected? No. We will soon see that only one combination will give the individual the most for his or her money.

FIGURE 5–4   Indifference Curves for Perfect Complements

THE BUDGET LINE

To determine which of the many possible combinations of imperfect substitutes will give the individual the most for his or her money, it is necessary to add or superimpose a budget line on the indifference curve diagram. The budget line shows the various possible combinations of two goods that cost a given amount of money.

Perhaps the easiest way to gain an understanding of a budget line is to construct one from a simple example. Let us continue to use the football and theater ticket example discussed in the preceding section. In constructing a budget line, two pieces of information are necessary: (1) the person's budget, or how much money he or she can spend on the two items under consideration, and (2) the price of each item. In this example, suppose you decide to spend $60 on football and theater entertainment for the upcoming season. Also suppose that the price of football tickets is $4 while theater seats cost $6.

To construct a budget line, determine where the line intersects the two axes. This can be accomplished by asking a couple of questions. First, how many football tickets could be purchased if you decided to spend your entire $60 entertainment budget on football if the price of each ticket were $4? The answer is 15 tickets. Now pose the same question for theater tickets. How many theater tickets could you purchase if you spent your entire $60 entertainment budget on the theater if the price of theater tickets were $6? In this case,

FIGURE 5–5   A Budget Line

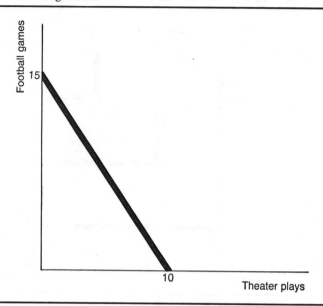

the answer is 10. We now have the two points where the budget line intersects the two axes. It intersects the football axis at 15 tickets and the theater axis at 10 tickets. To complete the budget line, draw a straight line between the two points that have been identified on the axes, as shown by Figure 5–5. The budget line is always a straight line regardless of the degree of substitution that exists between two goods.[1] This is because of the way the budget line is defined. All points on the line represent a given expenditure. At the point where the line intersects the football axis, $60 is being spent on 15 football tickets. At the 12 football–2 theater combinations, $48 is being spent on football and $12 on the theater. Moving down the line, you spend more on the theater and less on football, but you always spend $60.

MAXIMIZING UTILITY: INDIFFERENCE CURVE–BUDGET LINE APPROACH

We are now ready to combine indifference curves with the budget line to find out what combination of tickets would give you the most satisfaction for your $60. In Figure 5–6, we have imposed an indifference map on the budget line from Figure 5–5. First, let us choose any combination of tickets that totals $60, for example 12 football and 2 theater tickets. Will this combination give

---

[1] This is true as long as the prices of the two items remain constant at all points along the budget line which is the common situation for consumers.

FIGURE 5–6   Budget Line on Indifference Map

you the most satisfaction for your money? This question is answered by looking at Figure 5–6. Note that the highest indifference curve that can be reached with the 12 football–2 theater combination is I_0. But, a higher indifference curve can be reached by moving down the budget line, that is, by choosing a different combination of tickets that will be worth $60 (say, 9 football and 4 theater tickets). As you move down the budget line, you reduce your purchase of football tickets and increase the number of theater tickets you buy.

Remember that your overall objective is to reach the highest possible indifference curve within the constraint of the $60 you have to spend. The highest possible indifference curve you can reach is the one just tangent to the budget line, I_1 in Figure 5–6. Indifference curve I_2 could not be reached unless you wanted to spend more than $60. Thus, the general rule is that satisfaction will be maximized when you select that mix of goods on the budget line that enables you to reach the highest possible indifference curve.

In this example, the combination that maximizes your satisfaction is 9 football and 4 theater tickets. The cost of this combination, $60, is the same as any other combination on the budget line, such as 12 football and 2 theater tickets, or 3 football and 8 theater tickets, but your level of satisfaction is the greatest only at the 9 football–4 theater ticket combination.

Thus, even though we can purchase many different combinations of goods and services for a given expenditure, there is only one combination that will maximize our satisfaction. That is the combination that corresponds to the point of tangency between the budget line and the indifference curve.

The indifference curves drawn in Figure 5–6 are an arbitrary representation of a person's tastes. The 9 football–4 theater ticket combination that maximizes satisfaction for the $60 resulted from how the indifference curves were drawn. We could have as easily drawn the curves to illustrate a tangency point at any other combination. For example, an avid football fan who has little time for the theater likely would exhibit a different configuration on indifference curves, causing the tangency point to occur at a combination that weighed more in favor of football, such as the 12 football–2 theater combination illustrated by Figure 5–7A. On the other hand, a theatergoer would exhibit a set of indifference curves that would give rise to a tangency point favoring relatively more theater, such as the 3 football–8 theater ticket combination illustrated by Figure 5–7B. Again, each person has unique tastes and therefore exhibits a unique set of indifference curves between any given pair of goods.

In the preceding examples, we considered only one budget level—$60. The position of the budget line is determined in part by how large the budget is: the larger the budget, the farther to the right the budget line will be. For example, a $120 entertainment budget would cause the budget line to intersect the football and theater axes at 30 and 20 tickets, respectively. As a result, more of both items would be purchased, allowing one to reach a higher indifference curve, that is, a higher level of satisfaction. It can also be shown that changes in the price of each item also influences the position of the budget line and therefore affects the utility-maximizing combination, that is, the tangency point.

Although we have dealt with an example of imperfect substitutes (football and the theater), the same procedure applies to perfect substitutes and perfect complements. In the case of perfect substitutes, the utility-maximizing point will occur at one axis or the other if the slope of the budget line is different than the slope of the indifference curve. This means that the individual would buy only one of the two items, whichever is cheapest. This is reasonable to expect. If one item is as good as the other in satisfying one's tastes, why purchase any of the good that is more expensive? In reality, two goods that are perfect substitutes generally sell for the same price, otherwise no one would buy the good that offered less for the money. We will not be interested in two goods that are perfect substitutes and sell for the same price; essentially they are just one good. In the case of perfect complements, the utility-maximizing combination will occur at the corner of the indifference curve.

To summarize briefly, in this and the previous chapter we considered two approaches to the analysis of consumer behavior: (1) the marginal utility over price approach and (2) the indifference curve-budget line approach. Both approaches yield the same results. In the first approach, utility is maximized for a given expenditure when the consumption pattern is such that the marginal utility per dollar is equalized across all purchases. In the second approach, utility is maximized when the combination that is consumed corresponds to the

FIGURE 5–7   Illustrating Differences in Tastes

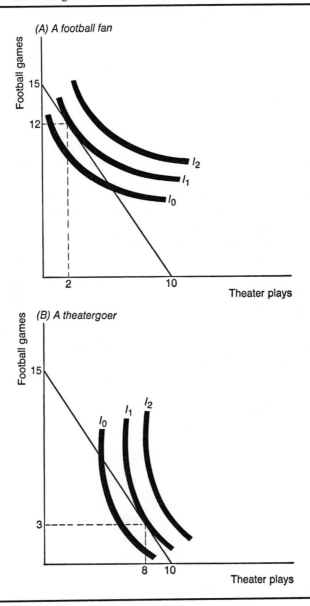

tangency point between the budget line and highest possible indifference curve. As shown in the appendix to this chapter, the marginal utilities per dollar of the two goods represented on the indifference curve–budget line diagram are equal for both goods only at the point of tangency

Both approaches have their place. The marginal utility over price approach is most useful for showing why additional utility can be gained by rearranging purchases until the marginal utilities per dollar of all items are equal. The indifference curve-budget line also shows this point, but in addition it is useful for illustrating differences in the degree of substitution between goods, as reflected by the shape of the indifference curves.

GLOSSARY

indifference curve   A line showing various combinations of two goods that yield a constant level of satisfaction or utility.

indifference map   A collection of indifference curves. Curves up and to the right show higher levels of satisfaction than those closer to the origin.

imperfect substitute   More of the abundant good must be obtained to give up successive units of the scarce good and remain equally satisfied. Illustrated by indifference curves that are convex to the origin.

perfect substitute   The amount of one good required to compensate for giving up successive units of another good remains constant at all combinations of the two. Illustrated by indifference curves that are straight, downward-sloping lines.

perfect complements   Goods that are used together in a fixed ratio. No substitution is possible. Illustrated by rectangular indifference curves.

budget line   A line showing various combinations of two goods that cost a given amount of money. Always straight, downward-sloping lines regardless of the degree of substitution between the two goods.

QUESTIONS

1. a. What is an indifference curve? An indifference map?
   b. What determines the shape of indifference curves?

2. Draw indifference curves for the following pairs of products and explain why you have drawn them in a certain shape:
   a. Paper and pencils.
   b. Pens and pencils.
   c. Baseball games and movies.

3. a. What is a budget line?
   b. Is a person equally well off at any point along a budget line? Explain.

4. a. Construct a budget line for a consumer who has $24 to spend on meat (beef and pork) for the week. Assume the price of pork is $2 per pound and the price of beef is $3 per pound.

   b. Add some indifference curves to the above diagram to indicate the combination of beef and pork that will maximize the consumer's satisfaction.

5. *a. Draw an indifference map for a person who likes olives better than pickles but considers the two items as good substitutes for each other.*
   b. Draw an indifference map for a person who likes pickles better than olives and considers the two items as poor substitutes for each other.

6. *Show that the utility maximizing rule presented in Chapter 4 is equivalent to the points of tangency of the indifference curve–budget line approach.*

APPENDIX: PROOF OF THE EQUIVALENCE OF THE UTILITY–MAXIMIZING RULE AND THE POINTS OF TANGENCY OF THE INDIFFERENCE CURVE–BUDGET LINE APPROACH

The purpose of this appendix is to show that at the point of tangency between a budget line and an indifference curve, the MU/product price ratios for two products (A and B) are equal.

Along a budget line:

$$\Delta TC = P_A \cdot \Delta A + P_B \cdot \Delta B = 0,$$

Where: ΔTC is the change in total cost of products A and B along the budget line. P_A and P_B are the prices of A and B. ΔA and ΔB are the changes in A and B purchased.

or:

$$\frac{\Delta A}{\Delta B} = -\frac{P_B}{P_A}$$

Since the slope of the budget line is $\dfrac{\Delta A}{\Delta B}$, its slope is also equal to $-\dfrac{P_B}{P_A}$.

Along an indifference curve:

$$\Delta U = MU_A \cdot \Delta A + MU_B \cdot \Delta B = 0$$

or:

$$\frac{\Delta A}{\Delta B} = -\frac{MU_B}{MU_A}$$

Since the slope of an indifference curve is $\Delta A/\Delta B$, its slope is also equal to $-\dfrac{MU_B}{MU_A}$.

At the point of tangency between a budget line and an indifference curve the slopes of the two lines must be equal. Therefore, at the point of tangency:

$$\frac{P_B}{P_A} = \frac{MU_B}{MU_A}$$

Rearranging the above expression, we obtain:

$$\frac{MU_A}{P_A} = \frac{MU_B}{P_B}$$

Therefore, at the point of tangency, the MU/P ratios are equal.

CHAPTER 6

Demand and Elasticities

OVERVIEW

The material in the previous two chapters is utilized to construct the concept of demand. Demand reflects the idea that consumers buy less of an item when it increases in price and they buy more when an item becomes cheaper. The second half of the chapter deals with consumer responsiveness to price changes.

DEMAND DEFINED

Demand is a negative *relationship* between price and quantity. The important thing to recognize about demand as used by economists is that it is not a set or fixed quantity but a relationship between price and quantity. To know what quantity a person or group of persons will demand, we must first know what price they will have to pay. For example, if you were asked what your demand is for football tickets, you would probably be reluctant to answer unless you knew what price you had to pay. The number of tickets you buy likely would be quite different if you had to pay $20 per ticket than if the price were $4. This chapter conceptualizes the relationship between the price of an item and the quantity people buy. We will begin by using the football ticket example.

In Figure 6–1, only two football tickets are demanded per season if the price is $8 per ticket; at a $4 price, six tickets are demanded; and at the bargain price of $2, nine tickets are demanded per season. By connecting the series of points on the graph, we obtain a curve that is known as a *demand curve*. A demand curve describes a relationship between price and quantity. If we establish a price, the demand curve tells us what quantity will be demanded. Or, if we specify a quantity, the curve tells us what price will be paid.

It is important to distinguish between demand and quantity demanded. Demand, as we have noted, refers to the relationship between price and quantity. However, quantity demanded refers to a particular quantity or point on the demand curve. Thus, when you wish to stipulate a particular quantity you can avoid confusion by calling it "quantity demanded" rather than "demand."

A second important characteristic about demand is that it reflects *wants*, not *needs*. If you tell me that you need six football tickets if the price is $4 per

FIGURE 6–1   The Concept of Demand (football ticket example)

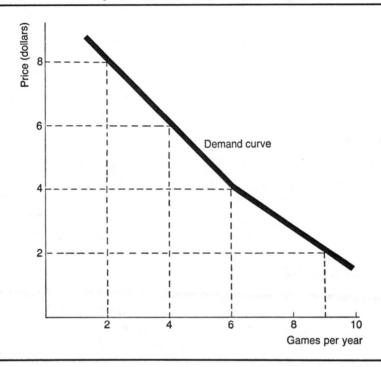

ticket, it would be easy to disagree with your statement. It could be argued that you do not need *any* football tickets because watching football is not necessary to sustain life. Or, you might say you need a new car or a vacation trip to a distant city. Again, neither is necessary to sustain life. On the other hand, if you said you *wanted* six football tickets or a vacation trip, this could not be disputed. Only you can determine what you want, and these wants are partly satisfied by the things you buy.

A third point about a demand curve is that it reflects what people actually would do if faced by certain prices rather than what they would like to do. Your favorite make of automobile may sell for $20,000, and you might like a new one every year, but that does not mean you would actually purchase one of these cars every year or even one in a lifetime. Demand is useful only if it reflects the actions of people, not what they would *like* to do. In other words, demand reflects wants that are translated into action, not mere intention or desire.

A fourth item to note about demand is that quantity is measured as an amount per unit of time. In Figure 6–1, the quantity of football tickets is measured in the number of tickets per year. However, there is no set time period that is always used. We can measure quantity as amount per week, per month, per year, and so forth. The time dimension that is chosen is often the one that is most useful in analyzing the problem at hand. When you change the time period, you also change the scale on the quantity axis.

The demand curve shown in Figure 6–1 is only an example. In this diagram, the demand curve is drawn with a slight curvature. This is not meant to imply that demand curves for all products look this way. Some may be straight, downward-sloping lines; others may have more curvature. For the moment, our main concern is with the downward-sloping characteristic rather than with the curvature of the line, or with how steeply it slopes down.

MARGINAL UTILITY AND DEMAND

Although the downward-sloping nature of a demand curve has an intuitive appeal, we can establish this characteristic more rigorously using what we learned about marginal utility and price in Chapter 4. A consumer maximizes satisfaction when the marginal utilities (MU) per dollar are equal for all the goods and services available. The following expression summarizes this idea:

$$\frac{\text{MU of good A}}{\text{Price of good A}} = \frac{\text{MU of good B}}{\text{Price of good B}} = \cdots = \frac{\text{MU of good Z}}{\text{Price of good Z}}$$

Recall also that marginal utility per dollar depends on both marginal utility and price. For a given marginal utility, the higher the price, the lower the marginal utility per dollar. For example, suppose a consumer is initially maximizing utility, as illustrated in the expression above. Now consider that just one of these goods, good A, changes in price as shown below:

	Initial situation	Price of A rises	Price of A falls
Marginal utility of A	20	20	20
Price of A	$4	$5	$2
Marginal utility per dollar	5	4	10

In the initial situation, all goods consumed by this person yield a marginal utility per dollar of five utils. When the price of good A rises, this good only yields four utils per dollar. In this case, it benefits the consumer to reduce the amount of good A purchased. One dollar less spent on A will reduce the person's satisfaction by four utils, but spending this dollar on something else that has not risen in price will yield close to five utils. Thus, the consumer can gain one util of net satisfaction by spending one dollar less on good A and one dollar more on one or more other goods.

As the consumer continues to reduce consumption of *A*, the marginal utility of *A* will increase (increasing the marginal utility per dollar of *A*). Also, as more other goods are consumed, the marginal utilities of these goods will decrease. Eventually the consumer will reach a new equilibrium where the marginal utilites per dollar are again equal for all goods. Note that as the price of a good rises, marginal utility per dollar declines, and this creates an incentive for the consumer to reduce purchases of the good in question. The end result is consistent with a downward-sloping demand curve, such as the curve in the preceding section, in which a higher price leads to a decreased rate of purchase.

Similar reasoning applies for a decrease in the price of *A*. Here, marginal utility per dollar increases, which provides an incentive for the consumer to increase purchases of *A* at the expense of other goods. This is consistent with the concept of demand.

INCOME AND SUBSTITUTION EFFECTS

It is reassuring to see that the downward-sloping nature of the demand curve that we obtained first by appealing to intuition also is obtained by the procedure we just used. It is useful to probe deeper into the relationship between price and quantity to fully understand why people buy more of a product when its price declines and buy less of a product when its price increases.

Economists have identified two major factors that explain why people behave this way: (1) the income effect and (2) the substitution effect. The income effect accounts for the fact that a change in the price of a good you buy changes the purchasing power of your income. It has the same effect as if you had a change in income. For example, as the price of theater tickets declines, your $60 entertainment budget can buy more tickets. It is as if your income has been increased. The opposite occurs if the ticket price rises; the $60 buys fewer tickets, so it is like a decrease in your budget or income. The substitution effect means that when the price of one good changes *relative* to another, there is an incentive to buy more of the lower-priced good and less of the higher-priced one. In other words, you try to substitute the relatively inexpensive good for the more expensive one.

The relative importance of the substitution and income effects depends on: (1) the degree and number of substitutes for the product and (2) the share of the item in the budget. The better the substitutes available, the greater the substitution effect. And, the larger the item's share in the budget, the greater the income effect. For example, if something you spend half your income on, such as rent, increases in price 10 percent, you notice it much more than the same percent price increase of something that is a small fraction of your budget—such as paper clips.

MARKET DEMAND

While we have been concerned with the demand curve of an individual consumer, the concept of demand is most useful when applied to a market situation—an entire group of consumers.

It is simple to develop the idea of a market demand from the demand of individual consumers. First, suppose that every consumer has a demand for every product. For some consumers, the demand will be large at a given price; for other consumers, the demand might be zero at the same price. No two consumers necessarily have the same demand for a product. To visualize the idea of market demand at each possible price, add up the quantity demanded by all consumers in the market. In other words, we obtain a horizontal summation of the demand curves of individual consumers. Figure 6–2 provides an example of how this is done.

FIGURE 6–2 Constructing Market Demand from Individual Demand (theater ticket example)

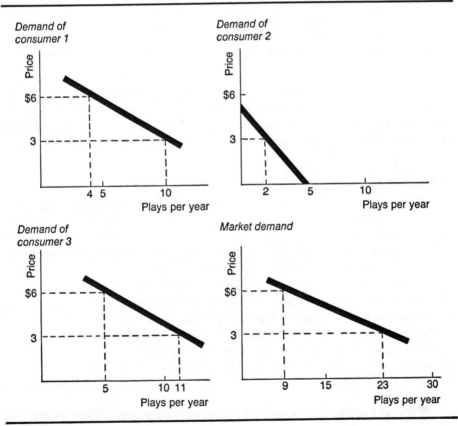

At $6 per ticket, consumer 1 demands 4 tickets per season, whereas at $3 per ticket, this person will buy 10 tickets. Consumer 2 is less of a theater fan. At $6 per ticket, consumer 2 would not attend the theater at all, and at the $3 price this individual will buy two tickets. Consumer 3 is a more ardent theatergoer than either Consumers 1 or 2. This person demands 5 and 11 tickets at the $6 and $3 prices, respectively.

To keep the example simple, assume that the market consists of these three demanders. The market demand curve is found by adding, at each price, the quantities demanded by all the consumers in the market, as shown in the following table. The market demand curve is plotted in the lower right frame on Figure 6–2.

| | | *Quantity demanded by consumer* | | | | | | *Market* |
Price		*1*		*2*		*3*		*demand*
$6		4	+	0	+	5 =		9
3		10	+	2	+	11 =		23

Notice in the above example that the increase in quantity demanded by the market as price declines comes from two sources: (1) the increase in quantity by the existing demanders in the market, and (2) the entrance into the market of new demanders when the price declines, as illustrated by consumer 2.

PRICE ELASTICITY OF DEMAND

The downward-sloping nature of a demand curve reflects the idea that people buy more of an item when its price declines and less when its price increases. However, this general relationship does not tell us anything about how responsive people are to price changes. One can show that people are relatively responsive to price changes by drawing a relatively flat demand curve as in Figure 6–3A. Conversely, a relatively small response to a price change can be illustrated by a steep demand curve, Figure 6–3B. The problem with using the shape of a demand curve to represent price responsiveness is that its shape can be changed simply by changing the units along one or both axes. For example, a demand curve is made steep by spreading the units of measure along the vertical axis and squeezing them together along the horizontal axis. This problem is eliminated by using price elasticity of demand to measure price responsiveness.

Price elasticity of demand is defined as the percent change in quantity

FIGURE 6–3   Differences in Response to Price Changes

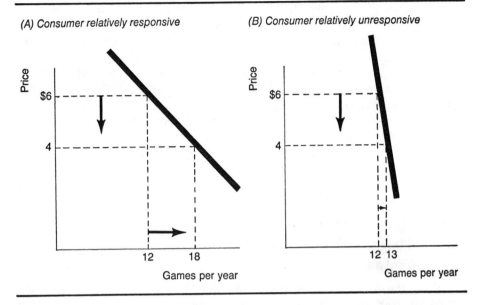

(A) Consumer relatively responsive

(B) Consumer relatively unresponsive

demanded resulting from each percent change in price. The price elasticity of demand formula is:

$$E_d = \frac{\% \, \Delta \, Q}{\% \, \Delta \, P}$$

where E_d is an abbreviation for price elasticity of demand, and the symbol Δ means "change in." For computation, this formula is written as:

$$E_d = \frac{\dfrac{Q_0 - Q_1}{Q_0}}{\dfrac{P_0 - P_1}{P_0}}$$

where Q_0 and P_0 are the beginning quantity and price, respectively, and Q_1 and P_1 are the ending quantity and price. To become somewhat more familiar with the formula, let us compute the price elasticity of demand for the change shown in Figure 6–3A. In this example, the Q_0 is 12, Q_1 is 18, P_0 is \$6, and P_1 is \$4. Thus, we have:

$$E_d = \frac{\dfrac{12 - 18}{12}}{\dfrac{6 - 4}{6}} = \frac{\dfrac{-6}{12}}{\dfrac{2}{6}} = \frac{-0.50}{0.33} = -1.5$$

In this example, a 1 percent decrease in price is associated with a 1.5 percent increase in quantity. Note that the price elasticity of demand is a negative number. This occurs because as we move along a demand curve, quantity and price change in opposite directions; when price goes down, quantity goes up, and vice versa.

Although the price elasticity measure is a negative number, when economists refer to a specific elasticity measure they often drop the negative sign and designate the number as an absolute value. For example, a price elasticity measure of −1.5 generally is referred to as 1.5. Once one is aware that the negative sign is implicit in the discussion, it is redundant to repeat it.

To facilitate discussion, economists have grouped the price elasticity measure, or *coefficient,* into three categories. Generally the groupings are made according to the absolute size of the coefficient (minus sign dropped). The elasticity coefficient categories are:

Less than 1 = Inelastic
Equal to 1 = Unitary elastic
Greater than 1 = Elastic

When the demand for a product is inelastic to price, we say that consumers are relatively unresponsive to a price change. In this case, the percentage change in quantity is smaller than the corresponding percentage change in price. If demand is elastic, on the other hand, we say that consumers are quite responsive to a price change. Here, the percentage change in quantity is greater than the percentage change in price. In the intermediate case of a unitary elastic demand, price and quantity both change in the same proportions.

The smallest possible value of the elasticity coefficient is zero. If E_d is zero, a price change will not result in any change in quantity. In this case, demand is perfectly inelastic. Demand that is perfectly inelastic is represented by a demand curve that is perfectly vertical (Figure 6–4).

The largest possible value of the elasticity coefficient is infinity. Here a slight change in price corresponds to an infinitely large change in quantity. In this situation, demand is perfectly elastic and is characterized by a demand curve that is perfectly horizontal (Figure 6–5).

FACTORS AFFECTING PRICE ELASTICITY OF DEMAND

The first and perhaps most important factor influencing the price elasticity of a good is the degree of substitution between it and other goods. The larger the number and the better the substitutes that exist for a good or service, the more elastic that particular good or service.

To understand the economic rationale of this generalization, consider a product that has many substitutes: pork chops, for example. When the price of pork chops rises, consumers have many alternative products to choose from—other cuts of pork; other meats, such as beef, poultry, and fish; as well

FIGURE 6–4 Perfectly Inelastic Demand

as other protein in place of meat, such as cheese or vegetables. A rise in the price of pork chops provides an incentive for consumers to reduce pork chop consumption and increase their consumption of alternative products. When pork chop consumption declines, it indicates that consumers are responding to the rising price of pork chops. This is the meaning of an elastic demand.

Products that have few or poor substitutes, on the other hand, tend to have an inelastic demand. Salt is the classic example of such a good. If the price of salt rises, consumers still have to buy it in about the same amounts since it has no satisfactory substitute. This means that consumers are not responsive to a

FIGURE 6–5 Perfectly Elastic Demand

change in the price of salt, which is another way of saying that salt has an inelastic demand.

The definition of a product also influences its elasticity. In general, the more broadly we define a product, the lower its price elasticity. This is because there are fewer substitutes for a broadly defined product than for a narrowly defined product. For example, the price elasticity for all pork would be smaller (less elastic or more inelastic) than it is for only pork chops. The substitutes for pork chops include pork loins, pork roasts, and pork substitutes, whereas the substitutes for all pork include only other meats or meat substitutes. Similarly, the demand for a particular brand of salt is more elastic than for all salt because brand X, for example, has substitutes in other brands of salt.

The second major factor influencing product elasticity is the proportion of the consumer's budget accounted for by the product. Products that take up a small proportion of the budget tend to be less elastic than products that rank high in the budget. For example, if the price of paper clips doubles, the impact on your budget's imperceptible; hence there is no strong incentive to reduce your use of paper clips. Yet, if something like the rent in a residence hall rises considerably, you might have to find an alternative place to stay, such as an apartment or a private home, and you might have to leave school. Thus, we would expect the demand for residence hall rooms to be more elastic than the demand for paper clips.

A summary of the effect of these two factors on the price elasticity of demand is presented in this table:

Factor	Effect on price elasticity
Many good substitutes	Increase
Large item in budget	Increase

PRICE ELASTICITY AND TOTAL REVENUE

One of the most valuable uses of price elasticity is that it helps predict what will happen to the total expenditure on a product by consumers, or the total revenue going to the product's sellers when its price changes. To understand how elasticity is related to changes in total expenditure or revenue, understand that a price change has two offsetting effects on total revenue or expenditure. Consider the case of a decline in price. Before the price falls, total revenue is defined as:

$$TR = P_0 \times Q_0$$

FIGURE 6–6   Price Reduction with Inelastic Demand

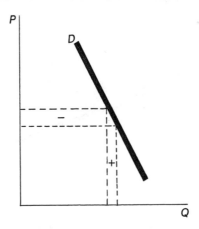

where *TR* is total revenue and P_0 and Q_0 are beginning price and quantity. After the price falls, total revenue is defined as:

$$TR = P_1 \times Q_1$$

where P_1 and Q_1 are the new price and quantity, respectively.

The reduction in price reduces total consumer expenditures or revenue. If the demand curve is downward sloping, however, the reduction in price leads to an increase in quantity sold, and the increase in quantity pulls total revenue back up. If demand is elastic, quantity increases by a larger percentage than price decreases; in this case, total revenue increases with a price reduction. The opposite occurs when demand is inelastic. In that case, a price reduction results in a decrease in total revenue because quantity increases by a smaller percentage than price decreases.

Figures 6–6 and 6–7 illustrate the relationship between price elasticity and total revenue or expenditure by means of demand curves. The area denoted by a minus sign represents a downturn of total revenue, whereas the plus area represents the augmentation of total revenue due to the price fall. In Figure 6–6 representing inelastic demand, the minus area outweighs the plus area, resulting in a reduction in total revenue. The opposite occurs in Figure 6–7, where the plus area outweighs the minus area because of the elastic demand.

We would observe the opposite change in total revenue if we considered a price increase. Here, an inelastic demand would create an increase in total revenue because price would increase more than quantity would decrease. Similarly, a price rise with elastic demand results in a decrease in total revenue. The relationship between price elasticity of demand and total revenue is summarized in the table on p. 74.

FIGURE 6–7 Price Reduction with Elastic Demand

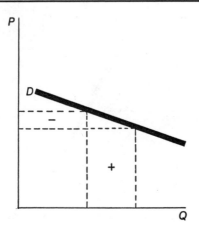

Price elasticity of demand	Change in total revenue or expenditure
Elastic demand	
Price fall	Increase
Price rise	Decrease
Inelastic demand	
Price fall	Decrease
Price rise	Increase

Notice that for an elastic demand, price and total revenue or expenditure change in opposite directions, whereas for an inelastic demand, they change in the same direction.

A CHANGE OR SHIFT IN DEMAND

Remember that whenever a demand curve is conceived of or drawn, everything that might influence the relationship between price and quantity is assumed to remain unchanged. This restriction is necessary in using a two-dimensional diagram; in other words, only two items can be considered at a time. With demand, these items are price and quantity. The world, of course, is never so kind as to hold everything constant other than the two items we are interested in. There are a number of factors that influence the price-quantity

FIGURE 6–8   Shifts in Demand

relationship by shifting the entire demand curve from one position to another. Before we consider these factors, it is useful to illustrate the two possible shifts in demand.

Think of D_1 in Figure 6–8 as a demand curve for a good or service during some time period. Then suppose that the demand changes position, say to D_2. This represents an increase, or an upward shift, in demand. One way of interpreting this shift is that buyers will take more off the market at any given price. For example, with the original demand, D_1, quantity Q_1 is demanded at price P_1. Now, with D_2, demanders will buy a larger quantity, Q_2, at price P_1. A second way of looking at an increase in demand is that buyers are willing to pay a higher price for a given quantity. With the increase in demand, buyers will pay price P_2 for quantity Q_1. At the original demand, buyers would pay P_1 for this quantity.

The meaning of a decrease in demand, as illustrated by D_0, is strictly parallel to an increase. At a given price, say P_1, the quantity demanded declines from Q_1 to Q_0. Or, looking at it the second way, the price buyers will pay for quantity Q_1 declines from P_1 to P_0.

There are five major factors or demand shifters that can cause the demand curve to shift from one position to another. They include changes in:

1. Money incomes of consumers.
2. Prices of related goods.
3. Consumer expectations regarding future prices and incomes.
4. Tastes and preferences.
5. Number of consumers.

A more thorough discussion of how and why they shift the demand curve is provided in Chapter 11.

INCOME ELASTICITY OF DEMAND

As noted above, changes in consumers' money incomes is an important demand shifter. To measure the responsiveness of consumers to income changes, economists have developed the concept of income elasticity. *Income elasticity* is defined as the percent change in demand resulting from each 1 percent change in money income. This concept is related to price elasticity of demand. The difference is that price elasticity measures the responsiveness of consumers to price changes as one moves up or down along a given demand curve, while income elasticity measures the responsiveness of consumers to income changes as the demand curve shifts from one position to another as illustrated by Figure 6–9. The increase in demand from D_0 to D_1 is assumed to have been caused by an income increase, I_0 to I_1. The resulting quantity change, Q_0 to Q_1, is measured at a given price, say P_0. The income elasticity formula is:

$$E_I = \frac{\% \ \Delta \ \text{quantity}}{\% \ \Delta \ \text{income}}$$

where E_I stands for income elasticity. Notice that it is similar to the price elasticity formula except % Δ P is written in the denominator. For computational purposes, the above formula is written as:

$$E_I = \frac{\dfrac{Q_0 - Q_1}{Q_0}}{\dfrac{I_0 - I_1}{I_0}}$$

It may be helpful to insert actual numbers in this formula to illustrate how income elasticity is computed. Suppose a family increases its purchase of beef from 200 to 225 pounds per year as a result of an increase in annual income

FIGURE 6-9   Income Elasticity Illustrated

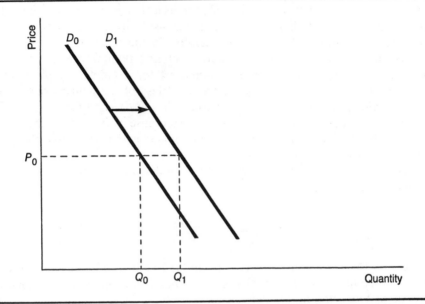

from \$14,000 to \$15,000. In this formula, Q_0 would be 20, Q_1 225, I_0 \$14,000, and I_1 \$15,000. In this example, income elasticity is 1.76, as shown by the following computations. The 1.76 means that this family increases its beef consumption by 1.76 percent when its income increases by 1 percent.

$$E_I = \frac{\dfrac{200 - 225}{200}}{\dfrac{14,000 - 15,000}{14,000}} = \frac{\dfrac{-25}{200}}{\dfrac{-1,000}{14,000}} = \frac{-0.125}{-0.071} = 1.76$$

An increase in money income can cause a demand curve to either increase, decrease, or remain constant. If demand increases when income increases as in the above example, income elasticity is a positive number. Such goods are referred to as *superior* or *normal* goods. Most items fit this description. However, there are some goods that exhibit a decrease in demand when income increases. In this case, income elasticity is negative. An example might be starchy foods; people tend to buy fewer starches as they become more affluent, buying instead more fresh vegetables and meat. It is possible that demand may not shift at all when income increases; Income elasticity is zero. Food, as a composite commodity in a high-income nation, is frequently used as an example of a good with a zero-income elasticity. People can eat just so much; with higher incomes, they usually don't eat more food.

CROSS ELASTICITY OF DEMAND

The second of the major demand shifters is a change in the price of related goods. There are two kinds of related goods—substitutes and complements. Two goods are substitutes when an *increase* in the price of one causes an increase in the demand for the other. Beef and poultry are examples of substitutes. When the price of beef increases, for example, people tend to increase their consumption of poultry and eat less of the higher-priced beef. This behavior is represented by an increase in the demand for poultry. The responsiveness of poultry consumption to an increase in the price of the beef is measured by the cross elasticity of poultry demand with respect to a change in the price of beef.

The formula expressing cross elasticity of demand is similar to price and income elasticity formulas:

$$E_{cd} = \frac{\% \, \Delta \, Q_i}{\% \, \Delta \, P_j}$$

where E_{cd}, the cross elasticity coefficient, is found by dividing the percent change in the quantity of good i by the percent change in the price of good j, i and j being two different goods.

To illustrate how E_{cd} is computed, consider a situation where the price of beef increases to $2.25 per pound from $2 per pound. Suppose this causes a family to increase poultry consumption, say, from 100 pounds to 125 pounds per year. The cross elasticity of demand for poultry with respect to a change in the price of beef (E_{cd}) is calculated as follows:

$$E_{cd} = \frac{\dfrac{100 - 125}{100}}{\dfrac{\$2.00 - 2.25}{2.00}} = \frac{-\dfrac{25}{100}}{-\dfrac{0.25}{2.00}} = \frac{-0.25}{-0.125} = 2.0$$

The E_{cd} coefficient of 2.0 means that the quantity demanded of poultry changes by 2 percent for each 1 percent change in the price of beef. The cross-elasticity coefficient for substitutes is a positive number reflecting that when the price of a substitute good increases, consumers will buy more of the good in question and less of the substitute.

The diagram illustrating cross elasticity is essentially the same as Figure 6–9, which illustrates income elasticity. The only difference is that the increase in demand for poultry is caused by an increase in the price of a substitute, beef, rather than income. Also note that the change in quantity of poultry resulting from the increase in the price of beef is measured at a given price of poultry, such as P_0 in Figure 6–9.

Two goods are complements if an *increase* in the price of one causes a *decrease* in the demand for the other. Bacon and eggs are complements. If the price of bacon increases, for example, people tend to buy less bacon and, as a result, they may have eggs for breakfast less frequently. Consequently, there is a decrease in the demand for eggs. The calculation of the cross-elasticity coefficient for complements is exactly the same as for substitutes except now the answer is negative.

To summarize the elasticity discussion, there are three elasticities that are commonly used by economists in the general area of demand:

1. Price elasticity of demand.
2. Income elasticity of demand.
3. Cross elasticity of demand.

GLOSSARY

demand   A negative relationship between price and quantity.

market demand   Summation at each price of the quantities demanded by all buyers in the market.

price elasticity of demand   Percent change in quantity resulting from a one-percent change in price.

income elasticity of demand   Percent change in demand resulting from a one-percent change in money income.

superior goods   Goods that people buy more of when their incomes increase; they exhibit a positive income elasticity.

inferior goods   Goods that people buy less of when their incomes increase; they exhibit a negative income elasticity.

cross elasticity of demand   Percent change in demand resulting from a one-percent change in the price of a related good.

substitutes   An increase in the price of one good causes an increase in the demand for the other good. They exhibit a positive cross elasticity of demand.

complements   An increase in the price of one good causes a decrease in the demand for the other good. They exhibit a negative cross elasticity of demand.

QUESTIONS

1. What is demand?

2. Is the downward-sloping demand curve consistent with the utility maximizing rule? Explain.

3. *What are the two factors which underlay the negative relationship between price and quantity along a demand curve?*

4. a. *What is price elasticity of demand?*
   b. *Define elastic and inelastic demand.*
   c. *Compute the price elasticity of demand from the following diagram and explain what the coefficient means:*

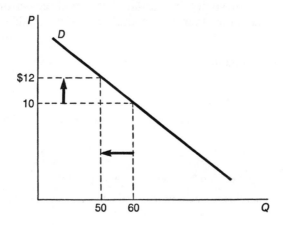

5. a. *Which would likely be more elastic: the demand for all cars as a group or the demand for Volkswagens? Explain.*
   b. *Which would likely be more elastic: the demand by students for paper clips or the demand for student housing on campus? Explain.*

6. *On most weekdays during the baseball season, professional baseball teams tend to play to less than sellout crowds. Assuming that the demand curve for baseball tickets is downward sloping, wouldn't the baseball teams take in more money by lowering their ticket prices to fill their stadiums? Explain.*

7. a. *What is income elasticity of demand?*
   b. *Compute the income elasticity of demand from the information on the accompanying diagram and explain what the coefficient means. Assume D_0 corresponds to a $20,000 annual income and D_1 to $24,000.*

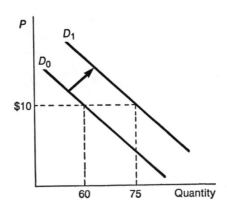

8. a. *What is cross elasticity of demand?*
   b. *What are goods called that exhibit a positive cross elasticity of demand? A negative elasticity?*

PART THREE
Producer Choice

CHAPTER 7

Cost Minimization

OVERVIEW

In this chapter and the following three chapters, techniques similar to the previous three chapters are applied to producers and supply. This chapter presents the cost-minimizing rule—how producers can produce a given level of output at the least possible cost. The law of diminishing returns, an important concept relating to production and supply, also is presented.

We turn our attention from the consumer to the producer. Just as the theory of consumer behavior is based on the assumption of utility maximization, the cornerstone of production theory is profit maximization. This assumption is not intended to cast the producer as a greedy, self-serving individual interested only in his or her own welfare. Business people are probably no more greedy or self-serving than any other group in society. Consumers try to do the best they can with the knowledge and resources at their disposal; business people have similar aspirations.

For a business to maximize profits, it must first minimize the cost of producing each unit of output. The rule for minimizing costs has much in common with the utility maximizing rule of Chapter 4. But, before presenting the cost-minimizing rule, it is necessary to lay the groundwork with some basic production relationships. We begin with the concept of production.

PRODUCTION DEFINED

Production is defined as any activity that creates present and/or future utility. This all-inclusive concept of production includes the activities of conventional businesses. The output of the automobile manufacturer yields utility because of the transportation services it provides. The auto dealer provides utility by making the product more accessible to car buyers. If a business did not produce as much utility as its consumers thought it was worth, it would soon go out of business. Most other activities also involve production as defined above. The dentist who fills a tooth may not create present utility, but the act does create future utility by preventing a toothache. The artist, in painting a picture, creates present utility for himself or herself and future utility for others who view the work. The symphony orchestra and vocalist create utility by the production of harmonious sound. The author creates future utility for others who learn from and/or enjoy reading his or her works. The typist creates utility by making words readable for others.

The activities of homemakers represent a large and important form of production. Utility is created by the preparation of meals, the rearing of children, and the many other activities homemakers perform that enhance their lives and their families. Students take part in a production process by studying and attending classes. The knowledge and experience that are acquired or produced impart both a present and a future utility. Present utility is created by the satisfaction of learning something new or gaining new experiences. Future utility stems from an increased awareness and understanding of the world, as well as from widened economic opportunities made possible by increased earning power. Teachers also perform a production activity by facilitating the assimilation of knowledge by students. Even sleeping creates utility and, as a result, it is a production activity. Production characterizes just about every activity of our lives.

While it is not correct to limit the concept of production to only items we can package, pile up, or count, there are activities that should not be classified as production as far as society is concerned. The arsonist, for example, may derive some satisfaction from burning down a building, but such an activity usually reduces utility for other people. The same is true for the thief. Activities that destroy property or human beings or forcibly transfer wealth from one person to another are better described as destructive rather than productive.

INPUTS IN PRODUCTION

In any production activity, there must be inputs that are either transformed or utilized in some way to produce an output. In economics, inputs are also referred to as resources or factors of production. All three names apply to the same thing.

In a modern, economically developed economy, most inputs are the product of some other production activity. For example, the steel in automobiles is an output of the steel industry. Even the human input in production has been modified or improved by some past training, whether it be formal schooling or informal knowledge gained from family, workers, or experience. Knowledge also is the output of a production activity, as we will see in Chapter 24.

Most production utilizes several inputs at the same time or in some time sequence. In fact, it is difficult to think of an example where production occurs with just one input. One example that comes close is the production of sound by a vocalist. But even this is not strictly correct, since the singer utilizes energy obtained from food, which should also be considered an input.

For descriptive purposes, inputs can be grouped or classified in several ways. One common classification is that of land, labor, and capital. Land can be seen as the resource provided by nature, including the minerals, petroleum, and water found therein. It is recognized, that land is seldom used in its natural state, except perhaps in the production of utility as a wilderness area. Labor is the services provided by human beings. Capital generally is defined as durable, reproducible resources such as buildings, machines, and tools. However, both land and labor also include considerable capital or man-made improvements. We will see in Chapter 22 that education involves the production of human capital. Land may have to undergo considerable change such as clearing, leveling, or draining before it can be used as an input. In the production of nonagricultural products, land is often treated as a capital input, resulting in two main types of inputs: labor and capital.

It is useful to group inputs into two other categories: fixed and variable inputs. In most production processes, it is possible to identify certain inputs that contribute to production that, for the period under consideration, cannot be increased or decreased to change the level of output. These are called *fixed inputs. Variable inputs*, as the name implies, can be varied according to the desired level of output. For example, in manufacturing, the building is considered a fixed input because it cannot be readily changed to a different size; and variable inputs include labor, materials, and fuel. Over a long period, the building can be changed in size or a new one can be constructed, so eventually even a fixed input can become variable. We will emphasize the distinction between fixed and variable inputs and the importance of time to this classification in the discussion that follows.

PRODUCTION WITH ONE VARIABLE INPUT

In developing basic concepts of production, it is easiest to begin with the simplest case: production with one variable input. It is impossible to visualize a realistic example of production using just one input. But, it is possible to imagine a situation in which one or more *fixed* inputs such as land or some physical facility are combined with one *variable* input, such as labor, in the production of an output.

As a specific example of such production, consider a small manufacturing establishment engaged in the production of cookies. Assume there is one variable input—labor—and everything else such as machines, tools, and the building is fixed, except the raw materials and energy to manufacture the cookies, which we will assume are available in unlimited quantities. The relationship we are interested in is between the input of labor and the output of cookies.

Production Function

A production function is a physical relationship between inputs and output. If you know the production function and you specify the amount of the input, it tells how much output is forthcoming. It is imperative, therefore, that the owner or manager of a business have a good idea of the firm's production function. Without this information, it is impossible to minimize costs and maximize profits.

TABLE 7–1   Production Function

(1) Labor input (days)	(2) Cookie output (TPP)	(3) Marginal physical product (MPP)	(4) Average physical product (APP)
0	0	—	—
10	100	10	10
20	800	70	40
30	2000	120	67
40	2900	90	73
50	3600	70	72
60	4200	60	70
70	4600	40	66
80	4800	20	60
90	4800	0	53
100	4500	−30	45

A. Total Physical Product.   The production function stating the relationship between the labor input and cookie output is given in columns 1 and 2 of Table 7–1. Assume these are weekly figures. As the labor input increases up to the 90th labor day, the output of cookies also increases. The figures in column 2 are called total physical product (TPP). Notice that TPP increases rapidly at first, then continues to increase at a decreasing rate, and finally begins to decline after the 90th day of labor.

The relationship between labor input and TPP is also shown in Figure 7–1. As labor is increased, the TPP curve increases at an increasing rate up to 30 days of labor. Between 30 and 90 days of labor, TPP still increases but at a decreasing rate. TPP reaches a maximum at 90 days and then begins to decline.

This general relationship between labor and output is typical for most production activities. When a small amount of labor is available, it has to do a variety of jobs. Therefore, no person becomes proficient at any one job. Or, people may have to do tasks they are not trained to do. As more labor is added, in this example, up to 30 days per week, greater specialization is possible, and perhaps all the machines are working at least eight hours per day. Thus, output increases more rapidly than labor increases.

As more labor is added, holding constant the size of the building and the number of machines, output can still increase—but not as rapidly as initially. Crowding occurs. People have to wait to use a piece of equipment or occupy a space. At some point, as more labor is added, people begin to get in each

FIGURE 7–1   Physical Product Curves

(A) Total physical product

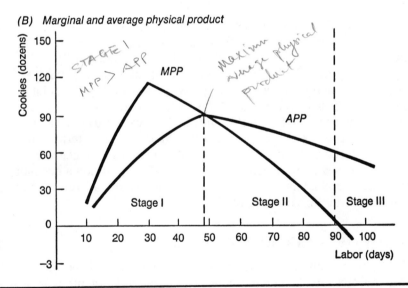

(B) Marginal and average physical product

other's way. The crowding problem can become so severe that total output declines. In this example, such a point is reached after 90 labor days per week.

B. Marginal Physical Product.   The exact relationship between increases in labor input and output can be measured more precisely by marginal physical production (MPP). MPP of an input is defined as the additional output obtained by adding one more unit of the input holding constant all other inputs. MPP is calculated by the following formula (Δ means change in):

$$MPP = \frac{\Delta \text{ output}}{\Delta \text{ input}}$$ *Slope of curve*

The MPP of labor in the production of cookies in this example is presented in column 3 of Table 7–1. Notice that MPP first increases, reaches a maximum, declines over a wide range of output, becomes zero, and then turns negative when total output declines as more labor is added. MPP describes the rate and direction of change of TPP.[1]

C. Average Physical Product.   Average physical product of an input (APP) is total output (TPP) divided by the total unit of the input used up to that point.

$$APP = \frac{\text{output}}{\text{input}}$$ *y/x*

The relationship between APP and MPP is shown in Figure 7–1. When MPP is above APP, APP is increasing. When MPP is below APP, APP decreases. Thus, MPP must intersect APP at the maximum APP.

The easiest way to understand the relationship between MPP and APP is to think of your grade point average (GPA). Say your overall grade point average is 3.0 out of a possible 4.0. If your GPA for the present term turns out to be above 3.0, your overall GPA will be pulled a little over 3.0 after including this term's grades. Conversely, if you earn less than a 3.0 this term, after these grades are factored in, your overall GPA will be pulled a little below 3.0. Thus, the marginal or last quarter pulls your overall GPA up or down depending on whether the marginal is above or below the overall average. The same relationship is true for APP and MPP.

THE LAW OF DIMINISHING RETURNS

Economists define the law of diminishing returns as follows: As more of a variable input is added, holding constant the quantity of other inputs, the additional output forthcoming from each additional unit of that input will lessen beyond some point.

---

[1] For persons who have had calculus, MPP is the first derivative of TPP.

This definition refers to a decrease in the MPP of an input. The law of diminishing returns is nothing more than the phenomenon of decreasing MPP.

The law of diminishing returns is to production what diminishing marginal utility is to consumption. These two propositions are the bedrock of all microeconomics—diminishing marginal utility on the consumer and demand side, and diminishing returns on the production and supply side.

Because of the importance of the law of diminishing returns to economics, how can we be sure that it exists? The best proof is the absence of any counter examples. If the law of diminishing returns did not exist, the world's production of cookies could occur in an 8' × 10' room, and the world's supply of wheat could be produced in a flower pot. We do not see such absurd conditions, which is evidence that the law of diminishing returns is a valid proposition.

The Three Stages of Production

Economists classify the levels of input use into three stages of production. As shown in Figure 7–1B, Stage I includes the area of increasing returns and extends to the point where the MPP curve intersects the APP curve. At this point, APP is at a maximum. Notice that Stage I includes a portion of the MPP curve that is declining. The distinguishing characteristic of Stage I is that MPP is greater than APP. As long as the marginal unit is greater than the overall average, the average will always increase.

The distinguishing characteristic of Stage II in Figure 7–1B is that MPP is everywhere less than APP. This results in the continual decline of APP. Stage II ends at the point where MPP becomes negative. Stage III begins where the MPP curve crosses the horizontal axis and extends to the right indefinitely as the negative MPP continues to pull APP down, approaching zero but never reaching it.

The significance of the three stages of production will be clearer when we relate them to the concept of supply in Chapter 10. For now, we have to settle for an intuitive explanation of their importance. No producer would want to be in Stage III. This is evident from the example in Table 7–1. By adding the 100th day of labor, total output actually declines. A person would be better off to go fishing or to stay in bed than to put in a day of work that brings negative results.

No producer would want to operate in Stage I, although the reason why is less clear than for Stage III. Consider the region of increasing returns. If it paid to produce any quantity at all, it would always pay to increase the level of the variable input until the product was past the level of increasing returns. As long as a producer is in the region of increasing returns, each additional unit of input adds more to output. Thus, the more input that is added, the more efficient production becomes, and the cheaper it is to produce the added output. Consequently, it would be foolish to stop adding the variable input when in the region of increasing returns.

We have established that a rational, profit-maximizing producer would add enough of the variable input to go past the region of increasing returns but would stop adding before entering Stage III, the region of negative marginal physical product. Thus, a producer will always produce in the region of diminishing returns. Moreover, if it pays to produce at all, a producer will always avoid Stage I, even though this stage may contain a small region of diminishing returns (as shown in Figure 7–1B). For the moment, we will assert this and wait until Chapter 10 to show why it is true. Note that production always occurs in Stage II.

PRODUCTION WITH TWO VARIABLE INPUTS

Although the example of production with one variable is a useful starting point to develop the basic concepts of production, all production activities involve two or more variable inputs. Because our main interest in this chapter is choosing the mix of inputs that yield a given output for the least possible cost, we must expand the original example to focus on this decision. We can retain the cookie example by allowing machines to be a variable input with labor. The building size is still held constant, and we continue to assume that the raw materials and energy to produce the cookies are available in unlimited quantities.

We will also assume that it is possible to use various alternative combinations of labor and machine hours. For example, if few or no machine hours are utilized, a large amount of labor would be needed to produce a given amount of output, whereas with more machine inputs the same output could be obtained with less labor. Having two or more variable inputs that can be used in different proportions brings us face to face with the main question of this chapter: What mix of inputs will produce a given level of output at the least possible cost?

COST–MINIMIZING RULE

To answer this question, we need two pieces of information: (1) the MPP of each input at the various input levels and (2) the price of each input. The MPP of an input is the units of output resulting from the use of one more unit of that input. Because of the law of diminishing returns, the MPP of each input eventually becomes smaller as more of the input is added. In measuring the MPP of an input when there are two or more variable inputs, it is necessary that the quantity of all other inputs is held constant—except the one being varied. The MPP of one input will likely be influenced by the level at which the other input is held constant, however. We will return to this point in Chapter 18.

The decision of how much of each input to use to produce a given level of output also depends on the price of each input. Even if an input contributes a lot to output (has a high MPP), it may cost so much that it does not pay to use much of it. Thus, a producer must consider both the MPP of each input and its cost in deciding how much of each to use in producing a given level of output. It makes sense to utilize a relatively large amount of an input that exhibits a high MPP (for a given input and output level) and is relatively cheap. This notion is made more specific when placed in the context of the *cost-minimizing rule*. To minimize costs at any given level of output, the inputs should be used such that the ratio of the price of each input to its MPP is equal for all inputs, as indicated below:

$$\frac{P_a}{MPP_a} = \frac{P_b}{MPP_b} = \cdots = \frac{P_z}{MPP_z}$$

It is easiest to see why the cost-minimizing rule holds true if we choose a situation where the above equalities are not met. Suppose the P/MPP ratios for labor and machines in the production of cookies are as follows:

Labor

$$\frac{P}{MPP} = \frac{\$60}{30} = \$2 \text{ per dozen.}$$

Machines

$$\frac{P}{MPP} = \frac{\$500}{400} = \$1.25 \text{ per dozen.}$$

The labor ratio tells us that another unit (day) of labor costs $60 and that this labor can produce 30 dozen cookies. Thus, the cost of producing one more dozen by adding a little more labor is $2. The P/MPP ratio for machines has the same meaning. Here, the cost of producing another dozen by adding a machine costs $1.25.

Suppose that labor and machines can be varied in small units. Enough machines can be added to produce one more dozen and labor can be reduced slightly to produce one less dozen. Now see what happens:

Produce one less dozen by labor: saves $2
Produce one more dozen by machine: adds $1.25

After making this adjustment, the same number of cookies are produced as before, but at a seventy-five cents savings in cost, for the last dozen. Therefore, if the P/MPP ratios are not all the same, it is always possible to reduce unit costs of production by using a little more of the low-ratio inputs and a little less of the inputs exhibiting high ratios.

How does this adjustment reestablish a cost-minimizing equilibrium? By using more of the low-ratio input, its MPP declines because of the law of diminishing returns. This, in turn, causes the size of the P/MPP ratio to increase. Conversely, using less of the high-ratio input causes its MPP to increase which, in turn, causes its P/MPP to decline. At some point, the two ratios will converge and costs for a given level of output will be minimized. The cost-minimizing rule does not indicate the specific amount of each input to be used. This decision must be made by management. But the rule brings out the information that is necessary to make the decision.

Notice the similarity between the utility maximizing rule of Chapter 4 and the cost-minimizing rule just presented. Both require the equality of ratios—MU/P for utility maximization and P/MPP for cost minimization.

GLOSSARY

production   Any activity that creates present and/or future utility.

production function   A physical relationship between inputs and output.

total physical product (TPP)   Physical units of output.

marginal physical product   The additional output obtained from one additional unit of the input.

average physical product   Output divided by the input.

law of diminishing returns   Diminishing marginal physical product.

stage I   MPP exceeds APP, and APP is pulled up.

stage II   MPP less than APP, and APP is pulled down.

stage III   MPP is negative.

cost-minimizing rule   All P/MPP ratios are equal.

QUESTIONS

1. a. What is production?
*   b. In each of the following activities, identify what is being produced and the major inputs:*
*   (1) Baking a cake.   (3) Eating.*
*   (2) Attending college. (4) Sleeping.*

2. a. What is marginal physical product (MPP)?
*   b. From the figures below, calculate the MPP of labor for each level of labor input:*

Labor	Output
0	0
1	100
2	190
3	160

3. *In what units is the marginal physical product of labor measured in the production of:*
   a. *Wheat*   c. *Houses*
   b. *Haircuts*   d. *Dental services*

4. a. *What is the law of diminishing returns?*
   b. *What evidence is there to suggest that it exists?*

5. *Delineate the three stages of production using the MPP and APP curves.*

6. *Will increasing a variable input in its region of diminishing returns lead to an increase or a decrease in total output? Explain. (Assume the input is in Stage II.)*

7. a. *What is the cost-minimizing rule?*
   b. *What is the economic meaning of the input price/MPP ratio?*
   c. *Why is the cost of producing a given level of output using two or more inputs not at a minimum if the rule is not met?*

8. *Consider the following information:*

	MPP	Input price
Capital	25	$75
Labor	20	80

   a. *Is the given level of output being produced at the least possible cost? Why or why not?*
   b. *By what means is the high P/MPP ratio reduced and the low ratio increased when inputs are rearranged to satisfy the cost-minimizing rule?*

CHAPTER 8

Substitution among Inputs

OVERVIEW

When the prices of inputs change relative to one another, producers have an incentive to substitute the cheaper ones for more expensive inputs. This chapter provides a framework for categorizing substitution possibilities among inputs. This framework is called isoquants. It has much in common with indifference curves.

ISOQUANTS

An *isoquant* is a line showing the possible combinations of two inputs that can be used to produce a given level of output. Since *iso* means equal, a more literal translation of the term is equal quantity. Returning to the cookie production example, consider the possible ways of producing a given level of output, say 500 dozen cookies. At one extreme, you might utilize a lot of labor and a small amount of machine services. This possibility is illustrated by the 60 labor—one machine combination in Figure 8–1. Or one could visualize the other extreme of using a large amount of machine services with a relatively small amount of labor, as indicated by the ten labor—seven machine combination. The first situation would be described as a *labor-intensive* method of production while the second would be called *capital-intensive*. Of course, there may well be many other possible combinations of inputs for producing the 500 dozen, such as the 30 labor and three machine combination.

Choosing a higher level of output such as 1,000 dozen would require larger amounts of one or both inputs. As shown by Figure 8–1, 1,000 dozen could be produced by 40 days of labor and $4\frac{1}{2}$ machine days. Whatever the level of output, each isoquant tells us the possible combinations of the two inputs that can be used to produce that output.

Substitution Possibilities

A. Imperfect Substitution. The particular shape of the isoquant is of interest at this point. Notice in Figure 8–1 that each isoquant is drawn convex to the origin. This implies that the two inputs are *imperfect substitutes* for one another in the production of cookies. They are called imperfect substitutes because it takes more of the abundant input to compensate for the loss of each successive unit reduction of the scarce input. As you move down along the labor axis, more machine days are required to compensate for the loss of each unit of labor. Moving from 60 to 50 days of labor requires only about one-half extra machine day to compensate for the loss of 10 days of labor. But moving from 20 to 10 days of labor requires about two and one-half extra machine days. The same relationship is true for increasing labor and decreasing machine time.

The necessity of using more of the abundant input to substitute for the loss of each unit of scarce input has intuitive appeal. The abundant input must be pressed into service on tasks for which it may not be well-suited. Hence, it takes a larger amount of the input to do the job. The distinguishing characteristic of inputs that are imperfect substitutes is the progressively increasing amount of the abundant input required to substitute for the loss of each unit of the scarce input. The isoquant is a close relative of the indifference curve presented in Chapter 5. Also, the meaning of imperfect substitutes is similar. One deals with goods and utility, the other one deals with inputs and output.

Before leaving imperfect substitutes, let's look at how to substitute machines (capital) for labor or vice versa. At first, one might argue that machines and labor have to be used together in a one-to-one ratio because it

FIGURE 8–1 Isoquants of Labor and Machine Inputs (cookie production example)

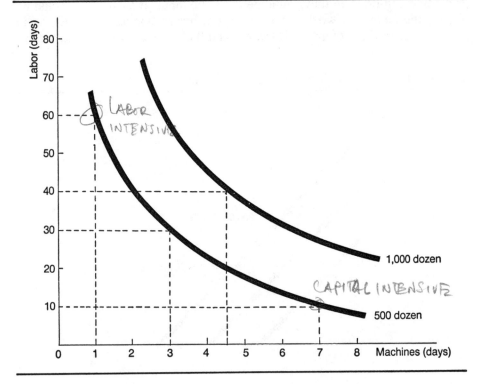

always takes a person to operate a machine. Although machines require operators, there are two ways that a substitution can occur. First, it is possible to utilize machines for an increasing number of tasks. In manufacturing, one can visualize labor-intensive, hand-crafted operations at one extreme and highly automated facilities where complex machines or robots do the work. A second way to substitute capital for labor is to utilize larger machines to accomplish a given task. Even though larger machines require an operator, the task is completed in a shorter time, which saves labor.

In the cookie production example, it is possible to envision a labor-intensive operation where the ingredients are mixed by hand and the cookies are baked and packaged by hand. A middle ground might be where a machine is used to mix the ingredients, form the cookies, and run them through an oven on a conveyor, with the packaging still done by hand. An even more sophisticated machine or machines might do all the tasks. Larger machines could turn out more cookies per hour with the same amount of labor—reducing the labor input per unit of output.

B.   Perfect Substitutes.   Perfect substitutes exist when the amount of one input required to compensate for a unit reduction of the other remains constant at all possible combinations. The ratio does not have to be one for one—just constant. It is difficult to think of realistic examples of inputs that are perfect substitutes; in practice they would be the same input. If such inputs could be found, the isoquants would be straight, downward-sloping lines such as in Figure 8–2. In this example, natural gas and fuel oil are perfect substitutes as

FIGURE 8–2   Isoquants Illustrating Perfect Substitutes

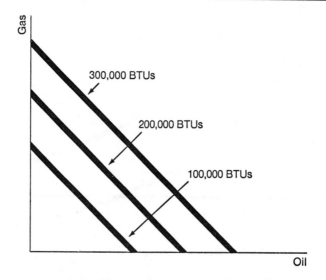

sources of energy for heat in baking cookies, as long as the equipment for using either or both fuels is in place.

C. Fixed Proportions. In this case, inputs cannot be substituted for each other. As the name implies, the inputs must be used together in a fixed ratio or proportion. Probably the most common examples of fixed proportions occur in manufacturing, where products require certain materials or ingredients. For example, a cotton shirt of a given size requires a certain amount of material, a certain number of buttons, etc. In a broader context, one can visualize substitution between different types of material, different buttons, and so on. The fixed-proportion case generally applies to inputs that are narrowly defined or in relatively short-run situations where it may not be possible or economically feasible to substitute one input for another.

Inputs that must be used in fixed proportions are represented by isoquants that are rectangular in shape, such as in Figure 8–3. This means that when more of one input is added, the other input cannot be decreased if the same level of output is to be maintained. Unless the other input also is increased, the input that is added is simply not used in the production process. Sugar and salt, shown in Figure 8–3, are examples of two inputs that are used in fixed proportions in cookie production.

Perfect substitutes and fixed proportions are the extreme or limiting cases of general imperfect substitutes. In the more general case, isoquants can vary in shape from a gentle curvature to a sharp curve. The less curvature of the isoquant, the closer it comes to the limiting case of perfect substitutes. Thus, an

FIGURE 8–3   Isoquants Illustrating Fixed Proportions

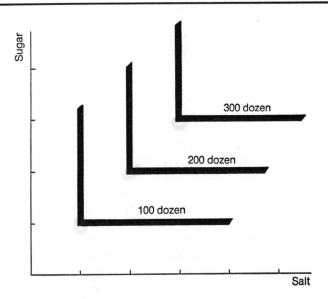

isoquant that exhibits a small amount of curvature represents the case of two inputs that can be readily substituted for each other. On the other hand, a sharply curved isoquant comes close to the case of fixed proportions, meaning that the possibility for substitution is limited.

ISOCOSTS

Although the isoquant is a useful device for representing the degree of substitution that exists between two inputs, it is also used to demonstrate the cost-minimizing rule. To do so, however, requires that we first construct the isocost line. An *isocost* line shows various combinations of two inputs that can be purchased for a given amount of money. As the name implies, it is a line showing equal costs.

To construct an isocost line, two pieces of information are required: (1) the price of each input and (2) the total amount of money to be spent on the inputs. If the total amount of money to be spent and the prices of the two inputs are known, the point of intersection between the isocost line and the two axes is easily determined. Consider a $1,000 sum of money. Also assume labor costs $50 per day, and machines cost $100 per day. If the entire $1,000 was spent on labor, 20 labor days could be purchased, $1,000/$50 = 20. If all the money was spent on machines, 10 machine days could be obtained, $1,000/100 = 10. The isocost line is always a downward-sloping straight line. Once the two end points are identified, the line can be drawn as shown in Figure 8–4. Larger and smaller costs are shown by higher and lower isocost lines, respectively.

Least–Cost Input Combination

The 500-dozen isoquant is superimposed on Figure 8–4. Compare this to the three isocost lines. The $600 isocost line does not come up to the 500-dozen isoquant. This means that it is not possible to produce 500 dozen with $600 worth of machines and labor. Next, consider the $1,200 isocost. For $1,200, it is possible to produce 500 dozen with various combinations of machines and labor ranging from the 10-machine 4-labor combination to the 4-machine 16-labor mix. But, it would be foolish to do so; The 500 dozen can be obtained in a cheaper way. The cheapest way to produce this level of output is determined by the point of tangency between the 500-dozen isoquant and the lowest possible isocost line, which is $1,000. The method entails the use of 5.4 machine days and 9.2 labor days. This combination costs $1,000.

In the preceding chapter, the cost-minimizing rule was presented using the P/MPP ratios. This rule is consistent with the point of tangency rule. Their equivalence is proven in the appendix to this chapter; the P/MPP ratios of labor and machines are equal only at the point of tangency. Therefore, we have shown the same concept with two techniques. The advantage of the isoquant-isocost technique is that it allows more precision regarding the degree of

FIGURE 8–4   Isocosts and Isoquants Showing Least-Cost Input Combination

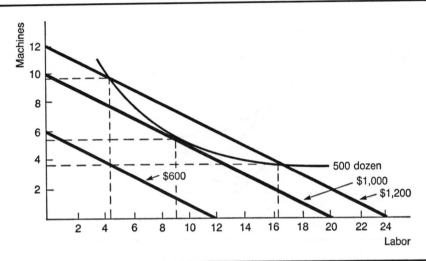

substitution and exact input combination that minimizes the cost of a given level of output.

Changing Input Prices

Another use of the isoquant-isocost technique is to show what happens to the least-cost input combination when the price of one input changes relative to the other input. In the example of Figure 8–4, suppose the price of labor increases to $100 per day, keeping the price of machines the same. This will cause the $1,000 isocost line to rotate in a clockwise fashion, intersecting the horizontal axis at a point closer to the origin. At the $100 price, $1,000 will purchase only 10 days of labor. The $1,000 isocost line still intersects the machine axis at 10 units because of the assumption that the machine price remains constant. The change in position of the $1,000 isocost line due to the increase in the price of labor is illustrated in Figure 8–5.

The increase in the labor price causes a steeper isocost line than the original and it is positioned down and to the left. Now, $1,000 will not be sufficient to produce 500 dozen cookies. The lowest possible isocost line that just touches or is tangent to the 500 unit isoquant is shown by the dashed line in Figure 8–5. It represents a higher cost—$1360 now (8 × $100 + 5.6 × $100 = $1,360).

Also notice that the least-cost input combination changes. Because of the increase in the price of labor, the least-cost combination now entails using more capital and less labor to produce a given output level. The previous combination that used to produce 500 units before the labor price increase now would

FIGURE 8–5   An Increase in the Price of Labor

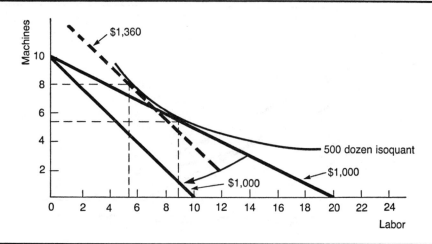

cost $1,460 (5.4 × $100 + 9.2 × $100 = $1,460). Thus, $100 was saved in the production of the 500 dozen by substituting machines for labor.

It should not be inferred from this example that the same level of output would continue to be produced when input prices change. The intention is to show how a change in input prices alters the cost-minimizing mix of inputs for a given level of output. In the next two chapters, we consider the profit-maximizing level of output and how this level changes when output and input prices change.

Notice the similarity between the material in Chapters 4 and 5 and 7 and 8. The consumer maximizes utility for a given budget by arranging his or her purchases such that the MU/P ratios are equalized, or the combination of goods consumed corresponds to the tangency point between the budget line and the highest possible indifference curve. The producer minimizes cost for a given level of output by utilizing inputs such that the P/MPP ratios are equalized, or the combination of inputs corresponds to the point of tangency between a given isoquant (given level of output) and the lowest possible isocost line. Both sets of decisions are similar.

GLOSSARY

isoquant   A line showing various combinations of two inputs that produce a given level of output.

imperfect substitutes   More of the abundant input must be used to compensate for each unit reduction in the scarce input to maintain a given level of output. They are represented by isoquants that are convex to the origin.

perfect substitutes The amount of one input required to compensate for a unit reduction in another input remains constant at all combinations of the two inputs. They are represented by isoquants that are straight, downward-sloping lines.

fixed proportions No substitution is possible. They are represented by rectangular isoquants.

isocost A straight, downward-sloping line that shows various combinations of two inputs that can be purchased with a given sum of money.

QUESTIONS

1. a. *What is an isoquant?*
   b. *What determines the shape of an isoquant?*
   c. *How is it possible to substitute capital for labor, and vice versa, if each machine must have an operator.*

2. *Draw isoquants for the following pairs of inputs in the production of automobiles, and explain why you have drawn them in a given shape.*
   a. *Capital and labor.*
   b. *Wheels and tires.*
   c. *Steel and aluminum.*

3. a. *What is an isocost line?*
   b. *Draw a $100 isocost line for two inputs assuming the price of input 1 is $10 and the price of input 2 is $25.*

4. *Using an isocost-isoquant diagram, illustrate the cost-minimizing mix of inputs for a given level of output.*

5. a. *What happens to the slope of an isocost line if the input represented on the horizontal axis increases in price?*
   b. *What happens to the cost of producing a given level of output when the price of an input increases?*
   c. *What happens to the cost-minimizing mix of inputs when the price of the input on the horizontal axis increases in price?*

APPENDIX: PROOF OF THE EQUIVALENCE OF THE COST-MINIMIZING RULE AND ISOQUANT-ISOCOST POINTS OF TANGENCY

The purpose of this appendix is to show that at the point of tangency between an isocost line and an isoquant, the input price/MPP ratios for the two inputs (X_1 and X_2) are equal.

Along an isocost line:

$$\Delta TC = P_{X_1} \cdot \Delta X_1 + P_{X_2} \cdot \Delta X_2 = 0,$$

Where: ΔTC is the change in total cost P_{X_1} and P_{X_2} are the prices of inputs X_1 and X_2, and ΔX_1 and ΔX_2 are the changes in inputs X_1 and X_2.
or:

$$\frac{\Delta X_1}{\Delta X_2} = - \frac{PX_2}{PX_1}$$

Since the slope of the isocost line is $\dfrac{\Delta X_1}{\Delta X_2}$, its slope is equal to $- \dfrac{P_{X_2}}{P_{X_1}}$.

Along an isoquant:

$$\Delta Q = \mathrm{MPP}_{X_1} \cdot \Delta X_1 + \mathrm{MPP}_{X_2} \cdot \Delta X_2 = 0,$$

or:

$$\frac{\Delta X_1}{\Delta X_2} = - \frac{\mathrm{MPP}_{X_2}}{\mathrm{MPP}_{X_1}}$$

Since the slope of an isoquant line is $\dfrac{\Delta X_1}{\Delta X_2}$, its slope is also equal to $- \dfrac{\mathrm{MPP}_{X_2}}{\mathrm{MPP}_{X_1}}$.

At the point of tangency between an isoquant and isocost line, the slopes of the two lines must be equal. Therefore, at the point of tangency:

$$\frac{P_{X_2}}{P_{X_1}} = \frac{\mathrm{MPP}_{X_2}}{\mathrm{MPP}_{X_1}}$$

Rearranging this expression, we obtain:

$$\frac{P_{X_1}}{\mathrm{MPP}_{X_1}} = \frac{P_{X_2}}{\mathrm{MPP}_{X_2}}$$

Therefore, at the point of tangency, the input price/MPP ratios are equal.

CHAPTER 9

Profit Maximization

OVERVIEW

In the last two chapters, the main question was how to produce a given level of output at the least possible cost. This chapter presents the profit-maximizing rule—how much output a firm should produce to maximize its total profits. To accomplish this objective, one must understand the various kinds of costs and profits. Hence, these concepts are discussed at the outset.

THE CLASSIFICATION OF COSTS

Explicit and Implicit

For descriptive purposes, production costs are commonly grouped into two categories: explicit and implicit. *Explicit costs* include all cash or out-of-pocket expenses incurred in production. Some examples of explicit costs are wages paid to hired labor, interest paid on borrowed money, rent on buildings, and the cost of supplies and raw materials purchased. These are the costs paid for purchased inputs—whether they are fixed or variable.

Implicit costs are the charge that should be made to the resources provided by the owner(s) of the firm. This charge can be measured by how much the resources could earn in the next best alternative use, that is, by their opportunity cost. Implicit costs are especially important for small owner-operated enterprises where the owner provides much or all of the labor and a good share of the capital. Just because a firm can earn enough to cover its explicit or out-of-pocket expenses for purchased inputs does not imply that the firm is making a profit.

Implicit costs also are important for corporations. In these firms, the stockholders are the owners. Therefore, the total cost to the firm should include the return that the money tied up in the firm's stock could earn in the next best alternative.

Fixed and Variable

Costs can also be classified according to whether they are fixed or variable. As mentioned in Chapter 7, inputs are commonly grouped according to these two categories. Since the purchase of inputs (including one's own time or facilities) is what gives rise to costs, it is reasonable to also classify costs by the same categories. Fixed costs are costs that do not change at various levels of output. Examples of fixed costs include depreciation on capital that occurs regardless of whether it is used; rent on property that must be paid regardless of use; and real estate taxes. Variable costs are costs that vary with the level of output. Examples include the cost of raw materials, fuel, and hired labor.

The items included in each category depend on the time period allowed for adjustment. In the short run, a greater proportion of all costs will fall in the fixed category than in the long run, where agreements and contracts expire, and the decision to purchase the inputs can be made anew. In the long run, all inputs become variable and all costs are variable.

PROFITS

Profits is a word that is used loosely and often means different things to different people. Because profits play an important role in production and supply, it is necessary to define what is meant by profits. In accounting, profits are defined as income minus expenses. (Depreciation on buildings and machines is included in expenses.) Most people think of profits in this way. Economists, however, define profits in a different manner. They begin by dividing profits into two categories: (1) normal profits and (2) pure profits.

Normal Profits

Normal profits are defined as the minimum return to the labor, capital, or other inputs contributed by the owner(s) of the firm needed to keep the inputs in a given production activity. By and large, normal profits are the same as implicit costs. They are exactly the same if resource owners are indifferent to where their resources are employed. However, owner-operators of small firms may like what they're doing or prefer to be their own bosses. In this case, they may be willing to accept a lower return from their own firms than they would earn as employees or stockholders of other firms. In this case, normal profits are less than implicit costs.

Pure Profits

Pure profits are defined as the return above all costs (explicit plus implicit). Pure profits exist because no one has perfect knowledge or knows the future with certainty. If knowledge was perfect and the future was certain, resources would gravitate to where they could earn the highest returns. As resources moved into the areas where returns were highest, the increase in production would cause output prices to decline along with the returns to resources. Conversely, as resources moved out of low-returns activities, the decrease in output would cause output price to increase along with the compensation to resources. When the earnings of each resource became equal in all activities, every resource would earn what it could in the next best alternative. Hence, there would be no pure profits.

Because knowledge is imperfect and the future uncertain, the possibility of pure profits provides the incentive for entrepreneurs and investors to take risks. Whenever there is risk, the possibilities of loss and gain exist. If there were no possibility of gain (pure profits), there would be no incentive to risk a possible loss. Pure profits also provide a source of funds to invest for increased output when an endeavor is successful. In such cases, it pays producers to increase output. As a source of investment funds, pure profits benefit society by making it possible to increase the output of goods and services that are most highly demanded.

Although pure profits have suffered from a bad press over the years, they play a beneficial role in society by providing an incentive to bear risk and as a source of investment funds. This is not to say that entrepreneurs and investors should be relieved of paying their share of taxes out of pure as well as normal profits. But, it generally is not in the best interest of society to regard pure profits as unnecessary or undesirable.

In the discussion on firms in Chapters 13 through 17, normal profits will be included in production costs unless otherwise stated. When we refer to profits in these chapters, we refer to pure profits—any earnings in excess of explicit plus implicit costs.

PROFIT RATES OF U.S. CORPORATIONS

There are two common methods of measuring and presenting profits. One is to divide the firm's annual accounting profits by its net worth (equity capital) to derive a rate of return on equity capital. This figure has the same interpretation as the rate of return on a savings account or money market fund. For example, a 10 percent return on equity capital means that each dollar invested in the firm by its owners earns 10 cents per year on the average after expenses. The second way is to divide accounting profits by the firm's sales. The resulting figure (multiplied by 100) indicates how many cents profit are earned on each dollar of sales. The after-tax profit rates of U.S. manufacturing corporations computed under both methods are presented in Table 9–1. Remember that these accounting profits represent a payment to the firm's resources—mainly capital.

From 1949 to 1986, the rate of return, after income taxes, on equity capital earned by U.S. manufacturing corporations averaged 11.7 percent. These firms earned, on the average less than five cents per dollar of sales. However, not all profits are paid out as dividends to stockholders. Some are returned to the firms to finance new investment. From 1946 to 1986, more than half the funds used for new investment came from internal sources, also called *retained earnings*.

TABLE 9–1 Profit Rates of U.S. Manufacturing Corporations after Income Taxes, 1949–1986

Year	Rate of return on equity capital (percent)	Profits per dollar of sales (cents)
1949	11.6	5.8
1954	9.9	4.5
1959	10.4	4.8
1964	11.6	5.2
1969	11.5	4.8
1974	14.9	5.5
1979	16.4	5.7
1984	12.5	4.6
1985	10.1	3.8
1986*	9.9	3.9
Average 1949–86	11.7	4.8

* First three quarters.

SOURCE: Economic Report of the President, 1987, p. 347.

The figures shown in Table 9–1 are overall averages for the country. In any given year, the rates of return vary considerably between industries. During the 1982–83 recession, several industries, including steel and motor vehicles, experienced negative rates of return on equity capital. One should not conclude that such differences will persist year after year. Demand and cost conditions change, which change profit rates. Even if these market conditions did not change, profit rates would begin to equalize because capital would move out of low-profit industries and into industries that offer more attractive returns. As capital moved out of low-return industries, profit rates would increase because of the decrease in output and the resulting price increase. Similarly, as capital moved into the high-return industries, their output would increase—causing price and profit rates to decline.

MARGINAL COST

Marginal cost is defined as the additional cost incurred by producing one more unit of output; or it is the amount saved by reducing output by one unit. The information required to calculate marginal cost is obtained from the firm's production function. The first two columns of Table 9–2 reproduce the cookie production function presented in the first two columns of Table 7–1.

TABLE 9-2 Total and Marginal Cost

(1) Output (TPP)	(2) Labor (days)	(3) TVC	(4) TC	(5) MC
0	0	0	1,000	—
100	10	$1,000	2,000	$10.
800	20	2,000	3,000	1.43
2,000	30	3,000	4,000	.83
2,900	40	4,000	5,000	1.11
3,600	50	5,000	6,000	1.43
4,200	60	6,000	7,000	1.67
4,600	70	7,000	8,000	2.50
4,800	80	8,000	9,000	5.00

Since output is rarely increased by just one unit at a time, MC requires a computational formula:

$$MC = \frac{\Delta TC}{\Delta Q} = \frac{\Delta TVC}{\Delta Q}$$

where TC is total cost (fixed plus variable) and Q is total output. Because MC is derived from changes in cost, fixed costs do not influence its level. The same answers are obtained using the change in total cost (ΔTC) or the change in total variable cost (ΔTVC) in the numerator. In this example, labor is priced at $100 per day, and fixed costs are assumed to be $1,000.

Relationship between Marginal Cost and Marginal Physical Product

Notice that MC begins at a high figure, declines rapidly, reaches a minimum, and then increases. This behavior is due to the law of diminishing returns (diminishing MPP). In the early stages of production, output increases more rapidly than inputs. This means that MPP is increasing. The rapid increase in efficiency causes production costs (MC) to decline. After production enters the regions of diminishing returns and MPP begins to decline, the cost of producing each additional unit of output (MC) increases. The relationship between MPP and MC is shown on Figure 9-1. They are mirror images of each other. MC reaches its minimum at the point where MPP is at a maximum.

FIGURE 9–1   Relationship between Marginal Physical Product and Marginal Cost

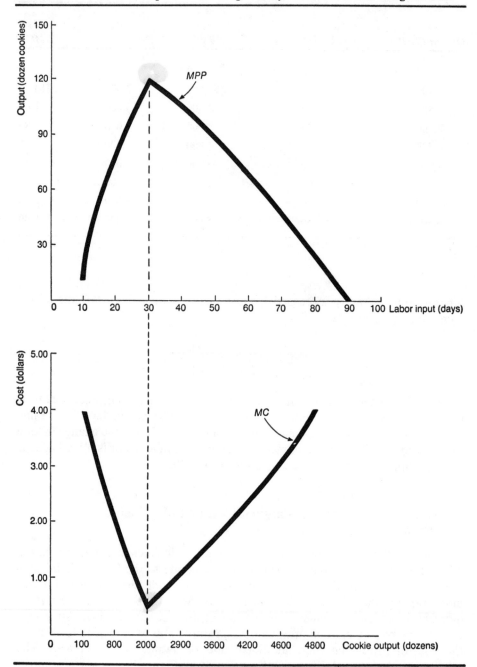

AVERAGE COSTS

To determine if a firm is making a profit, one must know about average costs. We will consider three types of average costs: (1) average fixed costs (AFC), (2) average variable costs (AVC), and (3) average total costs (ATC). Each of the average costs is calculated by dividing the corresponding total cost figure by output. Averaged fixed cost is found by dividing total fixed cost by the level of output, and average variable cost is obtained by dividing total variable cost by output. Average total cost can be calculated in two ways: (1) dividing total cost by output or (2) summing AFC and AVC.

These measures become more meaningful by calculating their values from the cookie production example. The values of ATC, AVC, and AFC for this example are shown in Table 9–3. Labor is priced at $100 per day, and fixed cost is assumed to be $1,000.

Looking briefly at these average costs, AFC becomes smaller at larger levels of output. We might expect this, since fixed cost is spread across more units at larger output levels so each unit bears a smaller share of the cost. Perhaps most interesting is the behavior of AVC and ATC. Note that AVC declines over a range of output or inputs, reaches a minimum point, and then increases. The same pattern is observed for ATC, only these figures continue to decline until a slightly larger output is reached before they increase.

RELATIONSHIP BETWEEN MARGINAL AND AVERAGE COSTS

To understand the concept of supply, one must understand the relationship between marginal and average costs. They are easiest to see represented by a diagram. In Figure 9–2, the ATC and AVC curves and the marginal cost curve are superimposed on the same diagram.

TABLE 9–3   Average Costs

Output (TPP)	Labor	ATC	AVC	AFC
0	0	—	—	—
100	10	$20.00	$10.00	$10.00
800	20	3.75	2.50	1.25
2000	30	2.00	1.50	.50
2900	40	1.72	1.38	.34
3600	50	1.67	1.39	.28
4200	60	1.67	1.43	.24
4600	70	1.74	1.52	.22
4800	80	1.88	1.67	.21

FIGURE 9–2 Relationships between Marginal and Average Costs

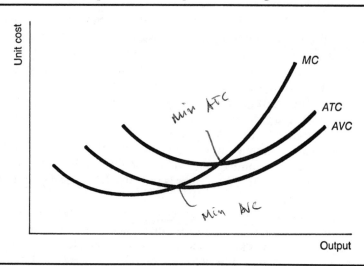

Perhaps the most important characteristic is that MC intersects both AVC and ATC at their minimum points. The explanation of this characteristic is the same as that for MPP intersecting APP at its maximum point: If the marginal unit is below the average, it pulls the average down; if it is above the average, the average will rise. The effect of this quarter's or semester's grade point average on your overall grade average is an example. If this quarter's grade average (the marginal quarter) is above the overall average, the overall average will improve, and vice versa.

The same reasoning applies to marginal and average costs. Marginal costs will pull AVC and ATC lower as long as MC is below the averages. Notice that MC can be increasing during this time, as it is just left of the intersections with AVC and ATC. To the right of the intersections, MC is above the averages and pulls them up. It also follows that MC must intersect AVC and ATC at their minimum points.

The most important thing about the AFC curve is that it is not important. Thus, it is not shown in Figure 9–2. If AFC were plotted on a graph, it would slope down and to the right—coming close to the horizontal axis but never reaching it.

You might have noticed that the three cost curves are drawn in a U-shaped configuration. This common shape of the marginal and average cost curves stems from the law of diminishing returns. At the point where MPP begins to decline, MC rises. When MC rises, the points where AVC and ATC begin to increase are not far behind.

PROFIT–MAXIMIZING RULE

In establishing the *profit-maximizing rule,* visualize a firm that produces varying quantities of a product at a given or constant price. This may not be true for the cookie firm, but such a firm comes close to this situation. In Chapter 14, we will look at a firm that meets this criterion exactly.

To maximize profits, a firm should produce a unit of output only if the additional revenue obtained from its sale is at least as large as the additional cost incurred by producing it. The additional revenue obtained by selling one more unit of a product is called *marginal revenue* (MR). For the firm that can vary the quantity it sells without having to change the price of its product, marginal revenue is the same as product price. If the firm sells an extra dozen cookies for $2, MR is $2.

A firm will maximize its profits by increasing its output up to the point where:

$$MR = MC.$$

An easy way to see why profits are maximized only where MR = MC is to select an output level that does not correspond to this point and then see what happens. In Figure 9–3, suppose the firm produces Q_0 output. At this output

FIGURE 9–3 Maximization of Profits Where Marginal Revenue Equals Marginal Cost

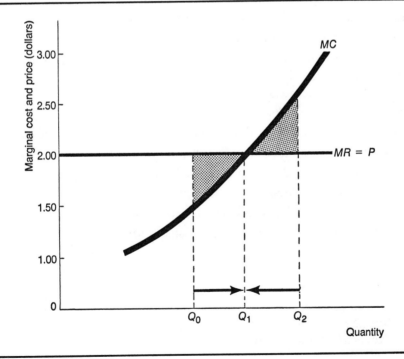

level, MC is $1.50. However, MR or price of the product, is $2. Thus, if the firm produced $Q_0 + 1$ units of output, it increases its profits (or decreases its losses) by 50 cents. (Figure 9–3 does not provide enough information to tell if the firm is making a profit or a loss at Q_0; This information is added in the next chapter.) If the firm is interested in maximizing profits, it will produce $Q_0 + 1$. At this output level should $Q_0 + 2$ be produced? The answer is yes—because MR again exceeds MC—the extra unit brings in more than it costs to produce it. The question will continue to be answered in the affirmation as long as the actual quantity produced corresponds to a point where MR exceeds MC.

If the output level corresponds to a point where MC exceeds MR, to the right of Q_1 on Figure 9–3, profits will be increased by reducing output. For example, at Q_2, MC is $2.50 and MR equals $2. Thus, a one-unit reduction of output at Q_2 will reduce costs by $2.50 and reduce sales by $2. In this case, profits are increased (or losses decreased) by fifty cents by reducing output by one dozen. The same rational is true between Q_2 and Q_1.

Total profits are maximized at the output corresponding to the point where MC = MR. If the firm is one unit to the left of this point, profits can be increased by increasing output. At one unit to the right, profits will be increased by decreasing output.

GLOSSARY

profits The excess of total sales over total costs.

explicit costs Out-of-pocket expenses.

implicit costs The charge to the firm for the resources provided by the owner(s) of the firm.

fixed costs They remain constant at all levels of output.

variable costs They vary with the level of output.

marginal cost The additional cost incurred by producing one more unit of output.

average total cost Total cost divided by output.

average variable cost Total variable cost divided by output.

average fixed cost Total fixed cost divided by output.

marginal revenue The additional revenue obtained by selling one more unit of output.

profit-maximizing rule Produce that level of output where MR = MC.

QUESTIONS

1. *Distinguish between:*
   a. Explicit and implicit costs.
   b. Fixed and variable costs.

2. *a. What are normal profits?*
   b. How will the total amount of normal profits of a firm be related to who owns the assets utilized by the firm?

3. *People who own and operate small firms have willingly earned less in their firms than what they could earn working for someone else.*
   a. Is this rational behavior?
   b. For these firms, are implicit costs greater or smaller than normal profits? Explain.

4. *a. What are pure profits and why do they exist?*
   b. What role do pure profits play in a market economy?

5. *a. What is marginal cost?*
   b. How is marginal cost related to MPP?

6. *a. The MC, ATC, and AVC curves are drawn in a U-shaped pattern. Why?*
   b. If MC is increasing, ATC and AVC will be increasing. True or false? Explain.

7. *a. What is the profit-maximizing rule?*
   b. Explain why any level of output that differs from the point where MR = MC will not maximize profits.

Supply and Elasticities

OVERVIEW

Chapter 10 combines material from the last three chapters to construct the theory of supply. The main idea is that producers place more of a product on the market when its price is high than when it is low. The second half of the chapter focuses on the responsiveness of producers to price changes.

SUPPLY DEFINED

Supply is defined as a positive relationship between price and quantity, as in Figure 10–1. Other things equal, the higher the price of a good, the greater the quantity supplied. Just as with demand, it is important to distinguish between supply and quantity supplied. Supply is the entire price–quantity relationship. Quantity supplied refers to a particular quantity on a specific supply curve—such as Q_0 or Q_1 in Figure 10–1.

The positive relationship between price and quantity along a supply curve stems from the profit-maximizing goal of producers. When the price of a product increases, holding constant all other output and input prices, the profitability of producing the good also increases. This prompts producers to shift resources from the production of less profitable products into the more profitable good.

Marginal Cost and Supply

The marginal cost curve becomes a supply curve by imposing the assumption of profit maximization. This is shown in Figure 10–1. Recall that profits are maximized when quantity produced corresponds to the point where MR = MC, or P = MC. If price equals P_0 the profit-maximizing quantity will be Q_0. At P_1, quantity supplied is Q_1, and so on. Thus, the MC curve coupled with the profit-maximization assumption is a supply curve.

AVERAGE COSTS AND SUPPLY

The idea that the MC curve also is a supply curve has a qualification; only a portion of the MC curve can be interpreted as supply. Only the portion of MC contained in Stage II of the three stages of production is supply. To see why, it

FIGURE 10–1 Supply

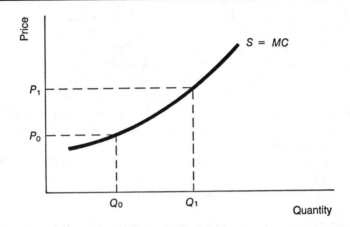

is necessary to reintroduce the average variable cost (AVC) and average total cost (ATC) curves discussed in Chapter 9. Recall that each is calculated by dividing the corresponding total cost figure by output. The U-shaped ATC and AVC curves, along with MC, are shown again in Figure 10–2.

Now we can see why production only occurs in Stage II. First, MC cannot be drawn in Stage III. Recall that in Stage III, output declines when an input and cost increase. Thus, Figure 10–2 only includes Stages I and II. If price is P_2, output will be Q_2 if the firm maximizes profits. At P_2, the firm is earning

FIGURE 10–2 Marginal Cost, Average Costs, and Supply

pure profits because product price exceeds ATC. The ATC curve tells us how much it costs to produce each unit on the average. Thus, if price exceeds ATC, the firm earns a pure profit. If price is below ATC, the firm incurs a loss.

If price is P_1, output will be Q_1. However, in this case, the firm will not cover all costs because price is below ATC. The firm makes all its variable costs but not all its fixed costs. In this case, the firm incurs a loss. Will the firm produce at price P_1? It will if the firm cannot get out of paying its fixed costs. This situation can occur if contracts or agreements must be fulfilled. In the long run, the firm would not produce if price is below the minimum ATC unless it was willing to accept a lower return on its resources than they could earn in an alternative occupation or use.

If price is below P_0, the firm will not produce. In this region, which is Stage I, the price is so low that the firm does not even make back its variable costs. It is like paying a person $2 to produce a good that sells for $1; it is better not to produce the good.

Now we can identify the supply portions of the MC curve. The dotted-line portion below the AVC curve is not supply. This is in Stage I. The dashed-line portion between AVC and ATC can be supply in the short run if fixed costs cannot be avoided or if the firm is willing to settle for less than maximum return on its resources. The portion of MC above ATC is always supply. The relationship between the stages of production, the MC, and average cost curves is summarized in Figure 10–3.

FIGURE 10–3   Relationship of Stages of Production and Cost Curves

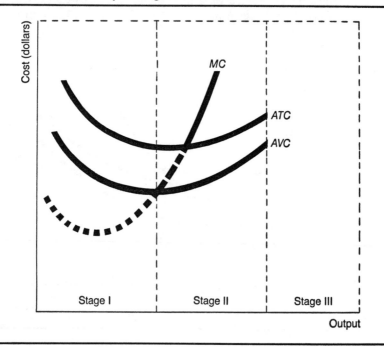

SUPPLY OF PREVIOUSLY PRODUCED GOODS

Not all goods supplied to markets have been produced in the period immediately preceding their sale. Examples include land, vintage automobiles, and old paintings. What does the market supply of these products look like? In these cases, the sum of the MC curves cannot be used as a market supply because production costs are nonexistent for natural resources or irrelevant for items produced years ago.

One might conjecture that the supply of such goods will be perfectly vertical because there is a fixed quantity of each. But that is incorrect. A vertical supply curve implies that people who own such goods will place the same quantity on the market at a low price as at a high price, which is unreasonable. If you owned a vintage '55 Chevy and someone offered you $100 for it, most likely you wouldn't sell. If someone offered you $10,000, you would be more likely to sell. Thus, the quantity you placed on the market at a high price will be greater than at a low price.

We can infer, therefore, that the supply of goods no longer being produced also is upward sloping. The higher the price, the greater the quantity that owners of these assets will place on the market per unit time.

MARKET SUPPLY

Although it is necessary to focus on the individual producer or firm to derive supply, the concept is most useful when applied to the entire market. *Market supply* is obtained by summing the quantity supplied by all producers in the market at the various possible prices. For example, suppose there are three producers in the market. Each has a specific supply curve as shown by the first three frames of Figure 10–4. To obtain the market supply curve shown in the fourth frame, we sum the three quantities at each price as indicated in this table:

| | *Quantity supplied by producer:* | | | *Market* |
	1	*2*	*3*	*supply*
Price				
$4	30 +	40 +	0 =	70
8	40 +	60 +	30 =	130

The increase in quantity placed on the market when price increases comes from two sources. First, there is an increase in the quantity supplied from existing producers in the market as illustrated by producers 1 and 2. Second, the price increase is likely to bring new producers into the market as illustrated by producer 3.

FIGURE 10–4   Deriving Market Supply

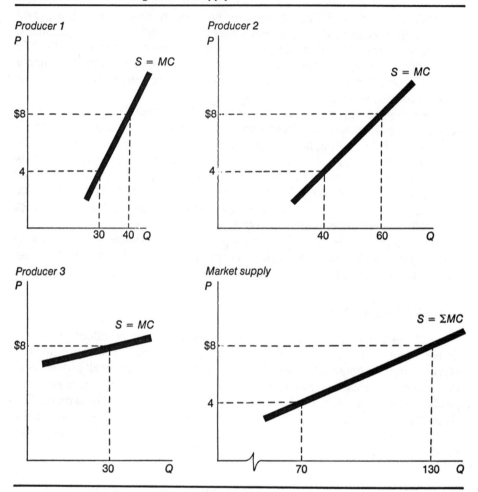

ELASTICITY OF SUPPLY

Thus far, we have indicated only that product supply is an upward-sloping line, meaning that producers are willing to produce larger amounts when they expect higher prices. We have not considered how responsive producers are to a price change. Economists use a concept known as *elasticity of supply* to measure the responsiveness of producers to a price change. We will see that this concept is similar to price elasticity of demand—presented in Chapter 6.

Elasticity of supply (E_S) is defined as the percentage change in quantity supplied resulting from each percent change in price. The formula for computing E_S is the same as the price elasticity of demand formula:

$$E_S = \frac{\dfrac{Q_0 - Q_1}{Q_0}}{\dfrac{P_0 - P_1}{P_0}}$$

In computing E_S, however, the quantities Q_0 and Q_1 refer to the beginning and ending quantities supplied rather than quantities demanded.

A simple example is worked out by inserting the numbers in Figure 10–5 into the E_S formula. Let \$4 be the initial price, P_0; \$5 the new price, P_1; 100 the initial quantity, Q_0; and 150 the new quantity, Q_1:

$$E_S = \frac{\dfrac{100 - 150}{100}}{\dfrac{4 - 5}{4}} = \frac{\dfrac{-50}{100}}{\dfrac{-1}{4}} = \frac{-0.5}{-0.25} = 2$$

The elasticity coefficient of 2 in this example means that quantity changes by 2 percent for each 1 percent change in price. Supply elasticity is useful because it tells us the change in quantity supplied resulting from a given percent change in price. For example, if E_S is 2, a 10 percent increase in price will result in a 20 percent increase in quantity supplied.

Since the formula for computing E_S is the same as the formula for finding the price elasticity of demand, it suffers from some of the same problems. First, it is a "point" elasticity formula, so it should be applied to only small changes in price and quantity. In measuring E_S for actual products, economists use a statistical technique that measures small changes. This technique is studied in intermediate level statistics courses and also in a specialized area or economics known as *econometrics*.

FIGURE 10–5   Elasticity of Supply Computation

Economists classify E_s similarly to E_d. If E_s is less than 1, it is inelastic whereas a supply elasticity coefficient greater than 1 is elastic. As E_s approaches zero, a vertical supply curve, E_S is described as highly inelastic. Similarly, when it approaches infinity, a horizontal supply curve, E_S is described as highly elastic.

Factors Affecting Elasticity of Supply

All products or producers do not exhibit the same elasticity of supply. Some products exhibit a highly elastic supply; a slight price change brings a large change in quantity. For others, supply is highly inelastic; a price change has little effect on the quantity supplied. Why are there differences in the size of E_S?

There are two major factors that influence the size of the elasticity of supply of a product: (1) the availability of substitute inputs that can be taken from other uses and (2) the time allowed for adjustment to occur. Regarding the first factor, if the production of a product utilizes inputs that are commonly used to produce other products, it will tend to have a more elastic supply than if it uses specialized inputs suited only for its production. In cookie production, for example, the resources used are widely available. Thus, one expects the supply of this product to be elastic.

The second factor, time for adjustment, is important because most production activities cannot be changed in scale overnight. If price increases, for example, some additional output will likely be forthcoming from increasing the amount of variable inputs; for instance, more labor can be hired and machines and facilities can be used more intensely by operating two or three shifts. However, relatively large changes in output usually cannot be attained until the level of fixed inputs can be changed, and it takes time to construct facilities and manufacture machines.

The ability to adjust outputs differs among industries. For example, changes in retail trade, where temporary facilities can be set up are likely to take less time than changes in the output of heavy industry where specialized plants and equipment are required. In any given industry, the longer the time that elapses after a price change, the greater the change in output that is physically possible and the more elastic the supply will be.

In addition to the purely physical constraints on changing output, particularly increasing it, the economic aspects are important. Even if it is physically possible to adjust output, it may not be profitable to do so immediately after a price change. The major consideration is the length of time the price change is *expected* to remain in effect. If the price change is expected to be temporary, there is little incentive for a producer to change the level of output substantially because changes in output usually involve additional expense. To increase output, it may be necessary to purchase new equipment, buildings, and so forth; or to decrease production one might have to let fixed inputs remain idle but still bear the fixed cost. Unless producers expect the price change to remain in effect for a time, it may not pay to incur the expense necessary to adjust output. As an analogy, you generally do not bother to put on a heavy coat to pick up the morning paper on your doorstep on a cold day, but when you are out for an hour, putting on a heavy coat is worth the effort.

No producer has a crystal ball to accurately predict whether a price change will be temporary or long run in nature. Most producers have an opinion on the duration of a price change based on information about the market, but none can be absolutely sure. The longer a price change remains in effect, the more information producers will have and the more certain they will be as to the duration of the change. As a result, we should not expect to observe much change in output resulting from short-run, month-to-month fluctuations in output price. Rather, we expect producers to respond mainly to changes in the overall average level of prices that exists over a period of time.

A CHANGE OR SHIFT IN SUPPLY

The supply curve can shift from one position to another—the same as demand. Representing the supply curve by a two-dimensional diagram makes it necessary to hold constant the other factors that can affect supply. If these factors do not remain constant, which is usually the case, there will be a shift in the supply curve from one position to another. Both an increase and decrease in supply are illustrated by Figure 10–6.

An increase in supply, illustrated by a shift from S_1 to S_2 in Figure 10–6, can be interpreted in two ways. First, at a given price, say P_1, producers will offer a larger quantity on the market: Q_2 instead of Q_1. A second way of interpreting a supply increase is that producers will supply the same quantity, say Q_1, at a lower price. Both ways of looking at a supply increase have the same meaning.

The meaning of a decrease in supply, as illustrated by S_0 in Figure 10–6, is strictly parallel to an increase. At a given price, say P_1, the quantity supplied declines from Q_1 to Q_0. Or, looking at it the second way, the price suppliers will require for quantity Q_1 increases from P_1 to P_2.

There are five major factors or supply shifters that apply to most products. A change in one or more of these shifters can cause the entire supply curve to shift from one position to another. A more thorough discussion of how and why they shift the supply curve is presented in Chapter 11. They include changes in:

1. Prices of alternative products that can be produced.
2. Prices of inputs used to produce the product.
3. Producer expectations of future prices.
4. Technology.
5. Number of producers.

FIGURE 10–6 Shift in Supply

CROSS ELASTICITY OF SUPPLY

Cross elasticity of supply (E_{cs}) is defined as the percent change in the supply of one good in response to a one-percent change in the price of an alternative product. It is computed with the following formula:

$$E_{cs} = \frac{\% \, \Delta \, Q_i}{\% \, \Delta \, P_j}$$

The change in quantity is taken at any price—such as the difference between Q_0 and Q_1 at price P_1 in Figure 10–6.

The value of the cross elasticity coefficient can be negative or positive. It is negative for most pairs of products. This means they are substitutes in production. For example, a leather goods firm might produce belts and basketballs. If the price of belts decreases, other things equal, basketballs become more profitable, so the firm allocates some of its resources away from belts toward basketballs. Thus, the relationship between the price of belts and the quantity of basketballs is negative.

A positive cross elasticity implies that the two goods are complements in production. By complements, we mean two goods that are produced together, such as gasoline and diesel fuel. If the price of gasoline increases, more petroleum is refined, which causes an increase in the supply of diesel fuel.

GLOSSARY

supply A positive relationship between price and quantity.

quantity supplied Refers to a particular quantity on a specific supply curve.

market supply The summation, at each price, of the quantities supplied by all the producers or suppliers in the market.

elasticity of supply Percentage change in quantity supplied resulting from a one-percent change in price of the product.

decrease in supply Shift to the left of the supply curve.

increase in supply Shift to the right of the supply curve.

cross elasticity of supply Percentage change in the quantity supplied of one product resulting from a one-percent change in the price of another product.

QUESTIONS

1. *Differentiate between supply and quantity supplied.*

2. *a. What is the economic meaning of an upward-sloping supply curve?*
   b. Why do producers or suppliers behave in this fashion?

3. *a. What assumption is required for the MC curve to also be a supply curve?*
   b. What portion of the MC curve is supply?

4. *a. Compute the elasticity of supply from the following data:*

	Price	Quantity supplied
Initial situation	$10	1,000
New situation	15	2,000

   b. What does the elasticity coefficient mean?

5. *a. Why is time for adjustment an important factor influencing the elasticity of supply?*
   b. What are the two sources of an increase in quantity supplied in a market when price increases?

6. *a. What is meant by an increase in supply? A decrease?*
   b. When drawing a supply curve what factors are assumed to remain constant?
   c. What happens when one or more of these factors change?

7. *a. What is cross elasticity of supply?*
   b. When will the cross elasticity be negative? Positive?

PART FOUR
Product Markets

CHAPTER 11

Demand and Supply

OVERVIEW

This chapter combines material from the previous seven chapters to construct the framework for price determination—demand and supply. After deriving equilibrium price, the second half of the chapter deals with the factors that cause the demand and supply curves to shift, which in turn cause changes in equilibrium price.

PRICE DETERMINATION

The first step is to superimpose the demand and supply curves on the same diagram, as shown by Figure 11–1. This is possible because both curves have price on the vertical axis and quantity on the horizontal axis. When the two curves are superimposed, they intersect. The price that corresponds to the point of intersection is the *equilibrium price,* while the corresponding quantity is the *equilibrium quantity. Equilibrium* is defined as a state of stability or balance where there are no forces causing movement, or there are equal opposing forces. If price is not at equilibrium, forces in the market will push price toward the equilibrium. This can be seen most easily if we choose a price that is not at equilibrium and see what happens. Consider price P_1 in Figure 11–1. At this high price, a small amount is demanded, Q_0^s in the diagram. On the other hand, a large amount is supplied, Q_1^s in the diagram. Thus, at price P_1, the quantity supplied is greater than the quantity demanded. Hence, there is a surplus in the market; more goods or services are offered for sale than are bought, and inventories pile up or people who offer the services remain underutilized. The inevitable result of this situation is a downward pressure on price. Sellers attempting to dispose of the surplus, are forced to take a lower price. To make money, suppliers must sell what they produce. Some sellers, therefore, will begin to cut price to entice buyers to buy from them rather than from other sellers. When some sellers cut price, others must follow to remain competitive. Of course, buyers also are likely to exert pressure, which reminds sellers who are reluctant to cut their price of the existing surplus and price reductions taking place. Thus, if price is above the equilibrium, the resulting surplus causes downward pressure on price and pushes it toward the equilibrium.

What happens if price is below the equilibrium, such as P_0 in Figure 11–1?

FIGURE 11–1   Demand and Supply, Showing Equilibrium Price and Quantity

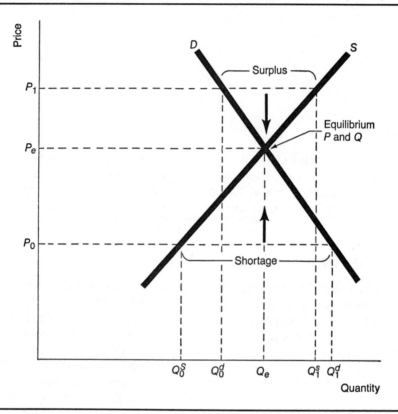

At price P_0, quantity demanded, Q_1^d is greater than the quantity supplied, Q_0^s. At such a low price, there is an incentive for people to buy more of the good, but at the same time, there is little incentive for producers to supply it. Consequently, there is a shortage; the product disappears from shelves, inventories fall, or people who provide the services are swamped with customers. The inevitable result is an upward pressure on price. Some buyers will not be able to obtain as much of the product as they would like, and they are likely to offer sellers a higher price if they will sell to them rather than to someone else. Other buyers, to remain competitive, must also offer higher prices. Sellers, seeing the shortage and realizing they can sell all they produce at a higher price, are likely to cooperate happily in the process by asking for higher prices. Thus, if price is below the equilibrium, there is an upward pressure on price caused by the resulting shortage. Only at price P_e will buyers take off the market exactly what sellers place on the market, that is, there will be neither a surplus nor a shortage.

DEMAND SHIFTS

As explained in Chapter 6, an increase in demand means that people wish to buy a larger quantity for any given price or will pay a higher price for a given quantity. An increase in demand is illustrated by an increase or shift to the right by the demand curve, as shown by the shift from D_1 to D_2 in Figure 11–2. Notice here that both the equilibrium price and quantity increase. A decrease in demand, illustrated by the shift in demand from D_1 to D_0 in Figure 11–2, results in a decrease in the eqilibrium price and quantity. Also, recall from Chapter 6 that there are five main demand shifters. Let us consider each demand shifter to see how they affect price and quantity in the product market.

DEMAND SHIFTERS

1. Change in Money Incomes

An increase in consumers' money incomes results in an increase in the demand for many products. Some of the increase comes from using the product more frequently, such as having eggs more times per week or from additional

FIGURE 11–2   The Effects of Shifts in Demand on Equilibrium Price and Quantity consumers in the market. For example, people tend to enter the luxury car market as their incomes approach the $60,000 to $70,000 per year bracket. The more people in this income bracket, the greater the demand for luxury cars. Economists refer to goods that increase in demand with higher incomes as *superior goods*. This name does not necessarily imply that such goods are made better or last longer than other goods. It is a name for the category of goods or services that exhibits an increase in demand as incomes increase.

There are examples of other goods or services that decrease in demand as incomes increase. For example, people tend to buy fewer starchy, high-calorie foods as their incomes grow. With higher incomes, they buy more meat, fruit, fresh vegetables, and convenience foods. Thus, the demand for starchy foods declines, or shifts to the left, as incomes increase. Economists refer to these goods or services as *inferior goods,* again without any intention to describe the durability or quality of the good.

It is possible to name goods whose demand does not change at all with an increase in consumer incomes. One example is the aggregate demand for all food in the United States. Because of the relatively high incomes enjoyed by a large part of the U.S. population, food consumption for most people is already at a maximum. Thus, with a continued increase in incomes, people tend to buy about the same quantity of food while increasing purchases of other amenities.

2. Change in Prices of Related Goods

A. Substitutes.   An increase in the price of a substitute has the effect of shifting the demand curve for a good to the right, as illustrated by the shift in demand from D_1 to D_2 in Figure 11–2. For example, if the price of Volkswagens increases, car buyers begin to substitute lower-priced Japanese- and American-built cars in their place. As a result, there is an increase in the demand for Japanese and American autos. Consequently, the equilibrium price and quantity of the goods in question both increase. As people switch from the higher-priced substitute toward the good depicted in Figure 11–2, the demand for the good increases and, as a result, consumers pay more for it while they increase the amount purchased. The increased demand for the good causes its price to increase.

The opposite occurs if a substitute decreases in price. As people turn to the lower-priced substitute, the demand for the good in question decreases. This is illustrated by the shift from D_1 to D_0 in Figure 11–2. Consequently, the price of the good in question decreases along with the decrease in the quantity exchanged. In this case, it is the decreased demand for the good that causes the price to decline.

Shifts in demand resulting from changes in the price of a substitute cause the price of the good to move in the same direction as the substitute. Thus, the prices of two or more goods that consumers regard as close substitutes tend to rise and fall together.

B. Complements. An increase in the price of a complementary good causes the demand for the good in question to decrease, as illustrated by the shift in demand from D_1 to D_0 in Figure 11–2. The increase in the price of the complementary good causes people to buy less of it, and as a result, they also buy less of the good depicted in Figure 11–2. For example, an increase in the price of gasoline, which can be considered a complement to automobiles, will decrease the demand for automobiles, especially those that offer the lowest gas mileage. In this case, the price of the good in question (gas-guzzlers in this example) decreases along with a decrease in quantity exchanged.

The appearance of completely new products on the market may change the demand for existing products. If a new product is a substitute for an existing product and offers consumers more for their money (more MU per dollar), the demand for the existing product will decline. In this case, the entry of the new substitute product on the market has the same effect as a decline in the price of an existing substitute. Similarly, the appearance of a new complement increases the demand for a given product. It is as if an existing complement decreased in price. Thus, we can treat new products as if there was a decrease in the price of substitutes or complements, providing the new products offer more for the money than products already on the market.

3. Change in Consumer Expectations Regarding Future Prices and Incomes

Since no one knows the future with certainty, our present actions are influenced by what we expect the future to bring. This is important in product demand. If, for example, you expect a product to be scarce and high-priced in the future, you will likely increase your purchases (demand) now to avoid the higher future price. An expected higher price will result in a shift to the right in demand, as illustrated by the shift from D_1 to D_2 in Figure 11–2. Expecting a lower price in the future has the opposite effect; present demand will decrease, such as the shift from D_1 to D_0 in Figure 11–2, as buyers wait for more favorable prices.

Anticipated changes in income also affect present demand. If you expected a rich uncle to leave you $1 million dollars in one or two years, you would likely be more liberal in your spending habits even now—well in advance of the date you actually receive the money. Thus your demand for many products or services would shift to the right, as shown by D_2 in Figure 11–2. Or, if you expected your present income source to dry up, you would become more frugal, your demand for some items would shift to the left.

It is important to realize that current demand depends heavily on your long-run expected income. College students illustrate this idea well. They tend to enjoy a higher standard of living while in college than people with similar incomes who do not have much hope of substantial income growth in the future.

4. Changes in Tastes and Preferences

There are a few products and services whose demand is influenced by the changing whims of consumers. These items are fads that often change in style. For example, there is not much demand nowadays for high-button shoes. On the other hand, there has been a resurgence in demand for blue jeans. In economic terms, the demand for goods that are "out" shifts to the left, as in D_0, whereas the demand for items that are "in" shifts to the right, D_2 in Figure 11–2.

When attempting to explain changes in consumer purchasing behavior, it is tempting to ascribe too much importance to a change in tastes and preferences. Except for fads or fashions, tastes of large groups of people (markets) are quite stable. Before relying on changes in tastes and preferences to explain consumer behavior, it is good to exhaust all other possibilities. Be careful to include changes in price as a possible reason for changes in consumer behavior. For example, it used to be argued that Europeans had different tastes than North Americans regarding small cars. But during the 1950s and 1960s, gasoline prices in the United States were between one fourth and one third the prices that existed in Europe because of high taxes on gasoline there. When gasoline prices increased to high levels in the United States, U.S. consumers also switched to smaller, more fuel-efficient cars. The reason is the relative increase in the price of gasoline—not a change in tastes.

5. Change in Population

Since the market demand for a good or service is the sum of all individual demands, the greater the number of individuals in the market, the greater the market demand. Population growth, therefore, is an important factor in shifting demand to the right, such as D_2 in Figure 11–2. It is about the only factor shifting the demand for all food to the right, for example. In fact, the demand for most goods and services is shifted steadily to the right because of growth in population size.

Although these five demand shifters are the major economic factors that influence the position of the demand curve, there are other special circumstances that also can shift the demand curve. For example, as discussed in Chapter 12, passing a law that restricts or forbids the purchase of an item will decrease demand for that good or service.

To fully understand demand and the behavior of consumers, it is as important to be aware of the possible demand shifts as it is to know about the downward-sloping nature of the demand curve. Without a knowledge of these shifts and the factors that can cause them, it is not possible to understand consumer behavior. For example, if the demand curve for an item shifts to the right, consumers will increase their purchases at the same price or at a higher price. To the uninformed, it appears that price has no relationship to quantity demanded. But if one knows why the demand curve has shifted, the observed changes in price and quantity are reasonable and expected.

SUPPLY SHIFTS

As explained in Chapter 10, an increase in supply means that producers are willing to place more on the market at any given price or are willing to sell the same quantity for a lower price. An increase in supply is illustrated by the shift from S_1 to S_2 in Figure 11–3. Note that the equilibrium price decreases but quantity increases. A decrease in supply, illustrated by the shift in supply from S_1 to S_0 in Figure 11–3, results in an increase in the equilibrium price and a decrease in quantity. Also, recall from Chapter 10 that there are five main supply shifters. Let us consider each supply shifter to see how they affect price and quantity in the product market.

SUPPLY SHIFTERS

1. Change in the Prices of Alternative Products

Most firms produce or have the capability to produce more than one product. The decision of how much of each product to produce depends on the price (profitability) of the other(s). There are two categories of related goods: substitutes and complements.

FIGURE 11–3   The Effects of Shifts in Supply on Eqilibrium Price and Quantity

Two products are substitutes in production when an increase in the price of one product causes a reduction in the supply of the other product. Belts and basketballs were examples in Chapter 10. Two products are complements in production when an increase in the price of one product causes an increase in the supply of the other product, such as gasoline and diesel fuel. Complements usually are products that are produced together, or one is a by-product of the other product.

2. Changes in Prices of Inputs

As noted in Chapter 10, product supply is the same as marginal cost. Thus, anything that changes production costs eventually changes supply. If, for example, there is an increase in the price of labor, the total variable cost of a given output increases, which will increase the marginal cost—the added cost of an extra unit of output. Thus, an *increase* in input prices or cost *decreases* supply, shifting it upward and to the left, as shown by S_0 in Figure 11–3. Conversely, a decrease in input prices increases supply, shifting it to the right (S_2 in Figure 11–3).

A change in input prices causes the opposite change in supply. In graphic terms, this is easy to show. If the price of labor for the cookie firm increases to $100 from $50 per day, the marginal cost at any level of output is higher. Graphing the MC curve, where labor is priced at $100, results in a line above and to the left of the original curve. In terms of supply, this is a decrease. Thus, an increase in costs causes a decrease in supply, and vice versa.

From an economic standpoint, this relationship is reasonable. When input prices increase, producers must obtain a higher price for output to cover the higher cost of production. This means that supply decreases.

3. Change in Producer Expectations of Future Prices

Since producers are human beings and therefore cannot know the future with certainty, many present production decisions are based on what they believe will happen in the future. If producers have a reason to expect changes in future prices, either in the prices of the product they presently produce or in prices of products they could produce, they will likely begin to adjust their production capacity accordingly. However, it is not possible to generalize across all situations the effect of, say, an expected increase in price. Each situation must be analyzed separately. For example, if the product can be stored, an expectation of higher future prices may lead to a reduction in the present supply as producers build up their inventories to have more to sell when they expect prices to be higher. The expected price increase must at least compensate for storage costs. For products that cannot be stored, the expectation of higher future prices may lead to an increase in the present supply as producers begin to expand capacity for the future.

Another important item is the expected duration of a price change. If producers expect only a temporary rise in future prices, they will be less willing to make extensive changes in productive capacity than if they expect higher prices to prevail for many years. Thus, the magnitude of the supply shift depends on the length of time the price change is expected to stay in effect. If the expected duration is short, the supply shift will be small, and vice versa.

4. Change in Technology

In general, new technology makes presently used inputs more productive by improving their quality or by creating new inputs that are more productive than the old ones; both result in higher productivity. We can define higher productivity as decreasing the cost of a given level of output, say Q_1 in Figure 11–3, or increasing the level of output for a given cost, such as P_1 in Figure 11–3. Both of these changes describe an increase in product supply. Thus, new technology always increases supply. If new technology did not reduce costs, producers would have no incentive to adopt it.

5. Change in Number of Producers

Other things being equal, an increase in the number of producers of a given size at any price causes the supply curve of a product to increase. The same phenomenon can occur if the average size of the firms in the market increases. As more firms come into the market, supply shifts to the right, price declines, and quantity increases. The opposite occurs when the number or size of firms decreases. In later chapters, we will see that changes in the number of firms in response to pure profits or losses play a key role in either reducing pure profits or restoring normal profits.

Although these five supply shifters are the major economic factors that influence the position of the supply curve, other shifters may be important for certain products. For example, a change in the weather or growing conditions is an important supply shifter for agricultural products. A period of adverse weather may decrease the supply of certain products, while unusually good weather may increase their supply. Also, as discussed in Chapter 12, a law that prohibits the production or sale of an item will decrease its supply, particularly if the penalty is severe.

SIMULTANEOUS SHIFTS IN DEMAND AND SUPPLY

To simplify the preceding discussion, we considered only one shifter at a time. We have no guarantee that actual market situations will be so simple. One or more of the demand shifters may operate in the market at the same time as one or more of the supply shifters. For example, an increase in money incomes may cause an increase in demand at the same time as an increase in wage rates results in a decrease in supply. This condition is what occurs during inflation. Other combinations of demand and supply shifts also are possible. Therefore, it is useful to list and illustrate the possible combinations of demand and supply shifts to observe what happens to price and quantity under each circumstance. There are four possible combinations of demand and supply shifts: (1) demand increases, supply increases; (2) demand increases, supply decreases; (3) demand decreases, supply increases; and (4) demand decreases, supply decreases. Each of these shifts can be caused by any one (or more) of the five demand shifters and by any one (or more) of the five supply shifters. The four combinations are illustrated in Figure 11–4.

In panel *A* of Figure 11–4, an increase in both demand and supply causes quantity to increase. However, in this example, the upward pressure on price caused by the increase in demand is offset by the downward pressure exerted by the increase in supply. Consequently, price remains constant. One could construct the example so that price either increases or decreases. If demand increased more than supply increased, the price would rise, whereas price would decline if supply increased more than demand. Thus, only the direction of price movement in this case is uncertain; it may stay the same, increase, or decrease. This example depicts the long-run behavior of most goods. Demand for most items, at least large categories of goods, tends to increase over time because of the growth in income and population. Supply tends to increase because of the growth in the number or size of firms.

The same idea applies to the other three combinations. In panel *B* the demand increase and the supply decrease both exert an upward pressure on price so that it increases. But, they exert offsetting pressure on quantity, so it is not possible to say how quantity will change. As mentioned, this example depicts the behavior of markets during inflationary times because of the increase of money incomes and input prices.

In panel *C,* the decrease in demand and increase in supply both exert a downward pressure on price—causing a decrease in price. But, these shifts exert offsetting pressure on quantity, so it is not possible to say what happens to quantity; perhaps there will be no change as shown. Finally, the decrease in demand and decrease in supply shown by panel *D* cause a certain decrease in quantity, but the change in price cannot be predicted with certainty. The last two examples panels *C* and *D,* represent less common occurrences, although they can happen in specific instances.

SUMMARY OF PRICE AND QUANTITY CHANGES

It is evident that there is much more to demand and supply than the downward and upward slopes of the two curves and their interaction to determine the equilibrium price and quantity. Unless one knows the possible shifts that occur in demand and supply, there may appear to be no order to markets. Sometimes price increases while quantity decreases; at other times,

FIGURE 11–4   The Effects of Simultaneous Shifts in Demand and Supply on Equilibrium Price and Quantity

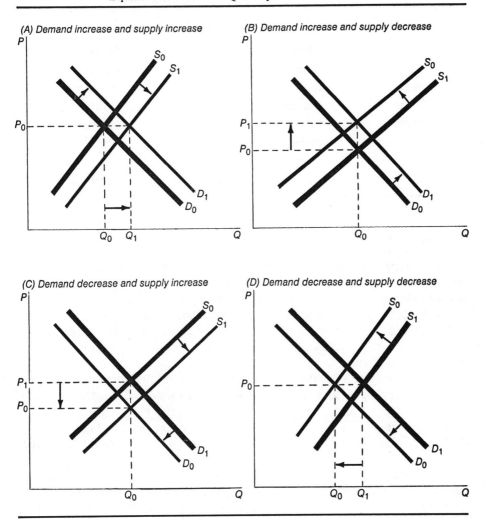

both price and quantity increase. Or, price may increase without any change in quantity. With knowledge of the demand and supply shifters and how they affect demand and supply and price and quantity, a person can explain why markets behave as they do and can predict future changes in the demand and supply shifters. Although it is better to utilize a diagram each time you wish to determine a price and/or quantity change rather than memorizing the changes, the following summary helps synthesize material from the preceding sections:

Change in:		Resulting change in:	
Demand	Supply	Price	Quantity
Increase	None	Increase	Increase
Decrease	None	Decrease	Decrease
None	Increase	Decrease	Increase
None	Decrease	Increase	Decrease
Increase	Increase	Uncertain	Increase
Increase	Decrease	Increase	Uncertain
Decrease	Increase	Decrease	Uncertain
Decrease	Decrease	Uncertain	Decrease

Time for Adjustment

The preceding discussion focused on the direction of change by price and quantity when demand and supply shifts occur. The magnitude of the price and quantity changes depends on the demand and supply elasticities. An important factor affecting these elasticities is time for adjustment. The longer the time that elapses after a price change, the greater the ability of people to adjust to it. Hence, price elasticities of both demand and supply are larger in the long run than in the short run.

On the demand side, consumers can search out lower priced substitutes, and producers have time to supply these substitutes. Consider a sudden decrease in supply. In the short run, price increases by a large amount, but the decrease in quantity is small. Then, as time goes by and demand becomes more elastic, the price increase is smaller but quantity adjusts downward by a larger amount.

The same thing occurs on the supply side. Consider a sudden decrease in demand. At first, when supply is inelastic, price declines by a large amount but quantity doesn't decrease much. Then, as time goes by and supply becomes more elastic, the price decrease is less but quantity decreases more.

GLOSSARY

equilibrium price   The price where sellers place on the market the exact quantity that buyers will take off the market. Corresponds to the intersection of the demand and supply curves.

surplus   Quantity supplied is greater than quantity demanded at that price; it occurs if price is above equilibrium.

shortage Quantity supplied is less than quantity demanded at that price; it occurs if price is below equilibrium.

increase (decrease) in demand Shift to the right (left) of the demand curve.

increase (decrease) in supply Shift to the right (left) of the supply curve.

superior goods Demand for these goods increases when income increases.

inferior goods Demand for these goods decreases when income increases.

substitutes in consumption Demand increases when the price of a substitute increases.

complements in consumption Demand decreases when the price of a complement increases.

substitutes in production Supply decreases when the price of a substitute increases.

complements in production Supply increases when the price of a complement increases.

QUESTIONS

1. a. *Define equilibrium price.*
   b. *If actual price is above the equilibrium, what will force it down?*
   c. *If actual price is below the equilibrium, what will force it up?*

2. *Water, one of the basic necessities of life, is in most places cheap, if not free. Diamonds, on the other hand, nonessential items in our lives, are expensive. Can you explain this perverse behavior of price?*

3. *State how the stipulated changes in each of the following demand shifters would change the equilibrium price and quantity of new U.S. cars? Assume all other shifters remain constant except the one under consideration:*
   a. *An increase in money incomes of the car-buying public. Assume new cars are a superior good.*
   b. *A decrease in the price of foreign cars, a substitute for U.S. cars.*
   c. *Consumers expect less unemployment in the near future.*
   d. *Consumers tastes shift in the direction of European styling.*
   e. *Population increases.*

4. *State how the stipulated changes in the following supply shifters change the equilibrium price and quantities of personal computers. Assume all other shifters remain constant except the one under consideration:*
   a. *A decrease in the price of typewriters—an alternative product that can be produced.*
   b. *A decrease in the price of silicon chips.*
   c. *Producers expect prices to be lower next year.*
   d. *Advances are made in electronics technology.*
   e. *There is a decrease in the manufacturers of this product.*

5. *For some goods, such as rooms at summer resorts, both price and quantity increase during certain times of the year. For other products, such as fresh strawberries, price is negatively correlated with quantity. Why does price increase when quantity increases for one good while price decreases when quantity increases for the other?*

6. a. *Is it possible for the equilibrium price of a good or service to change without a change in the equilibrium quantity exchanged in the market? (Assume that neither the demand nor supply curve is perfectly inelastic.) Explain.*

   b. *Is it possible for the equilibrium quantity of a good or service to change without a change in the equilibrium market price? Assume that neither the demand nor the supply curve is perfectly elastic. Explain.*

7. a. *Trace the short-run and long-run effects on price and quantity in the new automobile market of a sudden decrease in demand for new cars.*

   b. *Trace the short-run and long-run effects in the coffee market of a freeze in Brazil that kills many coffee trees.*

CHAPTER 12

Government in the Market

OVERVIEW

This chapter deals with the impact of government action on markets, particularly how it affects prices and quantities. Among other things, we see how government action can result in market shortages or surpluses.

The discussion in Chapter 11 on the determination of price and quantity and their changes focused on market-oriented factors. It is well-known that government at all levels intervenes in markets either through direct action, such as setting price, or through legal regulations that affect buyers and/or sellers. Much disagreement exists regarding the optimum amount of government intervention. People with a conservative political viewpoint tend to believe that markets can run themselves within the legal framework of society. People with a liberal view tend to prefer a greater amount of government intervention in markets. We will not argue one point of view over the other; instead, we will attempt to identify the major types of government intervention and evaluate their effects.

ESTABLISHING THE RULES OF THE GAME

Although we will not dwell at length on the legal aspects of markets, for any market to function properly, both buyers and sellers must obey certain rules. An important function of the government in any market is to establish basic rules of behavior and enforce them.

Perhaps the most basic rule is the law requiring buyers to pay sellers for goods purchased or services rendered. For many people, this rule would not be necessary; payment of one's debts is a matter of personal integrity. But for others, payment would not be forthcoming without the threat of legal action and punishment. Some people still attempt to gain ownership without payment. Without reasonable assurance of payment for goods or services, sellers could not remain in business. Sellers would have to charge higher prices so that the people who paid would cover the losses from those who did not pay. A market characterized by buyers' gross nonpayment would soon break down. Honest people would tire of paying for the goods and services consumed by dishonest neighbors.

A second important role of government in market operation is to provide information about products to buyers or to require that this information be available. As noted in Chapter 4, a consumer maximizes utility by equating the marginal utilities per dollar for all goods purchased. If information about the product or its price is lacking or wrong, it is not possible to compare the marginal utility per dollar of the product with the alternatives. Most of us have purchased goods or services that we would not have bought had we known their true characteristics or price. The truth-in-packaging and truth-in-lending legislation attempts to improve buyer information in the market. As a rule, it is easier and more successful to provide buyers with correct information and let competition take its course than to regulate sellers closely.

Government also is active in setting standards and testing products before they are put on the market. This is particularly important for potentially harmful products such as drugs and food. Harmful products eventually come to the attention of buyers and are forced off the market, but needless injury or death can be avoided if these products are identified beforehand.

MAINTAINING ENVIRONMENTAL QUALITY

The increase in pollution awareness and society's attempts to overcome it have necessitated government at all levels to establish and enforce environmental standards. In an open competitive market, each firm attempts to produce at the lowest possible cost to maximize profits and compete with other firms that also attempt to minimize costs. Consequently, in industries emitting pollution, each firm has an incentive to dispose of waste as cheaply as possible. Usually, this means disposing such materials into the water, soil, or air. Even if some firms would rather not pollute because of social conscience, firms that do pollute can drive the nonpolluters out of business by underpricing them in the market.

The tendency for individual firms to get rid of waste materials as cheaply as possible and pollute the environment has been called *market failure*. It is necessary, therefore, for government to establish environmental standards that must be adhered to by all firms. It costs money to install pollution-control devices or in some way capture the pollutants, and this increases production costs. As long as all firms have to meet the same standards, none has to go out of business. An exception are foreign firms located in countries that have less stringent pollution-control laws, which can undersell domestic firms because of lower costs. In a later chapter, we will see the effects of environmental quality regulations on the costs and product prices of firms.

In regard to maintaining environmental quality, the government monitors and regulates products that, when used by consumers, may be harmful to the environment or to people. Currently, extensive testing is required before potentially harmful products are placed on the market. Moreover, products that were developed before such testing was required are monitored for health or environmental damage. Examples of products that have been removed from the market include DES (a growth stimulant for cattle) and DDT (an insecticide used only by special permit). DES was suspected of causing cancer in humans, while DDT is not biodegradable. Consequently, DDT built up in the environment and living tissue—causing soft-shelled eggs in birds, which limited their reproductive ability; it was also suspected of harming humans. It is not that firms deliberately placed such products on the market knowing the damage they can cause. Rather, these firms do not always know the full impact of products that first appear to be beneficial. The objective of extensive testing is to discover any harmful side effects before they can take toll.

The need for government action to ensure environmental quality is not a problem specific to market or capitalist economies. Centrally planned economies also have pollution. The problem is one of property rights. Who is responsible for the pollutants, which are a special kind of *goods?* Perhaps it is more appropriate to call pollutants *bads.* If a *bad* is the opposite of a *good,* it should carry a negative price. To dispose of a pollutant, the seller should pay the buyer. The buyer, in the case of pollutants, is society. When pollutants are freely disposed into the environment, society unintentionally pays a high price for them. Restriction on disposal of pollutants through government action is a way for society to "purchase" fewer *bads.*

CEILING PRICES

There are times, generally during war, when society believes that the prices of certain goods or services are too high. This belief stems from the idea that excessive pure profits are earned in the production or supply of these items. Consequently, the government may enact legislation that establishes maximum prices of certain goods or services, which makes it illegal for suppliers to sell any regulated items for a higher price.

The established prices are known as *ceiling prices* because the selling price is not supposed to rise above the maximum. The ceiling price is below the market equilibrium price, otherwise it would not be a ceiling or have any effect on the market.

The consequences of a ceiling price are easily illustrated by the use of the traditional demand-supply diagram, as in Figure 12–1, where P_c represents the ceiling price, which is below the market equilibrium price, P_e. At P_c, the quantity demanded, Q_d, is greater than the quantity supplied, Q_s. At the price P_c, people want to buy more than what is offered for sale. Thus, some buyers have to settle for less than they would like. How should the available supply be allocated?

One option open to the government is to allocate the available quantity on a first-come, first-served basis. The problem with this approach is that it is wasteful. Countless hours are spent by people standing in line to obtain a portion of the scarce item. The total output of goods and services to society could be increased if people devoted their energies to production rather than to standing in line or attempting to bribe the product's distributors.

An alternative and more efficient method of allocating the available output is to issue ration stamps equally among the population. Although many people

FIGURE 12–1   Ceiling Price in a Market

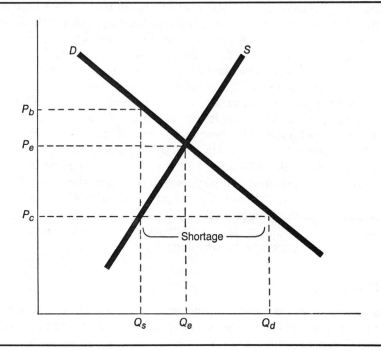

cannot buy as much as they would like under this scheme, at least there is a little for everyone, and it eliminates much of the wasted effort mentioned above. It is important to recognize that a ceiling price inevitably creates a shortage in the market and consequently makes it necessary to impose a rationing scheme.

A second side effect of a ceiling price is that it reduces the quantity produced of the already scarce commodity. In Figure 12–1, before the ceiling price, output is at Q_e, and after the ceiling is imposed, output declines to Q_s. This happens because the lower price provides an incentive for suppliers to reduce their production of the good or service in question—perhaps increasing their output of nonregulated items.

Because of food shortages and subsequent high food prices, the governments of numerous developing nations have set ceiling prices on food to hold down inflation. However, from our analysis of the effect of ceiling prices, it is evident that such a policy only makes the problem worse—because it further reduces the meager output of food. Low food prices also reduce the incentive for public and private research agencies to provide new technology for agriculture, and there is little increase (shift) in the supply curve of food.

A third effect of a government-imposed ceiling price is the creation of a black market where people who desire a larger amount than their quota are willing to pay a high price to obtain it. The black-market price can be determined from Figure 12–1. At quantity Q_s, the demand curve tells us that people are willing to pay the black-market price (P_b). This price is illegal because it is above the ceiling. Also, this price is substantially above the market equilibrium price, P_e. Thus, the black-market price is not a valid indicator of the price that would prevail without the ceiling.

SUPPORT PRICES

In other situations, society has decided that the prices of certain items are too low, and government action result's to keep prices above the market equilibrium. The motivation for this action stems from a belief that producers of the supported products suffer from low incomes and that raising the price of their products will raise their incomes.

The effect of a support price in the market is also seen using the demand-supply diagram in Figure 12–2. At the support price, P_s, the quantity supplied, Q_s, exceeds the quantity demanded, Q_d. As a result, there is a surplus in the market amounting to the difference between Q_s and Q_d. The only way the government can maintain the support price, therefore, is to buy the surplus and

FIGURE 12–2   Support Price in the Market

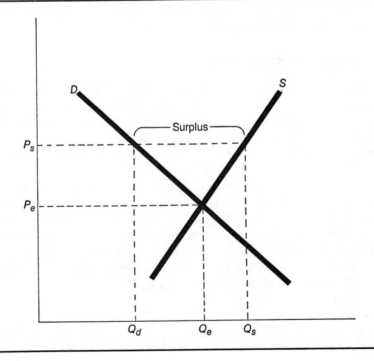

keep it off the market. Otherwise, the excess output will exert a downward pressure on price and drive it toward equilibrium.

The stocks of agricultural commodities accumulated by the U.S. government over the years, mainly grains and dairy products, are examples of surpluses resulting from support prices. Western European countries also have accumulated surpluses of agricultural commodities due to similar policies. At times, countries have attempted to dump surplus commodities on the world market at subsidized prices. But, this practice generally brings howls of protest from nations that normally export these products at nonsubsidized prices.

The existence of a support price provides an incentive for producers to produce even more of an overabundant product. At the equilibrium price, P_e, Q_e is supplied, whereas at the higher support price, P_s, Q_s is offered for sale. To reduce this surplus, the government has restricted the use of land by producers who wish to sell at the higher support price. Unfortunately, restricting land has not been a succesful means of restricting output because producers have increased output by increasing the use of inputs that substitute for land—particularly fertilizer, herbicides, and improved varieties of crops.

The ability of support price programs to substantially raise the income of producers who really need help is questioned increasingly. Support price programs have been ineffective as an income-supporting scheme because the low-income producers tend to be small producers. Doubling the price of wheat from $2 to $4 per bushel adds only $1,000 per year to the income of a 500-bushel-per-year producer, but it adds $40,000 per year to a 20,000-bushel producer. Thus, price support programs tend to help high-income producers more than low-income producers.

SALES AND EXCISE TAXES

Common methods of obtaining government revenue, both state and federal, are sales and excise taxes. These taxes are levied as a percentage of the selling price of the goods or services they cover. Some items, particularly items that society regards as luxuries or nonessentials, such as liquor or jewelry, may be covered by more than one tax. Other items, such as food and clothing, may be taxed at a lower rate or not at all.

The effect of sales and excise taxes is also evaluated by the simple demand-supply diagram. A convenient way of thinking about a sales or excise tax is that it increases the price of a given quantity of the item taxed. A sales or excise tax decreases the supply to consumers or shifts the market supply curve upward and to the left. Because of the tax, a given quantity will cost more to buy. The imposition of such a tax is illustrated in Figure 12–3, in which the supply curve after the tax is represented by S_0.[1]

---

[1] The supply shift is drawn to illustrate a tax of a given percent of the selling price. At higher prices the absolute difference between S_0 and S_1 is greater than at lower prices.

FIGURE 12-3   Effect of a Sales or Excise Tax

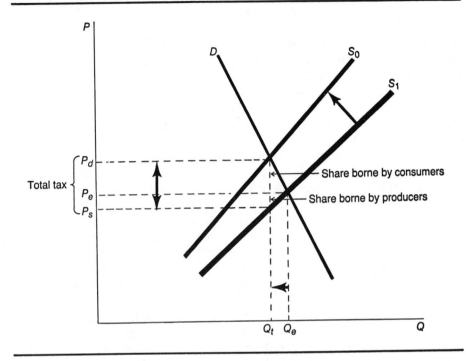

Notice that the market equilibrium price increases from P_e to P_d after the tax is imposed. Also, recognize that with a downward-sloping demand and an upward-sloping supply, the price rise to consumers is less than the amount of the tax. Figure 12-3 shows that the total tax at quantity Q_t is the same as the distance from P_s to P_d on the vertical axis. This is the amount that the supply curve has been shifted up because of the tax.

However, the price that producers obtain after the tax is reduced by the distance between P_e and P_s. Although producers (sellers) collect price P_d from buyers, they must relinquish an amount equal to the tax—leaving them with a lower net price than before the tax—as long as the demand curve is downward sloping. Producers are left with a lower new price after the tax than before because they do not decrease quantity enough to push the selling price up by the full amount of the tax. Even though producers suffer a reduction in profits due to the lower net price received, they would suffer an even greater reduction in profits by forcing the price up by the full amount of the tax. This results from the large decrease in quantity sold that would occur if the price were increased by the full amount of the tax. Profits depend on both price and quantity. We will see this more clearly in the following chapters.

Because of the price increase to consumers and the decrease in the net price received by producers, it is sometimes said that consumers bear part of the burden of the tax according to the price increase they must pay, while producers bear a part of the burden according to the decrease in the net price they receive. In Figure 12–3, consumers bear a greater share of the burden than producers. In the long run as supply becomes more elastic, an even greater share of the tax is borne by consumers. In this case, the more elastic long-run supply curve shifts up by the amount of the tax and raises the price paid by consumers by almost as much as the tax. If the supply curve is horizontal, that is, perfectly elastic, consumers bear 100 percent of the tax. In this case, producers have reduced output of the taxed items enough for the price to rise by the full extent of the tax.

Because of the reduction in the quantity of a taxed item demanded and supplied, the use of selective sales or excise taxes distorts the output mix of goods and services produced in an economy. The quantities of nontaxed or less heavily taxed items increase at the expense of items taxed at higher rates. This outcome has been of some concern to economists because it causes a reduction in the value of output to society from a given amount of resources used. An intuitive explanation for this outcome is that resources are pushed into the production of products that are less valued by society than the taxed items. We will say more about the effect of resource allocation on total value of output in Chapter 14.

Sales and excise taxes also have been criticized for being regressive, that is, for falling most heavily on low-income people. This occurs if low-income people spend a larger share of their income on the taxed items than their higher-income counterparts in the long run. An attempt is made to mitigate this problem by taxing nonessentials, such as alcoholic beverages, tobacco, and luxury items, at relatively high rates and not taxing such necessities as food and clothing—or taxing them at lower rates. However, this differential in tax rates still causes a distortion in the output mix of goods and services mentioned earlier.

ILLEGAL GOODS OR SERVICES

Most societies enact laws that forbid the use of certain goods or services. These laws stem from the belief that consumption of illegal items harms either the individual who consumes them or the people with whom the person comes in contact. Examples of currently illegal goods and services in the United States include mind-distorting drugs, pornographic literature, prostitution, and certain kinds of gambling. Unfortunately, passing a law against the use of a good or service does not eliminate the demand for it. Indeed, there would be no need for such a law if the demand for the good or service did not exist.

Just as for any other good or service, we can visualize both a supply and demand for the illegal item. We have no reason to believe that its demand curve will not slope downward and to the right, like any other market demand curve. There probably will not be as many demanders in such a market because most people do not buy illegal items. Moreover, as the equilibrium price increases, the number of people who buy in these markets will decline, as well as the quantity demanded per person.

Regarding the market supply of illegal goods, there is no reason to believe that higher prices would not bring forth additional quantities. As long as there is a demand for the item, there will always be entrepreneurs ready to supply it for a profit. As prices increase, so do profits; this provides more incentive for illicit suppliers.

Although the market demand and supply of illegal goods and services can be represented by the traditional downward-sloping and upward-sloping lines, there is one important consideration with such goods and services that is not present for their legal counterparts—the penalty for getting caught. The penalty is a demand shifter if it applies only to the person consuming the good or service. If the penalty applies only to the supplier, it is primarily a supply shifter. If it applies to both parties, we would expect the penalty to shift both demand and supply.

In general, the imposition of a penalty or an increase in the harshness of the penalty decreases (shifts to the left) the demand, the supply, or both. For example, imposing a suspended sentence will not decrease the demand for marijuana as much as a definite five-year prison term. Thus, we can expect that increasing the harshness of the penalty on buyers will shift demand to the left, reducing the market price and the quantity exchanged, as illustrated in Figure 12–4A.

On the other hand, if there is an increase in the penalty on suppliers, we can expect a decrease in supply. For example, many prostitutes would find alternative ways of making a living if the penalty for practicing their trade consisted of a $10,000 fine compared with a $100 fine. The effect of a penalty on suppliers is illustrated in Figure 12–4B.

Although a penalty on either the demander or supplier decreases the quantity of an illegal good or service, the price change depends on who is penalized. Goods or services for which only the supplier is penalized tend to have a higher price than in a free market. Most illegal goods or services fit this description. It is not clear why most socieites have penalized suppliers more harshly than demanders for dealing with illegal goods and services. Imposing a more severe penalty on consumers will lower the market price from what it would be in a free market, or from what it would be if only suppliers were penalized.

RATIONING

Rationing generally conjures up a scheme where the government issues ration coupons that allow consumers to purchase a specified amount of the good in question. This circumstance arises when the government places a control or ceiling on the maximum price sellers can obtain. Coupon rationing is most often used in times of national emergency such as wars, at least in the

FIGURE 12–4   Effects of Penalties in the Market for Illegal Goods and Services

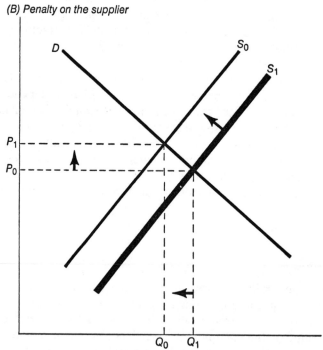

United States and other market economies. In more normal times, coupon rationing is rarely used in these countries.

One might ask, since every nation's ability to produce goods and services falls short of its citizens' desires, why isn't it necessary to always employ rationing to dole out the available output? The answer is that every nation employs a rationing scheme. The one most commonly used in market economies is market price. Recall that if there is a shortage in a market, the price will rise to the equilibrium level. At this level, buyers will purchase exactly what sellers place on the market. Hence, price is the rationing device.

That people rarely think of price as a rationing device attests to its success in this role. It works well because people impose rationing on themselves. If a good becomes scarce and its price rises, the MU per dollar received by consumers declines. This gives them an incentive to consume less of the item and substitute for it more of something that offers a higher MU per dollar. With coupon rationing, the limit of how much we can consume is set by an outside authority, the government. If the price is set low, causing MU per dollar to be high, people have an incentive to circumvent the regulation—attempting to buy more of the scarce item. Resources must then be employed to police people's behavior, and if they are caught breaking the law, more resources must be used to punish them.

Another undesirable consequence of coupon rationing is that the price ceiling reduces the incentive of producers to supply the already scarce goods—making them even more scarce. As time elapses and supply and demand become more elastic, the gap between quantity demanded and quantity supplied becomes wider. People then resort more to black markets until the official price becomes meaningless.

Even with coupon rationing, market price still performs part of the rationing task. The only time coupon rationing would perform 100 percent of the rationing function is when price is zero. As long as market price is some positive value, it contributes to rationing.

RESOURCE ALLOCATION

In any economy, millions of decisions must be made each day regarding how the nation's resources are used to produce the available output. How many resources will be used to produce food, how many for clothing, shelter, medical care, entertainment, or investment in capital goods?

There are two general methods of answering these questions: by a central planning authority or by the millions of participants in markets. The first method is utilized by communist societies, which is why they are often referred to as centrally planned economies. The second method is used by market economies.

In a communist society or centrally planned economy, all the nation's nonlabor resources are owned by the government and just about everyone works for the government. Thus, the people in charge of allocating resources, the central planning committee, have the authority to issue orders or quotas—

telling producers how much they should produce and by what means. The quotas may not always be met, but the resources generally go where the planning committee wants them. Labor must also receive permission from the authorities to change jobs and/or place of residence.

In a market economy, the resource allocation decisions are more diverse. The underlying source of information upon which these decisions are made is market price. Consider a situation where more of a good is produced than consumers want to buy at the prevailing market price. A surplus occurs and as a result, the price of the item declines. The lower price reduces the profitability of the item, which causes producers to look for other, more profitable products to produce. In turn, they reduce the output of the surplus item. Thus, resources are allocated away from the production of less popular goods and services toward more popular items. In this process, market price is both a source of information and an incentive mechanism. As the price of something declines, producers know it is amply supplied to consumers, and the decline in price and profitability gives them the incentive to act on this information. The opposite occurs when too little of a good or service is produced. The shortage causes an increase in the price and profitability of the good or service, giving producers the stimulus and the incentive to increase production. Hence, resources are allocated toward increasing the output of goods that consumers want.

Since market price allocates resources between alternative goods and services, government policies that change market prices, such as ceiling or support prices on selected items, also change the pattern of resource allocation in the economy. Consider a ceiling price. If the price of a good or service is maintained at an artificially low level, producers have an incentive to look for more profitable items to produce, and there is a tendency for resources to leave these areas in search of more profitable opportunities elsewhere.

Unfortunately, this outcome is the opposite of what we want. If the price of an item is relatively high, it indicates that the item is scarce relative to the demand of consumers. But the imposition of a ceiling price drives some resources away from its production, which makes the item more scarce than it was before the ceiling. An example of the effect of ceiling prices is rent control in New York City. Not only has a shortage been created for apartments, particularly in the central part of the city, but landlords also have little incentive to maintain their buildings, which hastens the deterioration of living units in the city. In the long run, resources that otherwise would have gone to repair the rent-controlled buildings have gone elsewhere in search of higher returns. A similar phenomenon occurred in the petroleum industry during the 1970s due to the ceiling price on this product. In this case, however, the shortage was neutralized by increased imports from other countries.

An opposite problem occurs when the price is set artificially high, that is, when there is a support price. In this case, the equilibrium price is low because the supply is large relative to the demand of consumers. The existence of a support price that is higher than the equilibrium price draws even more resources into the production of an already abundant good. Again, the result is the opposite of what we want.

Sales and excise taxes also have an impact on the allocation of resources. By driving a wedge between the prices that consumers pay and producers receive, a sales or excise tax reduces the profitability of producing the taxed item, and it tends to drive some resources away from its production. The higher price that consumers pay also discourages its use.

Market prices, in general, do not allocate resources to the production of public goods and services. Many products, such as roads, police protection, and the military, do not have a market price. The objective of people in charge of this allocation should be to produce the amount and mix of public goods and services that maximize the welfare of society—given the wishes of people for private goods and services. This is a difficult job, not only because no one knows what an optimal allocation is, but also because it differs for different people. For example, politically conservative members of society prefer a smaller proportion of all output to be public goods, or at least goods and services provided by government than their liberal counterparts. The anticipated benefits from public goods in relation to the amount of taxes one has to pay will also influence a person's desire for such goods. Few people like to pay for public goods and services that do not appear to be a good buy in relation to the private goods and services available. People who receive public goods without paying substantial taxes for them are not as likely to call them a bad buy.

As we saw earlier, market prices provide signals that enable producers to decide upon the amount and mix of private goods and services produced in the economy. The signals that guide public decision makers who allocate resources to public goods and services are more complex. Sometimes a shortage of such goods occurs as in the case of crowding in our national parks or congestion on our streets and highways. In other cases, the representatives of citizen groups, such as the Sierra Club or Common Cause, may petition public decision makers to reorder their priorities. Professional lobbyists representing special-interest groups also influence the amount and mix of public goods produced. It is also common for people with a special interest to demonstrate or picket a government agency in an attempt to change the allocation of resources. Sometimes the demonstrations become violent and turn into riots, which is a destructive way to reallocate resources.

In Communist economies, most of the resources used in the production of public and private goods are allocated by government orders. One drawback of allocating resources by political decree as opposed to price signals is that it often forces people to act against their self-interests, which hurts incentives. As an extreme example, you would not be happy if a government official ordered you to quit college or your job and take a job in the coal mines if there was a shortage of fuel. Nor would you be happy if you were ordered to use coal rather than fuel oil or gas to heat your dwelling. On the other hand, if the wages of coal miners rose substantially relative to other occupations, many people would voluntarily enter this occupation to increase their incomes. Similarly, if the price of oil and gas increased relative to coal, people would tend to voluntarily increase their use of coal while conserving oil and gas. Another problem of resource allocation by a central planning committee is that it is impossible for the committee to gather sufficient and accurate information to know where the resources would yield the greatest benefit to society. Hence, this type of economy is subject to making colossal mistakes of either producing too much or too little of various goods. Finally, political pressure may preclude making adjustments even when the committee knows that they should be made.

GLOSSARY

market failure   The discharge of pollutants into the environment without accounting for the cost to society.

ceiling prices   Maintaining the price of a good below the market equilibrium level. Sometimes called price controls; they cause shortages.

support prices   Maintaining the price of a good above its market equilibrium; they cause surpluses.

QUESTIONS

1. Cite the laws or regulations that improve the workings of markets.

2. a. A ceiling price, if it is below the market equilibrium price, will cause a shortage of the good or service in question. True or false? Explain.

   b. A support price, if it is above the market equilibrium price, will cause a surplus of the good or service in question. True or false? Explain.

3. a. Assuming upward-sloping supply and downward-sloping demand curves, a sales or excise tax raises price to consumers by the amount of the tax. True or false? Explain.

   b. In the long run, when supply becomes more elastic, will consumers or producers bear the major burden of such a tax? Explain.

4. The demand for mind-distorting drugs is inelastic. If so, should organized crime be in favor of tighter or looser controls over drug traffic? Explain.

5. Most illegal goods and services are high priced. Why?

6. a. Why is it necessary to ration every good and service?
   b. What are some alternative methods of rationing the available output?
   c. Why is price a desirable rationing device?
   d. How can government policies take away the rationing function of price?

7. a. How do market prices allocate the nation's resources to their most valuable users?
   b. How can ceiling and support price policies distort the allocation of resources?
   c. How are resources allocated in a communist or centrally planned economy?

PART FIVE

Market Structure

CHAPTER 13

Returns to Scale and Firm Size

OVERVIEW

This chapter and the next four chapters classify the firms in a market economy. This chapter explains why firms vary in size. The explanation is called returns to scale. *Returns to scale* are determined by the firm's long-run average total cost curve.

LONG–RUN AVERAGE TOTAL COST CURVE

The long-run average total cost (LRATC) curve of a firm is defined as an envelope of all possible short-run ATC curves. At any point in time, a short-run ATC curve can be drawn for a firm at a given level of fixed inputs such as land, buildings, and machinery. Because of the law of diminishing returns, each short-run ATC curve is U-shaped. When the firm is small, the minimum point on its short-run ATC curve corresponds to a small quantity. When the fixed inputs are small, output is small.

The short-run ATC curve for a small firm, say one with 1000 square feet of floor space, is denoted by ATC, in Figure 13–1. One can visualize similar ATC curves drawn for larger firms as denoted by ATC_2, ATC_3, and so on. As a firm's fixed inputs increase in size, the minimum point on its corresponding ATC curves occurs at successively large quantities. The curve that envelopes all the short-run ATC curves is the long-run ATC (LRATC) curve. Any point on the LRATC curve represents the lowest possible cost of producing a given level of output at the existing technology and input prices.

A. Economies of Scale

As the firm increases the size of its fixed inputs, building in this example, the minimum points on its corresponding ATC curves occur at lower levels, which is an expected outcome. The larger building can accommodate more people with each person better able to spend time on tasks that he or she does best. Also, the large space can accommodate larger and more efficient machines.

When the minimum points on successively larger ATC curves occur at lower levels, as shown by ATC_1–ATC_3 in Figure 13–1, the LRATC envelope will slope down and to the right. The reduction in LRATC at larger-sized firms is called *economies of scale*.

FIGURE 13–1 Long-Run Average Total Cost Curve

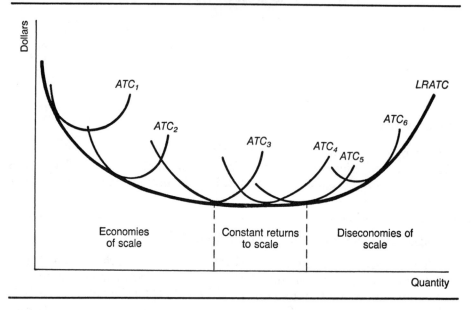

B. Constant Returns to Scale

After a firm reaches moderate size, it may not be possible to capture additional unit cost savings. Additional specialization of tasks may not be feasible, and machines are increased in number rather than becoming larger as the size of the firm increases. In this case, the minimum points on successively larger short-run ATC curves can level out at a constant level, as shown by ATC_3–ATC_5 in Figure 13–1. The LRATC envelope of such ATC curves is horizontal. This denotes *constant returns to scale*. No additional unit cost savings are attained as the firm becomes larger.

C. Decreasing Returns to Scale

As the firm increases in size, the minimum points on the corresponding ATC curves can become higher, indicating that unit costs increase as the firm grows. This phenomenon generally is attributed to management difficulties for large firms. Managers are further removed from the production process and have to obtain information second- or third-hand. This leads to inaccuracies and mistakes. As the firm grows, the increase in unit costs is called *diseconomies of scale*. The region of diseconomies of scale corresponds to the upward-sloping portion of the LRATC curve.

FIRM SIZE

Returns to scale is a long-run concept, enough time for firms to change the level of inputs that are fixed in the short run—land, buildings, and machines. It behooves a firm to grow to a size that enables it to capture any economies of scale but not so large as to encounter diseconomies. This size corresponds to the lowest possible point on the LRATC curve. Or, if the curve has a flat portion (constant returns), the firm should strive to be here. When average total cost is minimized, the firm has the best opportunity to earn pure profits—or at least escape losses.

The shape of the LRATC curve for the typical firm in an industry has an important bearing on the size of firms in an industry. If the LRATC curve turns upward at a small size, the average size of firms in that industry will be small. In such an industry, large firms exhibit higher unit costs and therefore cannot compete with small firms. In the long run, the price of the product will correspond to the lowest point on the typical firm's LRATC curve. If product price is higher than this, the existence of pure profits will attract new firms or resources. In turn, industry output increases and price declines. The opposite occurs if product price is lower than the minimum point on LRATC.

If the shape of the typical firm's LRATC curve is such that its low point occurs at a large level of output, the average size firm in the industry also will be large. In this case, small firms cannot compete with large ones. Product price will be competed down to the point where the most efficient, large firms can just cover their costs.

Another possibility is a LRATC curve that exhibits a relatively long, flat portion—constant returns to scale. In this situation, there can be a large difference in the size of firms. Small firms can coexist with large ones; neither has a cost advantage.

PRODUCTION COSTS: THE FIRM VERSUS THE INDUSTRY

A. Increasing Cost Industry

Although the preceding discussion of economies and diseconomies of scale focused on the individual firm, remember that a firm's production costs can be affected by other firms in the industry. This can happen through the price of resources. If just one or a few firms expand or contract, there will not likely be any change in the price of resources because they use a small part of the industry total. A change in output by all firms in the industry or a substantial change in the number of firms, however, might change the price of the resources used in this industry. A substantial contraction by the industry, for example, releases resources that must find alternative employment. To do this, they might be required to accept lower prices. On the other hand, if there is interest in attracting a substantial quantity of additional resources, their price might rise to draw them away from other industries.

In addition to resource price increases, expansion by the entire industry can affect the individual firm's cost curves through which economists call *technical diseconomies*. The most common example of these is waste disposal. If the industry is small and its firms are scattered, disposing of waste tends to be less costly than if the industry is large and highly concentrated. For example, one or a few small firms may pipe their wastes into a stream or body of water without causing public alarm. But with growth of the industry, each firm may have to construct costly waste disposal facilities, which increases the cost curves of all individual firms.

Economists refer to industries that experience a rise in costs, either through resource price increases or through technical diseconomies, as *increasing-cost industries*. As this kind of industry expands, the minimum point on each firm's LRATC curve increases so that the zero pure-profit price rises. Thus, as the industry grows larger, the long-run equilibrium price for the industry increases. The situation is illustrated in Figure 13–2A, in which it is assumed that the industry expands by adding additional firms.

B. Constant Cost Industry

Although increasing costs are expected in many industries, it is possible to visualize one that can expand its output without increasing costs. This could happen if the resources used by the industry make up a small proportion of the total employment of these resources. Cookie production, for example, employs a small proportion of the total land, labor, and other resources that are available in the economy. Also, no technical diseconomies are present. Economists refer to such an industry as a constant-cost industry because each firm's cost curves and the long-run equilibrium price do not change as the industry expands to large levels of output, as in Figure 13–2B.

C. Decreasing Cost Industry

There is a third possibility, a decreasing-cost industry, in which costs decline as the industry grows. This is less common than the first two cases. Decreasing costs can occur if the price of the industry's resources declines as the industry grows. This phenomenon usually occurs in new or developing areas. If only a few firms are present, many of the resources will have to be shipped in from distant places or produced locally on a small scale at high costs. If the industry is small and insignificant, there likely will be no public effort to establish institutions to serve it or to train people to work in it if special skills are required. On the other hand, an industry that becomes a significant part of an area's economy can expect to enjoy special advantages. Supporting

FIGURE 13–2 Long-Run Average Total Cost Curves for a Typical Firm in Increasing, Constant, and Decreasing Cost Industries

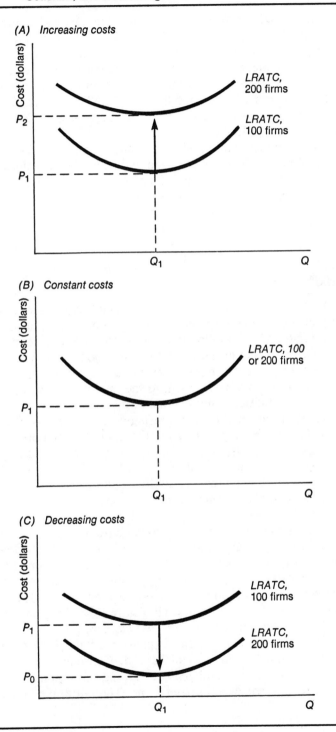

industries that can supply resources at a minimum cost will emerge; financial institutions will consider it a better risk and will loan money at a lower rate of interest; and public schools might offer special training to young people who want to find employment in the industry. Economists refer to these circumstances as *external economies*. In this case, the entrance of additional firms lowers costs for all firms. It is not totally unexpected, therefore, that industries tend to concentrate in specific areas rather than spread out. Decreasing costs are illustrated in Figure 13–2C.

An industry might exhibit all three situations at different stages of development. When an industry is young and becoming established, it might enjoy decreasing costs. Then, when it is moderate in size, it might expand with constant costs. Finally, as it becomes a major industry using a significant proportion of the resources it employs, it may have increasing costs.

LONG–RUN SUPPLY

In the long run, competitive forces make each firm in an industry produce the quantity of output that corresponds to the minimum point of its LRATC curve, Q_1 in Figure 13–2. If a firm does not produce at this point, other firms that succeed in producing at the minimum-cost point will produce at a lower cost and drive the high-cost firms out of business. This occurs because the price of the product will be competed down to the minimum point of the LRATC curve, and any firm that does not operate at this point incurs losses.

Consider what happens in an increasing-cost industry. At the low price, P_1, there are 100 firms of a given size in the industry, each producing Q_1, as shown in Figure 13–3. Thus, in the long run, the total output of the industry at price P_1 is 100 Q_1. This is illustrated by Figure 13–3. Now suppose the demand for the industry's product increases and the resulting short-run increase in the price of the product draws 100 more firms of equal size into the industry so that the industry doubles in size. If the growth of the industry causes the price of one or more of the industry's resources to increase, the LRATC curve for the typical firm will shift upward as shown in Figure 13–2A. In the long run, the price of the industry's product will settle at P_2. Thus, in the long run, the total output of the industry at price P_2 is 200 Q_1. This is also illustrated in Figure 13–3. Connecting the two points we have just derived yields an upward-sloping, long-run supply curve as shown in Figure 13–3. Thus, in an increasing-cost industry, the long-run supply is upward sloping.

In a constant-cost industry, the expansion of the industry leaves the LRATC curve of the typical firm unchanged. Consequently, product price remains at P_1 at both 100 Q_1 and 200 Q_1. Plotting these points on a diagram similar to Figure 13–3 yields a horizontal line. Therefore, the long-run supply

FIGURE 13–3   Long-Run Supply in an Increasing-Cost Industry

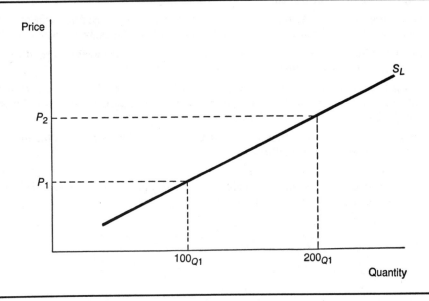

curve in a constant-cost industry is horizontal, or perfectly elastic. Finally, in a decreasing-cost industry, the growth in size from 100 to 200 firms lowers the LRATC curve to each firm, as shown in Figure 13–2C. Now, when output increases from 100 Q_1 to 200 Q_1, the price of the product declines to P_0 from P_1. Plotting these points yields a downward-sloping line. Consequently, the long-run supply for a decreasing-cost industry is downward sloping. Try to plot the long-run supply curves for the constant- and decreasing-cost industry cases on your own.

GLOSSARY

long-run average total cost (LRATC) curve   An envelope of all possible short-run ATC curves that shows the lowest cost of producing a given level of output.

economies of scale   A reduction in long-run average total cost as the firm expands in size; corresponds to the downward-sloping portion of the LRATC curve.

constant returns of scale   Long-run average total cost remains constant as the firm's size increases; corresponds to horizontal portion of the LRATC curve.

diseconomies of scale   Long-run average total cost increases as the firm increases in size; corresponds to upward-sloping portion of the LRATC curve.

increasing-cost industry   Long-run average total cost curve of the average firm shifts upward as the industry expands.

technical diseconomies   An increase in the LRATC of the individual firm as the industry expands due to increased technical difficulties such as disposing of waste material.

constant-cost industry   Long-run average total cost curve of the average firm does not shift as industry expands.

decreasing-cost industry   Long-run average total cost curve of the average firm shifts down as industry expands. Can occur because of a decrease in the prices of inputs as suppliers are able to capture scale economies.

external economies   A reduction in the LRATC of the individual firm as the industry expands due to lower input prices.

long-run supply   Consists of minimum points of the average firm's LRATC curve. Slopes up for an increasing-cost industry, is horizontal for a constant-cost industry, and slopes down for a decreasing-cost industry.

QUESTIONS

1. a. Why might the minimum points of a firm's short-run average total cost curves decrease as the firm expands?
   b. Why might the minimum points increase?

2. Define:
   a. Economies of scale.
   b. Constant returns to scale.
   c. Diseconomies of scale.

3. Under conditions of economies of scale, is it possible for a large firm that produces a small quantity to experience a higher average total cost than a smaller firm that produces a quantity at the lowest point of its ATC curve? Explain.

4. Illustrate the shape of the LRATC curve for the typical firm in an industry:
   a. Made up of small firms.
   b. Made up of large firms.
   c. Made up of large and small firms.

5. Define the following:
   a. Increasing-cost industry.
   b. Constant-cost industry.
   c. Decreasing-cost industry.

6. *a. What conditions give rise to increasing-, decreasing-, and constant-cost industries?*
   b. What kinds of firms would you find in each of the above industries?

7. *What conditions cause:*
   a. An upward-sloping, long-run supply curve?
   b. A horizontal long-run supply curve?
   c. A downward-sloping, long-run supply curve?

CHAPTER 14

Perfect Competition

OVERVIEW

This chapter focuses on the small end of the size distribution of business firms—perfect competition. After establishing the two characteristics common to all perfectly competitive firms, the discussion turns to the profit-maximizing behavior of such firms. The adjustment of a perfectly competitive industry to pure profits or losses is also considered.

PERFECT COMPETITION DEFINED

A *perfectly competitive* firm is one that has no power to alter the price it receives for its product. For this reason, the perfectly competitive firm is sometimes called a *price taker*. The firm takes the price of its product as determined in the market. The agricultural firm or farm is the only firm that meets this criterion. Therefore, agriculture is a perfectly competitive industry of perfectly competitive firms. The small size of each firm relative to the industry's size suggests a lack of significant scale economies.

CHARACTERISTICS OF A PERFECTLY COMPETITIVE FIRM

There are two basic reasons that a perfectly competitive firm must accept the price that is determined by the market: (1) it sells a product that is undifferentiated from the product of all other firms in the market and (2) it sells a small proportion of the total market.

That a perfectly competitive firm sells a product indistinguishable from what is produced by other firms in its market means that buyers have no preference for the product of one firm over another. Thus, every firm must sell its product at the price all the other firms obtain. Why should buyers pay $4.25 per bushel of wheat from farmer Jones if 10,000 other farmers are selling the same product for $4 per bushel? In other words, each producer must conform to the market price.

We also know that because of the downward-sloping nature of market demand curves, market price can be changed only if the quantity sold is changed; quantity must decrease to obtain a higher price, or any increase in the quantity demanded must be accompanied by a price reduction. But, because the perfectly competitive firm sells a minute fraction of the market, each firm cannot alter market price by producing more or less. For example, suppose farmer Jones decides that the market price of wheat is too low. What can he do about it? If he reduces his production by half (a drastic measure for any firm), the total market supply would remain unchanged, because taking a few hundred or thousand bushels from a market in which millions of bushels are traded has an imperceptible effect; it's like taking a handful of sand away from a beach. Thus, no matter what quantity the firms decide to produce, within reason, the market price remains the same.

Thus, the characteristic of an undifferentiated product requires each perfectly competitive firm to sell at the same price as all other firms, that is, the market price; and the characteristic of producing a small fraction of the market means that each perfectly competitive firm has no power to alter the market price.

DEMAND FACING A PERFECTLY COMPETITIVE FIRM

We can obtain a better understanding of the relationship between a perfectly competitive firm and the market in which it sells by diagrams. The traditional market demand and supply curves are depicted in Figure 14–1A. The equilibrium price and quantity that prevail in this market are denoted by P_e and Q_e. The price that each firm will face, therefore, is P_e, if the market is allowed to reach an equilibrium.

FIGURE 14–1   Relationship between the Market and the Perfectly Competitive Firm

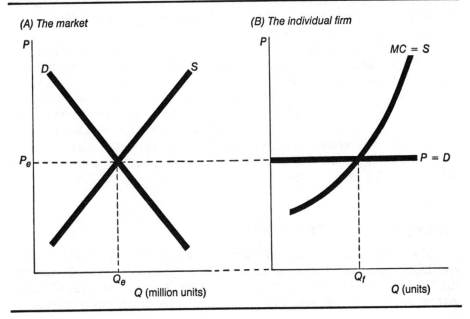

The individual perfectly competitive firm operating in this market is represented by Figure 14–1B. Its supply curve, as we know, is the marginal cost (MC) curve above the point where it intersects the average variable cost curve if it is already committed to its fixed costs. The price that the firm will receive for its product is P_e, as determined by market supply and demand. This price, P_e, is the demand facing this firm. The price line, P, is a demand curve in that it tells the firm what price it will receive for its product. The fact that the demand curve is a perfectly horizontal line (perfectly elastic) means that the firm can produce and sell any output within reason at this price. In other words, the market stands ready to buy any reasonable quantity from this firm at price P_e. Thus, the line showing the price is the demand curve facing this firm.

In an actual market situation, the prevailing market price need not be the equilibrium price. For example, if market demand had recently shifted to the right and the market price had not adjusted to the new, higher equilibrium level, the actual market price probably would be less than the equilibrium. However, as explained previously, forces then would occur and push the actual price up toward the new equilibrium. During the adjustment, the price line facing the individual firm would rise in accordance with the existing market price. In other words, we would not expect the price line to shift instantaneously from one equilibrium position to another.

From our discussion relating to product supply, we know that a producer of this nature maximizes profits by producing a quantity that corresponds to the point where price equals marginal cost. This quantity is represented by Q_f in Figure 14–1B. Notice that the units of measure on the quantity axis differ greatly between the market and the firm. The market quantity might be measured in terms of millions of units, whereas the firm's quantity might be measured in number of units. The units of measure on the price axes are the same for the market and the firm.

Let us summarize the three kinds of demand curves we have studied. The first is the demand of an individual consumer, represented by a downward-sloping line indicating that quantity increases as price decreases, and vice versa. The second demand curve is market demand—the sum of all individual demanders in the market. This is also represented by a downward-sloping line, as in Figure 14–1A. The third is the demand curve facing an individual firm. For the perfectly competitive firm this demand curve is a perfectly horizontal line, indicating that the market will take any reasonable quantity the firm wishes to sell at the going market price.

PRICE, COSTS, AND PROFITS

The perfectly competitive firm takes the price as determined in the market and decides whether or not it should produce; and if so, how much. Recall from the supply discussion in Chapter 10 that pure profits are earned only if price is greater than the average total cost at the quantity the firm chooses to produce.

FIGURE 14-2   Possible Profit or Loss Positions of Perfectly Competitive Firms

We also know that the profit-maximizing quantity corresponds to the point where marginal cost equals price.

The three diagrams in Figure 14–2 illustrate the three possible profit positions for perfectly competitive firms. The price, P_e, that is shown is determined by market demand and supply, as illustrated in Figure 14–1A. A firm that earns pure profits in its business is illustrated in Figure 14–2A. The resources (inputs) used in this production activity earn more than they could in other kinds of work. The total pure profits for the firm are represented by the shaded area. Notice that total profits are maximized at a level of output beyond the point where profit per unit is the largest, that is, the point where the distance between price and average total cost (ATC) is the greatest. Such an outcome is reasonable because the firm is interested in maximizing its total profits rather than profit per unit.

The situation depicted in Figure 14–2B, zero pure profits, is one in which the resources employed by this firm are earning just what they could earn in some other alternative occupation. This situation is the only one of the three shown in which the firm produces a quantity corresponding to the minimum point on its ATC curve. The case of a firm that is not covering its costs (implicit plus explicit) is shown in Figure 14–2C. In this example, the resources employed by the firm earn less than what they could in other occupations. This does not necessarily mean, however, that this firm's cash expenses are greater than its total sales because, as noted in Chapter 10, the ATC curve includes a charge for the resources owned by the firm as well as its cash expenses.

If we could measure perfectly the costs of individual firms at any point in time, we would probably observe all three of these situations in a given market or industry. There would be a few well-managed, low-cost firms making pure profits, as illustrated in Figure 14–2A. There would be other firms breaking even but doing as well as they could in any other occupation. There would also be a few firms making less than they could in other occupations, perhaps looking for a chance to sell their assets and begin another line of production.

Figure 14–2C need not depict a badly managed, slipshod enterprise. The costs for this firm might be high because it has better alternatives than the other firms in the market. For example, the owner of the firm might be a highly educated wheat farmer who has the opportunity of working in a nearby bank at a salary much higher than his neighbors could obtain in their best alternative occupations. Thus, a firm's cost might be high either because the owner is a bad manager or because the person has superior talents that are in demand elsewhere. It is not valid to conclude, therefore, that an industry in which the number of firms is decreasing is losing its least productive people. It may lose some of them, but at the same time, it can lose its most productive people because they have superior opportunities elsewhere.

LONG–RUN ADJUSTMENT

Economists have precise definitions for the terms *short run* and *long run* as they apply to production and supply. The short run is the length of time that is too short to change the level of fixed inputs used or the number of firms in the industry but long enough to change the level of output by changing variable inputs. Essentially, the marginal physical product curve and its mirror image, marginal cost, reflect short-run changes in production.

The long run is a period of time long enough to change either the level of fixed inputs used by firms or the number of firms. Unfortunately, it is impossible to designate a period of time that constitutes the long run for all types of firms or even for different situations. The length of this period differs among firms, depending on how difficult or costly it is to change fixed inputs. If production requires extensive fixed inputs, say extensive irrigation or drainage facilities, the length of time to reach a long-run adjustment will be longer than for firms that pursue production in small rented facilities, such as barber shops.

The length of time to reach a long-run adjustment also depends on how profitable it is to adjust. If it is profitable for a firm to expand its fixed inputs or for new firms to enter the industry, the adjustment time will be shorter than if it barely pays to change the level of output or to enter or leave the industry. For example, if it is profitable to expand facilities, most contractors will step up the completion date if they are paid to do so. A higher fee enables them to pay their employees for overtime work to finish the job more quickly.

In looking at long-run adjustment for a perfectly competitive industry in more detail, we will start where the market is in equilibrium, that is, where price corresponds to the intersection of supply and demand, as shown in Figure 14–3A. Suppose that the typical firm in the industry is making substantial pure profits, as shown in Figure 14–3B. Assume as well that each firm maximizes its profits by producing an output that corresponds to the point where price is equal to marginal cost, Q_f in Figure 14–3B. These two conditions—market price is at the point where the quantity demanded equals the quantity supplied and price equals marginal cost for each firm—constitute a short-run equilib-

FIGURE 14–3 Short-Run Market Equilibrium with Pure Profits Made by the Average Firm

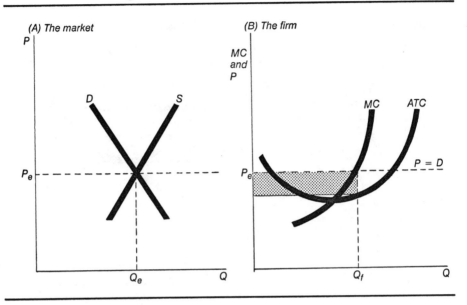

rium for an industry. This situation is illustrated in the two diagrams in Figure 14–3.

If each firm makes pure profits, however, we can expect that existing firms will expand their facilities (increase their fixed inputs) and/or additional firms will enter the industry to get a piece of the action. We need not assume that all firms are making substantial pure profits for this to happen. In fact, some businesses might be characterized by Figures 14–2B and C. All that is necessary is that a sizable portion of existing firms make pure profits.

Recall from the discussion on product supply that an increase in the number of firms or an increase in the size of firms shifts the market supply curve to the right, as shown in Figure 14–4A. An increase in supply reduces market price. As the market price falls, so does the price that faces each firm. Thus, as the supply shifts right and market price falls, the pure profits that each firm is making are competed away. This process is illustrated in Figure 14–4A and B.

This process of new resources coming into an industry to compete away pure profits is most noticeable at high levels of pure profits. Then, as price falls closer to the zero pure-profit point (P_0 in Figure 14–4), the entry of additional resources will slow down as the prospects for pure profits diminish, although it is not uncommon to observe situations where firms have built up optimism over time and continue to expand until price falls below the zero pure-profit point. As soon as this happens, some firms find more profitable opportunities elsewhere, move out of the industry, and contribute to a decrease in supply, which eventually pulls price up toward the zero pure-profit equilibrium.

FIGURE 14–4   Long-Run Adjustment to Pure Profits by Entry of Additional Resources or Firms

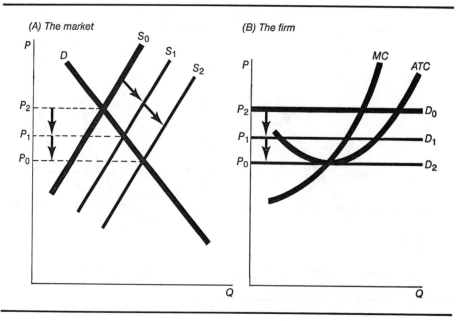

An opposite process of adjustment occurs if a large share of the firms in a market or industry are suffering losses or negative pure profits. Here, firms move to more profitable opportunities, decreasing the market supply, and raising market price.

The existence of pure profits or losses results in a long-run adjustment characterized by the corresponding entry or exit of resources or firms. It is also possible to observe adjustments on the cost side. In the production of wheat, for example, there may be a few firms that enjoy some special advantage, such as productive soil. The entry of new firms might push price down to the zero-profit position for every firm in the industry except the privileged few. They might continue to reap pure profits. Eventually, these unusually profitable firms will be sold to new owners, and the price paid for these firms reflects the pure profits that can be expected in the future. The new owners are willing to pay more for productive land than for poor land. With an increase in the land price, there will be an increase in the cost of production, mainly because of the increase in the interest charge (explicit or implicit) and taxes. If the sellers of these productive firms are shrewd bargainers, they will obtain a price that pushes average total cost (ATC) just about up to the expected future price as illustrated by Figure 14–5. Economists refer to this situation as a *capitalization* of pure profits into the value of land.

This phenomenon of cost adjusting to price has been particularly important in U.S. agriculture. As pointed out in Chapter 12, the government has attempted to increase incomes by establishing support prices of various

FIGURE 14–5 Long-Run Adjustment to Pure Profits by Increases in Cost of Resources to the Individual Firm

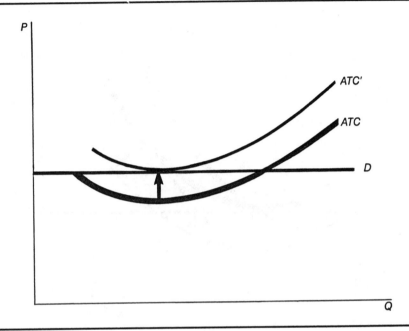

products. Prices are fixed, but over the years, pure profits have been eroded away because of the bidding up of land prices. Eventually, producers are forced back to the same zero pure-profit position that existed before support prices. The people who owned the land during its price rise, however, enjoyed a capital gain. Also remember that for this phenomenon to occur, a necessary condition is that the product price be maintained at the artificially high level, such as by price supports. Without the price support, competitive forces would drive the product price down to the zero pure-profit level, as illustrated by Figure 14–4.

Again, adjustment will not be instantaneous. Pure profits or losses exist for different firms at any point in time. But, if pure profits or losses exist, we can observe an adjustment toward a long-run zero pure-profit position in a perfectly competitive industry.

THE CONTINUAL SEARCH FOR LOWER COSTS

Even though all firms in a perfectly competitive industry face a common market price, there are substantial differences in *costs* among firms. High costs may be due to low productivity resulting from inept management, or they may stem from high-paying opportunities in other lines of work. A perfectly competitive firm has no control over the price of its product, and such a firm cannot alter the opportunities existing elsewhere. In fact, high implicit costs

FIGURE 14-6   Effects of a Cost Reduction

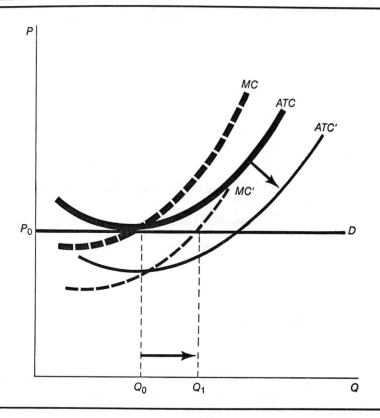

stemming from superior opportunities elsewhere are welcomed because they represent opportunities to increase income.

However, most perfectly competitive firms can do something about the efficiency of their production processes. The more efficient a firm is in transforming inputs into output, the lower its production costs and the higher its profits. Thus, most firms continually search for new cost-reducing inputs or techniques to increase profits. The effect of achieving a cost reduction in production is illustrated by Figure 14-6. Average total cost (ATC) is shifted downward, and marginal cost (MC) is shifted downward and to the right. If price is at P_0, than the firm can move from a zero pure-profit position to a position of positive pure profits after the cost reduction.

In addition to creating pure profits for the firm in this example, a second effect of a cost reduction is the shift downward and to the right of the MC curve. This tells us that the firms now can produce an additional or marginal unit more cheaply than before. But remember that the MC curve is also the firm's supply curve. At the original MC, Q_0 is produced by the firm, whereas at the new lower MC', Q_1 is produced. If a few firms find a way to reduce costs and shift their supply curves, there is no perceptible effect in the market. Increasing the production of wheat by 1,000 bushels, for example, will not be noticed in a market where millions of bushels are traded.

Although the increased production from a single firm has no appreciable effect on the market, similar action by many firms will shift the market supply curve to the right, which reduces the market price. Furthermore, the lower market price squeezes the newly created pure profits out of firms that have achieved lower costs.

Once a significant proportion of firms adopts a new cost-reducing input or technique and the market price begins to fall, the firms that have not reduced costs find their profit positions eroding, and consequently they must also adopt these inputs or techniques so they will not suffer losses or have to leave the industry. This process of the early adopters reaping pure profits and the subsequent erosion of profits to these firms (and losses to the remaining firms) is like a treadmill; each firm must run faster (decrease costs more and more) to stay even. Although each firm may not appreciate this continuous struggle, consumers and society generally gain from it, because more output is obtained from the nation's scarce resources.

ECONOMIC EFFICIENCY

A perfectly competitive industry frequently is used by economists as a standard by which to judge other industries. The reason is that a perfectly competitive equilibrium (short-run or long-run) results in maximum economic efficiency. At this point, resources are allocated such that the value of society's output is maximized. Three criteria are required to obtain economic efficiency. First, there must be maximum technical efficiency. This means that a physical output obtained from a given level of inputs is at its maximum. In other words, resources are not being wasted. For example, a given amount of labor and capital might produce only 20 bushels of wheat if time were wasted or the machines used inappropriately. But, if the inputs were fully and correctly utilized, 30 bushels might be produced. Technical efficiency also means that the firm is on the highest isoquant for a given input mix.

A second criterion necessary to obtain economic efficiency is that a given level of output is produced at the least possible cost. Recall from Chapter 8 that a given output can be produced by various combinations of inputs, but only one combination will result in the lowest possible cost. This is the combination that results in the equality of the P/MPP ratios or that corresponds to the tangency point between the isoquant and the lowest possible isocost line. This is the cost-minimizing condition. Actually, any firm, whether it is perfectly competitive or not, can meet these first two conditions; the attainment of maximum technical efficiency and the cost-minimization condition.

The third criterion necessary for maximum economic efficiency is that the level of output for each good corresponds to the point where the marginal cost of producing an extra unit is equal to the price of the good. This is the profit-maximizing level of output for each perfectly competitive firm. In the next three chapters, we will see that an imperfectly competitive firm will not produce this level of output. Hence, only perfect competition meets the three criteria required to reach maximum economic efficiency, i.e., the maximum value of output. The next question is: Why does the P = MC equality result in the maximum value of output given the amount of resources available to a country? To understand why, we must understand what price and marginal cost represent.

The price of a product is the value that society assigns to a marginal unit. For example, if the price of wheat is $4 per bushel, we can infer that society values an extra bushel of wheat at $4 or it would not choose to buy it for this price.

Marginal cost (MC), on the other hand, represents the cost to society in terms of other products given up to obtain an extra unit of this product. For example, if the MC of wheat is $4, to produce an extra bushel, $4 worth of another good or service must be given up, assuming that this other good is produced in an industry where price and MC also are equal.

It is easiest to understand why the equality of price and MC results in a maximum value of output if we first look at situations where price does not equal marginal cost. Suppose that, for some reason, the price of a bushel of wheat is $4 and its MC is $3. This means that society values an extra bushel at $4 and values the goods or services given up to produce this extra bushel at $3. Now, if one extra bushel of wheat is produced, society gains $4 and gives up $3, leaving a net gain of $1. Thus, it behooves society to increase the production of wheat under these circumstances, because the value of total output is increased using the same amount of resources. There is an underallocation of resources to the production of a good or service if its price is greater than its MC.

In the opposite situation, say price is still $4 but MC is $5. By decreasing the production of wheat by one bushel, society gives up $4 worth of wheat but gains $5 worth of other goods and services, resulting in a net gain of $1. Thus, if MC is greater than price, there is an overallocation of resources to the production of this product because by reducing its production, the total value of output is increased with a given amount of resources. The value of output is maximized only if price equals marginal cost because when this occurs, it is impossible to reallocate resources to increase the total value of output. Perfectly competitive firms attempt to produce at the point where price equals MC. Thus, an advantageous characteristic of perfect competition for society is that producers attempting to maximize their profits by equating price and marginal cost also maximize the value of output to society.

However, perfect competition is not the ultimate goal in all industries. We will see in the following chapters that the nature of most products precludes perfect competition in their production. However, the further removed an industry is from the perfectly competitive model, the greater the chance that society will suffer a significant reduction in the value of output for a given amount of resources.

The idea of competitive forces working for the good of society was introduced by the eighteenth-century Scottish economist and philosopher Adam Smith in *The Wealth of Nations,* published in 1776. He called this phenomenon the "invisible hand." Each firm that attempts to maximize its own profits also maximizes the value of output to society, as though guided by an invisible hand.

GLOSSARY

perfectly competitive firm   A firm that takes the price of its product as given. Such a firm sells a small share of the market and sells a product undifferentiated from the product of other firms in the industry.

perfectly competitive industry   An industry made up of perfectly competitive firms.

demand facing the perfectly competitive firms   A horizontal line corresponding to the market price of the product.

short run   Period of time too short to change the level of fixed inputs such as land and buildings or the number of firms.

long run   Period of time long enough to change the level of fixed inputs or number of firms.

capitalized   The increase in the price of an asset such as land due to expected pure profits in the future.

economic efficiency   Maximization of the value of output to society for a given amount of resources. Requires: (1) maximum technical efficiency, (2) minimum costs, and (3) output of each firm corresponds to the point where product price equals marginal cost.

QUESTIONS

1. a. What is a perfectly competitive firm?
   b. What are the two characteristics that give rise to such a firm?
   c. What industry comes closest to perfect competition?

2. a. Distinguish between the demand by consumers for a product produced by a perfectly competitive firm and the demand facing such a firm.
   b. What is the shape of the demand curve facing a perfectly competitive firm?
   c. What is implied by such a demand curve?

3. Wheat production in the United States is carried on by many firms, each selling a product undifferentiated from that of other firms in the market. Explain how the price of wheat is determined and how this price is related to the individual producer.

4. An increase in market supply, say because of favorable growing conditions, will cause a decrease in the demand facing the firm. True or false? Explain.

5. a. Differentiate between short-run and long-run adjustment to price changes.
   b. What are the two ways in which pure profits are competed away in a perfectly competitive industry?
   c. It is common practice for governments to set the support price of wheat at the average cost of production for the industry. What happens to the price of land that is more productive than the industry average? What happens to the industry average cost of production?

6. Plant breeders continually develop new varieties of wheat that yield more than old varieties.
   a. Explain the effect of a new variety on the costs and profits of the alert, early-adopting farmer.
   b. Explain the long-run adjustment of the wheat-producing industry to this new development.
   c. Explain what would happen to producers who do not adopt a new variety.

7. a. What is economic efficiency?
   b. What are the three criteria necessary to achieve economic efficiency?
   c. Why does perfect competition result in maximum economic efficiency?

CHAPTER 15

Pure Monopoly

OVERVIEW

The three types of firms discussed in this section, pure monopoly, monopolistic competition, and oligopoly, are commonly grouped in the broad category called imperfect competition. This chapter defines an imperfectly competitive firm, and then focuses on pure monopoly. A major consideration is the profit maximizing price that a monopoly would charge if it were free to do so.

IMPERFECT COMPETITION DEFINED

An imperfectly competitive firm is one that can exercise some control over the price it receives for its product. There are two main reasons a firm might have some control over the price it charges: (1) each firm produces a sizable share of the market and (2) each firm sells a product that is distinguishable from competitors' products. These two reasons are the opposite for a perfectly competitive firm. It is sufficient for a firm to fulfill either of these requirements to be imperfectly competitive. Some firms exhibit both characteristics.

In examining why these two characteristics allow a firm to have some control over the price of its product, consider a firm that sells a large share of the total market, such as U.S. Steel. If U.S. Steel reduced its annual output by 10–20 percent, we would observe a noticeable decline in total steel output in the United States and an increase in the price of steel, providing the market demand for steel is downward sloping. As a result of its production cutback, U.S. Steel could raise the price of its product by a small amount. Similarly, a comparable *increase* in output by U.S. Steel would add a noticeable amount to total steel output and result in at least a small decline in the market price of steel. In this case, U.S. Steel would have to accept a lower price for its product. The main point is that such a firm can manipulate the price it receives for its product by changing its level of output.

A firm that sells a product that differs somewhat from its competitors can also exercise some control over the price of its product. In the above example, we considered a firm that sells a large share of the market with a product that is the same as its competitors to keep the effect of product differentiation separate from share of the market. Now we will consider a firm that sells a small share of the market but whose product is slightly different from its competitors—say, the local Amoco station in your neighborhood. It might appear that such a firm's main product, gasoline, is the same as that sold by other Amoco stations. However, a retail firm's specific location and the kind of service it renders can result in some difference in its product. If some of the firm's customers prefer its product to the product of competing stations, the station in question probably could raise its price a few cents a gallon over its competitors without having its gasoline sales go to zero. The people who found the station a convenient place to stop or for some reason liked the service probably would continue to patronize it, at least for a time. On the other hand, if the station lowered its price a few cents below its competitors, it would attract additional customers. A firm that sells a product that is somewhat different from its competitor's products has some leeway in the price it charges.

DEMAND FACING AN IMPERFECTLY COMPETITIVE FIRM

The imperfectly competitive firm's ability to alter the price of its product is translatable to the demand curve facing such a firm. Chapter 14 showed that the perfectly competitive firm faces a perfectly horizontal (perfectly elastic) demand curve, reflecting the fact that it has no control over the price it receives. For an imperfectly competitive firm, its ability to raise the price and sell a smaller quantity, or lower the price and sell a larger quantity, means that the firm faces a downward-sloping demand curve. This is illustrated in Figure 15–1.

If the firm raises its price, say from P_1 to P_2, it is forced to reduce its sales from Q_1 to Q_0. Or, if the firm wishes to increase sales, say from Q_1 to Q_2, it must lower the price from P_1 to P_0. Thus, the demand curve of all imperfectly competitive firms is downward sloping. Remember, however, that even though this downward-sloping demand curve facing the individual firm resembles the market-demand curve for the product, it is not the same as market demand. (Pure monopoly, to be discussed shortly, is an exception.) As long as there is more than one firm selling in a market, the demand curve facing each firm is considerably more elastic than the market demand curve. For a pure monopoly, the demand curve facing the firm is the same as the market demand curve because there is just one firm.

MONOPOLY DEFINED

Pure monopoly exists when a single firm supplies a product. Private, unregulated monopoly is illegal in the United States. The firms that currently are closest to a pure monopoly include public utilities such as natural gas and electric companies. These firms have exclusive rights to operate in an area to capture scale economies and to avoid a duplication of facilities. The motivation for having such firms is to lower the product's cost for consumers from what it would be in an open, competitive market. In electric power, the main source of

FIGURE 15–1   Demand Curve Facing an Imperfectly Competitive Firm

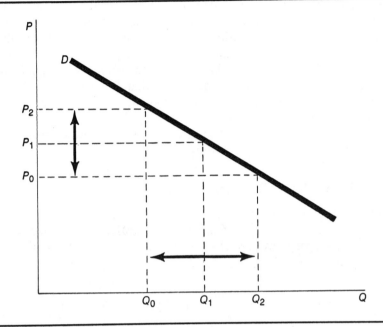

increased costs is the duplication of transmission lines. The same is true for natural gas supply.

The definition of monopoly depends on how one defines the industry. For example, an electric power company has a monopoly in selling electricity but not in selling all power. Fuel oil and gas are alternatives—although imperfect for lighting. Similarly, the post office has a monopoly in delivering first-class mail but not all mail or communication. Thus, to have a monopoly, one must narrowly define the industry.

A monopoly is not a natural economic phenomenon. To preserve a monopoly, the government must keep out competition by issuing licenses to existing firms. If there are profits to be made, other firms would be attracted and the monopoly would disappear.

What about small towns or rural areas where a single grocery store, service station, or barber shop serves the entire community? Aren't these firms monopolies in their communities? No. If a single firm in a small community started to charge unusually high prices, customers, especially persons living in the fringe area next to another supplier, could easily switch. Also, the threat of a competitor moving in if a firm becomes too greedy can temper a desire to monopolize. Thus, there is little concern over the apparent lack of competition for such firms.

Firms that hold licenses to operate free of competition in an area are closer to the pure definition of monopoly. For this reason, such firms are regulated by government agencies. Standards of performance and prices are established, and the firm's behavior is monitored. However, in recent years, an increasing amount of criticism has been directed at government-sanctioned monopolies, which has led to the deregulation of several industries such as airlines, trucking, telephones, and certain financial services. The evidence suggests that regulation actually increased the price paid by consumers. For example, during regulation, the airfare from Los Angeles to San Francisco, which was an intrastate route and not regulated, was about half the regulated fare from Chicago to Minneapolis–St. Paul, approximately the same distance. There is nothing like a little competition, even one or two competitors, to keep a firm efficient and innovative.

MARGINAL REVENUE AND PRICE

To determine the profit-maximizing price for a monopoly, it is necessary to reintroduce the concept of marginal revenue (MR). Recall that marginal revenue is the additional revenue obtained by selling one more unit of output. It is computed as:

$$MR = \frac{\Delta TR}{\Delta Q}$$

where ΔTR is change in total revenue and ΔQ is change in quantity of output sold.

For a firm that faces a perfectly elastic demand, such as perfect competition, marginal revenue is equal to product price. Selling one more unit of a product, say for $5, adds $5 to the firm's sales or revenue. For a firm that faces a downward-sloping demand curve, such as monopoly, marginal revenue will be less than the price received for the product. The reason is that the firm must sell all of its output at the same price. If the firm wishes to sell more, it must lower the price. This lower price must apply to all units sold. The firm cannot sell the additional output to its newest customers at a lower price than it charges old customers. Therefore, the slight reduction in price of all previous units sold causes the added revenue obtained from the additional units sold to be less than the price received for them.

For example, suppose an electric company wishes to increase sales. To do so, it must lower its price:

Initial situation:	price :	$10
	quantity:	100
New situation:	price:	$9
	quantity:	150

FIGURE 15–2   Monopoly Price Determination

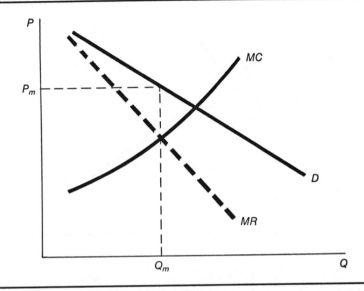

$$\text{Marginal revenue} = \frac{\Delta\ TR}{\Delta\ Q} = \frac{1,350 - 1,000}{150 - 100} = \frac{350}{50} = \$7$$

Although the price of the marginal unit is $9, MR is $7. The $1 reduction in price on the previous 1,000 units sold causes the MR to be $2 less than the new lower selling price of the product. Because MR is less than price at any given quantity, when the demand curve facing the firm slopes down, the line graphing MR lies below the demand curve, as in Figure 15–2.

Monopoly Price Determination

The profit-maximizing rule stated in Chapter 9, MR = MC, is true for all firms—including monopolies. To maximize profits, the monopoly firm should produce the quantity corresponding to the point where MR = MC. This is denoted as Q_m in Figure 15–2. The price that the firm charges is determined by the demand curve. At Q_m, the firm's customers are willing to pay P_m. Thus, the firm will set price at P_m. Any other price and quantity will reduce profits. At a smaller quantity and higher price, MR is greater than MC. This means that the firm can take in more than it lays out if it lowers price slightly and increases output. Conversely, if output is greater than Q_m, MC is greater than MR. Now the firm can do better by reducing more than sales. Quantity Q_m is the best place to be because at any other quantity profits can increase by moving toward Q_m.

FIGURE 15–3 Social Cost of Monopoly

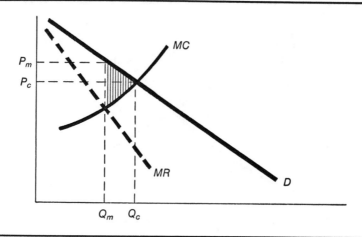

From the information in Figure 15–3, it is impossible to tell if the firm is making a pure profit. To do so requires that ATC be superimposed on the diagram. Pure profits will be earned if P_m is greater than ATC at Q_m. A loss will occur if P_m is less than ATC at Q_m.

Social Cost of Monopoly

Most people dislike monopoly, except persons who enjoy the privilege. The dislike stems from the knowledge that the price charged by a monopoly will be higher than what occurs in a more competitive market.

In addition, it can be shown that monopoly is undesirable because it causes a misallocation of resources in the economy. This results in a reduction in the value of output for society. The economic rationale for this reduction is easier to understand with a diagram—such as Figure 15–3. Notice that the profit-maximizing price exceeds marginal cost. Again, product price is an indication of how much consumers value an extra unit. Marginal cost reflects the value of alternative products given up to produce an extra unit (opportunity cost). Therefore, at the profit-maximizing price, the value of the marginal unit produced by a monopoly exceeds the opportunity cost of this unit. At first glance, this may appear desirable. But society could do better if the monopoly produced more and other industries produced less. Each additional unit of output past Q_m yields a net gain to society of the difference between the demand curve (price) and the MC curve. By moving to Q_c from Q_m, society gains the value of the shaded triangle in Figure 15–3. At Q_c, price is P_c. If the monopoly was, instead, a perfectly competitive industry and had the same costs as the industry, it would produce Q_c and have price P_c. Thus, the shaded triangle represents the social cost of monopoly as opposed to perfect competition.

A regulatory agency that wished to duplicate the perfectly competitive outcome would set price at P_c. At this price, the firm's customers would purchase Q_c output. If the firm makes normal profits, it should be willing to produce Q_c.

Any situation where price is greater than marginal cost causes a misallocation of resources, resulting in a smaller total value of output for society given the resources available. Therefore, the same criticism can be levied against any firm that faces a downward-sloping demand curve (i.e., imperfectly competitive). But economists have found that the loss of output in the U.S. economy because of a misallocation of resources from monopoly power of firms is small.[1] Also, politicians and the public are not very concerned about a misallocation of resources, probably because they do not envision the total value of output without the misallocation.

Monopoly Power

It is common to refer to the degree of monopoly power held by firms, particularly large corporations, even though private monopoly is illegal in the United States. Monopoly power, however, is a vague term. The most precise measure of monopoly power is the ratio of the product price to the marginal cost of producing the last unit of the product. Recall from Chapter 14 that in a perfectly competitive industry, each firm produces the quantity corresponding to the point where $P = MC$. In other words, the P/MC ratio for firms with no monopoly power (perfectly competitive) is equal to one.

With imperfect competition, each firm maximizes profits by producing the quantity that corresponds to the point where MR = MC. Because an imperfectly competitive firm faces a downward-sloping demand curve, its profit-maximizing price is greater than MC. Thus, the P/MC ratio for all imperfectly competitive firms is greater than one. This ratio becomes larger, the steeper (less elastic) the demand curve facing the individual firm. Given the elasticity of the market demand for the product, the greater the share of the market enjoyed by each firm (the closer it comes to a pure monopoly), the steeper the demand curve facing the firm and the higher the P/MC ratio. Thus, the size of the P/MC ratio is a precise measure of monopoly power.

The main difficulty in using the P/MC ratio to measure monopoly power is the lack of information on the marginal cost of firms. The next best monopoly power measure for the largest firms in a market or industry is market share. Given the market elasticity of demand for the product, the larger the share of the market, the greater the monopoly power of large firms. The market shares enjoyed by the four largest firms in selected U.S. industries are in Table 15–1. Although these figures do not give the P/MC ratios, they help identify industries where the potential for excessive monopoly power exists.

---

[1] See Arnold C. Harberger, "Monopoly and Resource Allocation," *American Economic Review*, May 1954, pp. 77–87.

TABLE 15–1 Percent of Total Industry Shipments Accounted for by the Four Largest Firms, Selected U.S. Industries, 1985

Motor vehicles	93%	Farm machinery	46%
Cigarettes	81	Bakeries	33
Organic fibers	78	Petroleum refining	30
Tires	70	Periodicals	22
Soap	59	Meat packing	19
Aircraft manufacturers	59	Sawmills	17

SOURCE: Statistical Abstract, 1985, p. 764.

These figures represent the market share accounted for by the *four* largest firms as a group. Even if the four firms' sales accounted for 100 percent of the market, on the average, each firm would have 25 percent. It is possible that the largest of the four firms would have more than 25 percent. These value-of-shipment figures include only U.S. firms. Consumers also have the option of buying imported goods. Imported products are especially important for automobiles, petroleum, steel, tires, shipbuilding, and radio and TV manufacturers. Foreign competition causes the demand curves facing large U.S. firms to be flatter (more elastic) than without it.

Monopoly Power and Inflation

During times of increased inflation, people tend to blame large firms for rising prices. Since businesses are raising prices, it is understandable why people come to that conclusion. Although a full explanation for inflation is best left to a macroeconomics course, each imperfectly competitive firm, regardless of its monopoly power, has only one profit-maximizing price for a given set of demand and cost curves. This price is read off the demand curve at the quantity corresponding to the intersection of MC and MR. If firms decided to raise prices without a change in their demand and cost curves, they would experience reduced profits, which would be irrational. Thus, we can be certain that the underlying cause of inflation is not due to a sudden increase in greed by businesses, for such behavior leads to lower profits. Indeed, there is no reason to believe that the desire for profits is any greater druing inflation than during periods of stable prices.

However, businesses do raise prices during periods of inflation. This behavior is the result of the desire to maximize profits or minimize losses (the latter also occurs during inflation). Price increases result from an increase in the demand facing the firm and/or an increase in the cost of production. The demand facing the firm increases because of consumers' higher money incomes, although not necessarily higher real incomes. Recall that a change in *money* incomes is a demand shifter. In addition, higher prices paid for labor, capital, and raw materials increase the firm's marginal and average cost curves–shifting them up and to the left. Both shifts result in a higher profit-maximizing price.

The shifts in the demand and cost curves that occur during inflation are out of the individual firm's control. If the firm had control over them, it would want to decrease costs to put more distance between price and ATC. The firm wants to experience an increase in demand for its product, but this desire is not limited to inflationary times. At any rate, the desired shifts in costs and demand, if the firm could control them, would not necessarily lead to an increase in product price. Thus, we should look for a reason other than the monopoly power of businesses for the underlying cause of inflation. This is a major topic in the macroeconomics course.

GLOSSARY

imperfect competition   Each firm has some control over the price it charges and faces a downward-sloping demand curve.

pure monopoly   A single firm sells the entire output of the industry.

demand facing a monopoly   It shows the quantities its customers will buy at various prices; it is the same as the market demand curve for the product sold by the monopoly.

marginal revenue   The additional revenue earned by selling one more unit of output; less than price for a firm facing a downward-sloping demand curves.

profit-maximizing quantity   It corresponds to the point where MR = MC.

profit-maximizing price   The point on the demand curve that corresponds to the profit-maximizing quantity.

social cost of monopoly   The loss in value of output to society because the value of the marginal unit sold by a monopoly exceeds its opportunity cost at its profit-maximizing quantity.

QUESTIONS

1. a. *How does an imperfectly competitive firm differ from one that is perfectly competitive?*
   b. *If an imperfectly competitive firm wishes to increase quantity sold, what must it do to price? What if it wishes to increase price?*

2. *What is monopoly and how does its definition depend on how the industry is defined?*

3. *At expressway service stops, a single gasoline company is generally given exclusive right to do business at one location. Is this service station a monopoly? Explain.*

4. *a. What is marginal revenue (MR) and why is MR less than price for a firm facing a downward-sloping demand curve?*

   b. Draw a demand curve facing an imperfectly competitive firm and its corresponding marginal revenue curve. Do the same for a perfectly competitive firm.

5. *a. Compare the profit-maximizing price and quantity for a monopoly with the values in a perfectly competitive industry. Assume the same marginal cost and demand for both.*

   b. In attempting to maximize profits, do owners of a monopoly act differently than owners of perfectly competitive firms? Explain.

   c. The higher the price charged by a monopoly the higher its total profits. True or false? Explain.

6. *Why is monopoly considered socially undesirable?*

7. *The United States and other market economies will always suffer from inflation because of the desire of large corporations having monopoly power to maximize profits. True or false? Explain.*

CHAPTER 16
Monopolistic Competition

OVERVIEW

Chapters 16 and 17 consider the majority of nonagricultural firms in a market economy. In numbers of firms, most are in the monopolistic competition group, the topic of this chapter. After establishing the two conditions common to all monopolistically competitive firms, their adjustment to pure profits or losses is considered. The discussion then turns to advertising, and the chapter ends with an explanation of why the marginal cost curve of an imperfectly competitive firm is not strictly a supply curve, which it is for perfect competition.

MONOPOLISTIC COMPETITION DEFINED

Monopolistic competition bears some similarity to both monopoly and perfect competition, but it is more closely related to the latter. The two distinguishing characteristics of monopolistic competition are: (1) there are many firms, each selling a small proportion of the market, and (2) each firm sells a product that is slightly different from competitors' products.

The characteristic of monopolistic competition that is similar to perfect competition is that there are many firms, each selling a small proportion of the market. However, the fact that each firm sells a product slightly different from its competitors results in a downward-sloping demand curve facing each firm. Because its product or service is slightly different from competitors, the firm has some control over the price it charges.

The multitude of firms engaged in retail trade are the best examples of monopolistic competition; service stations, barber shops, department stores, grocery stores, florists, and repair shops are examples. In addition, all of the small and medium-sized manufacturing firms fall into this category. In numbers of nonagricultural firms, the majority are monopolistically competitive.

It may appear strange to say that two retail outlets that sell the same brand of product, such as two Amoco service stations, sell a slightly different product. In retail trade, remember that the location of the firm is a part of the product sold. For example, an Amoco station located on a well-traveled, easily accessible location sells, in a sense, a different product from another Amoco station in a remote location. Other things being equal, the product that is more accessible to us is more desirable, and most people are willing to pay more for a more desirable product.

Another factor that distinguishes two seemingly identical products is service. Some people prefer to purchase their clothing in intimate little shops where the clerk is friendly and instantly available for assistance. Others buy their clothes in large department stores with little assistance and impersonal checkout counters. Even though the physical characteristics of the items sold in the two stores are identical, the customer who wants to consume more service along with the item will buy from the small, intimate shop.

However, providing services involves a cost, so we should expect to pay a higher price where more service is provided. For example, gasoline is cheaper at self-service pumps because you buy less service than at full-service pumps. As individual consumers, we must decide whether the marginal utility per dollar for these services is at least equal to the marginal utility per dollar of other things we buy.

Price Determination

The fact that the goods or services sold by monopolistically competitive firms differ in some respect, either physically or because of location or services, allows a particular firm flexibility in the price it charges. This does not mean that a service station could charge $1.75 per gallon for gasoline when other stations in the neighborhood are charging $1.15 to $1.20 per gallon without causing either a price war or losing most of its sales. If the station manager feels that the station can clear more net profit by a narrow-margin, high-volume operation, the manager will probably charge a bit less than the competition. If the manager thinks the station can make more with a wider-margin, lower-volume business, the price will be higher than average.

In monopolistic competition, the price range within the firm can operate is determined largely by the average price of its closest competitors. The individual firm may diverge slightly from the average market price, depending on the kind of business it wishes to operate. It is a mistake, however, to believe that just because a firm selling monopolistic competition places a price tag on its product that it can charge any price it pleases. Most firms in this kind of market are restricted to a narrow range of price. They have a bit more freedom, however, than the perfectly competitive firm, which has no leeway in the price it charges.

With perfect competition, we were more precise in determining the price and output for an individual firm. Recall that a perfectly competitive firm maximizes profits if it produces a quantity that corresponds to the point at which marginal cost is equal to market price. We illustrated this with a diagram. We can utilize a similar technique for monopolistic competition, only in this case, we must remember that the firm faces a slightly downward-sloping demand curve. Moreover, the marginal revenue of an additional unit sold is somewhat less than the price of this unit because the new lower price must apply to all units sold. There is no difference in the way costs are derived between perfect competition and monopolistic competition, so we can continue to apply the average and marginal cost concepts utilized in Chapters 14 and 15.

Like a monopoly, a monopolistically competitive firm maximizes profits if it sells a quantity that corresponds to the point at which marginal cost is equal to marginal revenue. Recall that marginal cost (MC) is the cost of producing or selling an additional unit of output, and marginal revenue (MR) is the additional revenue obtained from this extra or marginal unit sold. For example, if it costs a service station 90 cents to sell an extra gallon of gasoline, and the marginal revenue from this extra gallon is 95 cents, the station can increase its profits (or decrease losses) by 5 cents if it sells this extra gallon.

Moreover, it benefits the firm to increase output as long as MR is greater than MC. Why this is so is illustrated in Figure 16–1. Suppose we cut in at a quantity of output just short of the point where MC equals MR, Q_0. If we increase output by one additional unit past Q_0, our total costs increase by the distance from the horizontal axis up to the MC curve. However, our total revenue increase is shown by the distance between the horizontal axis and MR. The difference between these two distances represents the additional profit that the firm captures by producing this extra unit.

FIGURE 16–1 Profit-Maximizing Price and Quantity for a Monopolistically Competitive Firm

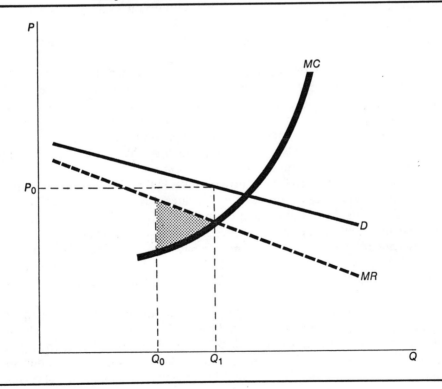

If we continue to increase output, the distance between MC and MR continues to grow smaller, but as long as there is any distance between them, total profits can be increased by increasing output. Total profits are maximized (or losses minimized) at the quantity where MR equals MC, Q_1 in Figure 16–1. To stop producing short of this point, say at Q_0, means that the firm needlessly forgoes profits (or incurs unnecessary losses) equal in value to the area of the shaded triangle.

Also, we can use Figure 16–1 to illustrate the profit-maximizing price that a monopolistically competitive firm charges. If the firm chooses to maximize profits and produce or sell Q_1, the demand curve facing this firm indicates that the price its customers are willing to pay is equal to P_0. The firm would not want to charge a lower price because in so doing it would throw away profits. On the other hand, it could not charge a higher price because its customers will pay only price P_0 for quantity Q_1.

Pure Profits or Losses

In Figure 16–1, there is no indication however, that the firm is making a pure profit or incurring a loss. All we can tell is that P_0 and Q_1 are the optimum price and quantity, respectively, meaning that either the firm's losses are minimized or its profits are maximized. To determine the profit or loss, we must know the average total cost (ATC). If ATC is below the price at the optimum quantity, the firm reaps a pure profit; if ATC is above the price, the firm incurs a loss.

Figure 16–2A illustrates a situation where the firm makes a pure profit, meaning that the resources used by the firm are earning more than they could make in some alternative activity or occupation. The total dollar value of the pure profit is illustrated by the shaded area. A firm can find itself in this enviable position for two reasons: (1) The firm is managed so well that its costs are low, or (2) the firm sells a desirable product so that the demand curve it faces is high relative to competitors' demand curves.

Figure 16–2B depicts a firm incurring a loss. In this situation, the resources used by the firm earn less than they could in alternative employment. The total dollar value of the loss is illustrated by the shaded area. A firm can be in this circumstance if its costs are high because of either high-paying alternative employment for its resources or poor management. Or, the firm can incur losses if the product it sells is not as desirable to consumers as the products sold by its competitors, so that the demand it faces for its goods is relatively low.

To summarize this procedure, we determine the profit-maximizing quantity for a monopolistically competitive firm by the intersection of the MR and MC curves. The profit-maximizing price is then determined by extending the vertical line drawn through the intersection of MR and MC up to the demand curve. The point where this vertical line touches the demand curve cor-

FIGURE 16–2 Profit and Loss Situations for a Monopolistically Competitive Firm

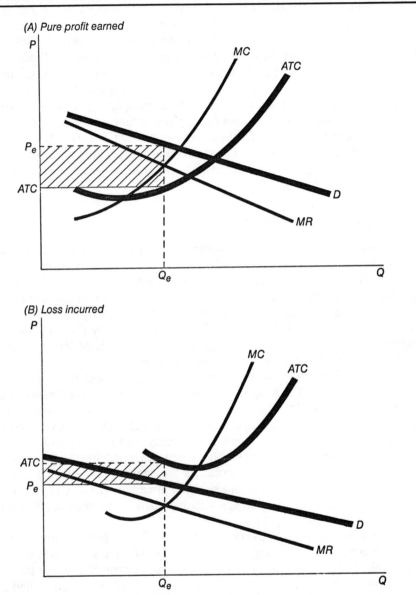

responds to the profit-maximizing price on the vertical axis. The price line is not drawn over from the intersection of MR and MC because the price is determined by the demand curve.

If price as determined by the demand curve is greater than the ATC at the profit-maximizing quantity, then the firm is making a pure profit. The average profit per unit is given by the distance between price and ATC at the profit-maximizing quantity. If we multiply this average profit per unit by the total units sold (the profit-maximizing quantity), we obtain the total pure profits. This is illustrated by the shaded rectangle in Figure 16–2A. Similarly, if price is less than ATC at the profit-maximizing quantity, losses will occur. The average loss per unit is equal to the distance between price and ATC, and the total loss is equal to the rectangle, as illustrated in Figure 16–2B.

In short, we use MR and MC to determine the quantity to produce and the demand to give us the profit-maximizing price at that quantity. The profit (or loss) is determined by the difference between price and ATC. This procedure applies to any firm that faces a downward-sloping demand curve, that is, any imperfectly competitive firm, including one that is monopolistically competitive.

LONG–RUN ADJUSTMENT

The existence of either pure profits or losses for a substantial number of firms in a monopolistically competitive market, will cause adjustments in the industry. For example, if a substantial share of firms reap pure profits, this is a signal for existing firms to enlarge their enterprises or for new firms to enter. In either case, the demand curve facing each firm begins to decrease, shifting downward to the left. A decrease in demand has two meanings: (1) the firm's consumers will now buy a small amount at a given price, or (2) its consumers will buy a given amount only if the price is lower.

This phenomenon is easier to understand if you visualize yourself as the owner of a restaurant that is making substantial pure profits. Seeing a good opportunity, another firm builds a restaurant across the street and begins to take some of your customers, perhaps by selling at a slightly lower price. As some customers leave, the demand curve facing your firm begins to decrease. You lower your price to compete with the new firm and adjust to the new lower demand and marginal revenue curves. As the demand curve facing your firm decreases (shifts left), the profit-maximizing price and quantity declines. As a result, your pure profits decline and you approach a zero pure-profit position, as illustrated in Figure 16–3A.

There is no reason why every monopolistically competitive firm has to end up at a zero pure-profit or tangency position. Some firms may continue to reap pure profits because they own or control certain specialized inputs that other firms cannot duplicate. In retail trade, each firm's location is unique, and some are more accessible to customers than others. The choice of a superior location may be due to the skill of the original owner or manager, to luck, or to circumstances beyond the firm's control, such as the construction of a housing development nearby. In other cases, a firm may have built up goodwill among its customers over the years, which cannot be duplicated by new entrants into the market. Also the owners of some firms may possess superior entrepreneurial ability that cannot be duplicated by competing firms.

FIGURE 16–3 Long-Run Adjustment by Individual Firms to Pure Profits in Monopolistic Competition

(A) Entry of new firms or resources

(B) Increase in asset value of profitable firms

Will the owners of such firms continue to reap pure profits? Yes and no. The fact that other firms cannot duplicate the firm's superior inputs means that the product price probably will not be bid down any further and that the firm can retain the profits. On the other hand, the market value of the profitable firm's assets will increase to reflect its superior profit position. We could expect potential buyers to pay more for the assets of a highly profitable firm than for the assets of a firm that earns normal profits or incurs losses. Economists would say that the pure profits are capitalized into the firm's value. If the owner correctly calculates implicit costs, mainly forgone interest on the increased equity value in the firm, the average total cost curve will increase as illustrated by ATC′ in Figure 16–3B. The pure profits disappear into the increased capitalized value of the firm. However, the current owner does not lose these profits because they have contributed to an increase in the value of the person's assets.

Since owners have finite life spans, profitable firms eventually change hands. If the original owner or seller is a shrewd bargainer, it is possible to obtain a price that will give the new owner a normal profit or a normal return on the investment. The phenomenon is the same for corporations, whose owners (stockholders) may number in the thousands, while the firm's equity value is reflected in the value of its stock certificates.

In any industry, circumstances continually change. Thus, it is unlikely that every firm is at a zero-profit, long-run equilibrium. It is more realistic to visualize a situation where there is continual movement toward equilibrium but few instances where it is ever reached. We would expect to observe at any time, a wide variety of profit positions by firms; some might enjoy substantial pure profits; others earn what is earned in other industries, and others incur losses.

We could do the same analysis for a case in which a substantial share of the firms in a monopolistically competitive market suffer losses. The opposite would occur, compared with the pure-profit situation. Firms would leave the industry—shifting the demand curve that faces the remaining firms to the right.

Persistent losses also can change the asset value of a firm. As an example, consider a service station or restaurant that is built on a busy two-lane highway that gives way to a new expressway that takes most of the highway traffic. The firm will suffer a major decline in sales and may go out of business. If the owner sells the structure, it will bring considerably less than it would have in its original use. The new owners may turn the service station into a bicycle repair shop, or the restaurant may be converted to a day-care center. If the new owners are shrewd bargainers, they will not pay any more for the structure than what assures them a normal profit in the new business.

Firms such as a service station, clothing store, or restaurant that realize losses often go out of business. After a few months of remaining vacant, they may open under new management in the same kind of business. If the previous owner could not make a normal profit, how can the new owners expect to do any better? They may have ideas on how to improve things, and it is likely that they have purchased the structure at a price that enables them to expect a normal profit. Or, if the new owner is a shrewd bargainer, the person may buy the property at a price low enough to yield pure profits, at least for a time.

A change in costs because of a revaluation of assets, either up or down, does not affect the price of the product sold or produced. Here, costs are *price-determined*. In a case where costs are changed because of changes in production technology or input prices, the market price will change because of a change in supply. In the latter case, costs are *price-determining*.

ADVERTISING

Advertising is common to all imperfectly competitive firms, particularly with monopolistic competition and oligopoly, although perfect competitive firms and public utilities also engage in this practice. It includes a wide range of activities. The homemade for sale sign on an automobile, the want ads in the newspaper, roadside signs, and radio and TV commercials are examples of advertising. Some advertising is done by buyers, such as help-wanted ads, although the majority is done by sellers.

Advertising is divided into two major types: informational and persuasive. Informational advertising informs prospective customers about what is for sale, its characteristics, and its price. An example of informational advertising is the grocery store newspaper advertisement telling the prices of items that can be bought at a particular store. Persuasive advertising, on the other hand, attempts to persuade people to buy one product rather than another. Most of the advertising on television and radio is persuasive, although such advertising also contains some information by making us aware of certain product characteristics.

All advertising attempts to accomplish one objective: increase the demand for the good or service being advertised. Advertising costs money; thus, when a firm or group of firms decides to advertise, we assume that the marginal revenue obtained from the extra products sold due to advertising is at least as great as the marginal cost (including advertising expense) of the extra units sold; otherwise, firms would not advertise.

Much disagreement exists about the merits of advertising. Most people, including economists, agree that informational advertising is beneficial. For consumers to maximize utility, they must know what is for sale, something about the good or service being sold, and the selling price. In addition, advertising increases competition between buyers and sellers and between different sellers of the same product. If buyers are informed through advertising that a given product is available at a lower price than what is asked by a particular seller, they can bargain with the seller to lower price or they will buy elsewhere. Similarly, if sellers see other sellers offering lower prices, they will follow to remain competitive. For example, the average price of eyeglasses in states where eyeglasses advertising is banned was more than twice the average price paid in states where advertising is not restricted.[1]

Much less agreement exists, however, about persuasive advertising. The advertising industry argues that advertising stimulates the economy by enticing people to spend. Others, particularly persons who have recently endured a nauseating commercial, argue that persuasive advertising is pure waste because the effect of one firm's advertising cancels out the advertising of other firms.

An objective appraisal of advertising, if possible, would rate it somewhere between these extreme views. Advertising stimulates spending on the item being advertised or it would not pay to advertise. But, it is less clear whether advertising makes people spend a larger share of their income. Expenditures on advertising have increased greatly during the past four decades, but on the average, people spend about the same proportion of their income today as they did 40 or 50 years ago. Nor is it clear that it is desirable for people to spend a larger share of their present income on consumer goods.

It has been suggested that the government ban persuasive advertising and allow only informational advertising. The problem, however, is to separate the two. One could argue, for example, that telling people product *A* is superior to all competitive products is really informational advertising. A ban on persuasive advertising also would result in much waste from lawyers' fees and court costs. The litigation cost would be borne by consumers through higher product prices and higher taxes.

MARGINAL COST AND SUPPLY

Throughout the discussion on imperfect competition thus far, use of the word *supply* has been avoided. This is because an imperfectly competitive firm does not have a supply curve as such. Recall that in perfect competition, the firm's marginal cost (MC) curve is its supply curve. The firm, faced with a given price, maximizes profits by producing up to the point where price equals MC. The MC curve, therefore, is the supply curve because it denotes the quantity that will be produced at a given price, or vice versa.

The MC curve of an imperfectly competitive firm, however, is not its supply curve, because for a given quantity, the price charged will depend on the demand curve facing the firm. Thus, we cannot determine both price and quantity from the MC curve alone. We have to know both MC and demand to determine the price and quantity for a firm operating in imperfect competition.

---

[1] Lee Benham, "The Effect of Advertising on the Price of Eyeglasses," *Journal of Law and Economics*, 1972.

However, the factors that shift the MC or supply curve of a perfectly competitive firm also shift the MC curve of a firm in imperfect competition. Moreover, the result of a shift in MC is the same as a shift in supply. For example, a shift to the left, or an increase in MC, reduces the quantity and increases the price in imperfect competition, which is the same as a decrease in supply in perfect competition. Remember from our discussion of product supply that an increase in costs results in a decrease in supply, and vice versa. Because of these similarities, we do not commit a gross error by referring to the *supply* of automobiles or gasoline, for example, even though these products are sold by imperfectly competitive firms.

GLOSSARY

monopolistic competition   An industry consisting of small or medium-size firms each selling a small share of the market and differentiated products.

product differentiation   Products that have different characteristics, different services attached, or are sold in different locations.

profit-maximizing quantity   It corresponds to the point where MR = MC.

profit-maximizing price   The price on the demand curve that corresponds to the profit-maximizing quantity.

long-run adjustment   The entry (exit) of new firms or resources in response to pure profits (losses).

price-determined costs   The revaluation of assets due to pure profits or losses.

price-determining costs   Changes in product price due to shift in the MC and ATC curves.

QUESTIONS

1. a. *What are the two characteristics that cause monopolistic competition?*
   b. *Give some examples of monopolistically competitive firms.*
   c. *How can two retail stores that sell the same brand of product be considered as selling differentiated products?*

2. *Suppose by lowering its price from $1.20 to $1.15 per gallon, a service station can sell 15,000 gallons of gasoline per week as opposed to 10,000. Can we infer from these figures that the marginal revenue of an extra gallon sold in this range of output is $1.15? Why or why not? What is MR in this case?*

3. a. *Using the appropriate diagram, illustrate the profit-maximizing price and quantity for a monopolistically competitive firm.*
   b. *Explain why any other price or quantity will not maximize profits.*

4. *Using the appropriate diagrams, illustrate the case where a monopolistically competitive firm is making:*
   a. *Pure profits.*
   b. *Just normal profits.*
   c. *A loss.*

5. *Describe the process of adjustment that would occur if a grocery store in an expanding resort area is making pure profits.*

6. *What are the two ways in which pure profits are competed away in a monopolistically competitive industry?*

7. a. *Why do firms advertise?*
   b. *Would society be better off if advertising was banned? Explain.*

CHAPTER 17

Oligopoly

OVERVIEW

This chapter deals with the market situation of oligopoly—where three or four large firms supply the major share of the market. Although the model for portraying an oligopoly is similar to the monopoly and monopolistic competition cases, a special problem is addressed—the possibility of collusion among firms to divide the market and set a higher than competitive price. The chapter ends with a discussion of the economic effects of pollution.

OLIGOPOLY DEFINED

Oligopoly is derived from the Greek word *oligos,* meaning few. This definition provides a hint about the kind of industry characterized by an oligopoly. An *oligopoly* is an industry in which a few firms, say three or four, produce the major share of the market. Oligopoly is commonly found in heavy industry or in products marketed nationally. Autos, steel, airplanes, drugs, construction equipment, minerals, petroleum, and computers are products produced by oligopolies.

Industries in which a few large firms produce the major share of the output occur mainly because large firms can produce the product more efficiently than small firms, that is, because of economies of scale. For example, it is hard to visualize the auto industry consisting of several thousand or even several hundred firms. Each firm would be too small to utilize the most efficient mass-production techniques.

Unlike monopolistic competition, the firms in an oligopolistic market do not necessarily produce a differentiated product. In fact, petroleum, steel, and minerals could all be classified as homogeneous products. A ton of steel produced by U.S. Steel is essentially the same product as a ton produced by Bethlehem Steel or Jones and Laughlin. There are oligopolies that produce differentiated products such as automobiles or appliances. Thus, the distinguishing characteristic of an oligopoly is the small number of firms in the market.

Price Determination

The fact that each firm sells a substantial share of the market or sells a differentiated product allows each firm to somewhat influence the price of its product. For example, if one of the large steel companies reduced its output, there would be a decline in the amount of steel on the market, providing that steel imports do not make up the difference. This would result in an increase in steel prices. Thus, each firm has some control over the price of the product it sells. In other words, each firm in an oligopoly faces a downward-sloping demand curve.

However, each firm's ability to influence the price of its product is limited by the substitute products available. Each firm, therefore, must sell its product at a price in line with the prices of competitors. Ford would not sell many cars if its price were several hundred dollars higher than comparable Chevrolet models. For homogeneous products produced in an oligopolistic market, it is even less likely for price differentials to exist. Disregarding transportation charges, no one would buy steel from U.S. Steel if it charged more than the other companies.

We should not be surprised, therefore, when all firms in an oligopoly market change their prices at about the same time. This indicates that consumers regard the products of firms in an oligopoly market as close substitutes. If a firm's price rises out of line with the prices of other firms, its customers soon discover substitute products that give them more for their money. If the products of firms in an oligopolistic market are close substitutes for one another, as in steel or petroleum, for example, there will be no price difference between the products. For products such as luxury automobiles, which consumers regard as less perfect substitutes, wider price differences between firms occur.

Also, all firms in a particular industry use about the same technology and resources. Therefore, if resource prices change, the MC and ATC curves for each firm will shift by about the same amount. Consequently, the profit-maximizing price will change by about the same amount for each firm.

In dealing with the prices of oligopolistic products, one must distinguish between the list price, the price on the window sticker for automobiles, for example, and the actual price that consumers pay. The difference between the two prices can be substantial for differentiated products. For example, during most years, the actual selling price of new U.S.-made cars is about 15 percent lower than the list or sticker price. In times of unusually low demand, or for certain models that are not selling well, the discount may be even greater, particularly at the end of the model year. On the other hand, in times of strong demand for certain makes or models, actual prices can exceed sticker prices. One should regard the actual price—rather than the list price—as the profit-maximizing (or loss-minimizing) price. When cars sell below list price, auto makers would like to obtain the higher price. But, in many cases, the demand is such that firms would end up with large, unsold inventories at the end of the model year and, as a result, earn lower total profits, or incur greater losses than if they cut the price and sell the extra units.

Oligopolistic price determination is illustrated with Figure 17–1. The same diagram used for illustrating the optimum price and quantity for a monopoly

FIGURE 17–1   Profit-Maximizing Price and Quantity for an Oligopoly

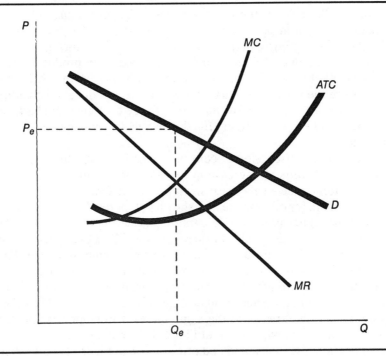

and a monopolistic competition firm can be used for oligopoly. We might expect, however, that an oligopoly would face a less elastic demand curve than a monopolistically competitive firm because by definition it sells a larger share of the market. It is risky to generalize about this because of differences in the degree of product differentiation between the two types of firms and because of possible differences in the elasticity of the market demand for the general category of product, such as steel versus cars. The demand facing an oligopolist selling a homogeneous product is more elastic than for someone selling a product different from its competitors.

The three types of firms, monopoly, monopolistic competition, and oligopoly, are similar in that the oligopoly also attempts to equate MC with MR to determine the most profitable output. The price charged by the firm is determined by the demand facing the firm at this output. This profit-maximizing price, shown in Figure 17–1, is actual price, not list price.

In this example, price is greater than average total cost, so the firm earns a pure profit. Of course, this is only an example. If the ATC curve was everywhere above the firm's demand curve, the firm would have to take a loss or shut down.

Interdependence of Firms

An inevitable result of the few firms in an oligopolistic market is that the action of any major firm significantly affects the sales and/or price of the other firms in the market. For example, suppose General Motors grants a wage increase to its employees, which leads to an increase in production cost, as shown in Figure 17–2A. We can see from Figure 17–2A that it is in GM's interest to raise the price of its cars from P_0 to P_1 and reduce the quantity sold from Q_1 to Q_0 to again equate MC and MR. If they continued to charge P_0 and sell Q_1, MC would be greater than MR; they would lose money on the marginal units produced.

Recall from our discussion of consumer demand that when the price of a good increases, there is an increase in demand for substitute goods. We can predict, therefore, that an increase in the price of GM cars will lead to an increase in demand for other makes, as shown in Figure 17–2B. Consumers will try to avoid the higher price of GM cars by purchasing more of other makes. But, an increase in the demand for other makes will lead to an increase in both price and quantity of these cars, as the other firms attempt to equate MC with MR, as shown in Figure 17–2B. We see, therefore, that an increase in the costs and price of products of just one of the major firms in an oligopolistic market leads to an increase in the price of other firms' products as well. The other auto firms eventually will experience the same increase in labor costs as GM, so everyone's cost curves will end up at about the same level.

Also, the increase in demand and price shown in Figure 17–2B will lead to a slight increase in demand for GM cars, resulting in a slightly greater increase in price for these cars than originally specified in Figure 17–2A. In fact, we can trace this process of cause and effect back and forth indefinitely. As a rule, however, the largest and most interesting changes come on the first round, so economists are not as concerned with the second- or third-order effects.

Price Searching

Although diagrams are helpful in providing a framework for thinking about the operation of an oligopolistic firm and market, we should not lose sight of the complexities involved, particularly regarding price determination by the individual firm. It is one thing to equate marginal cost with marginal revenue, follow the line up to the demand curve, and determine price and quantity. It is quite another thing to learn what these magnitudes are.

Each large oligopolistic firm has a staff of economists, cost accountants, market researchers, and the like to assess costs and market demand. But, there is still plenty of trial and error in price determination. This is particularly true for a new product or an entirely new firm. If there are similar products already on the market, the firm wants to set a price somewhere in line with established items. The firm also wants to compare such a price with its unit production costs. It will have a good idea of average costs and may have some idea of marginal costs.

FIGURE 17–2   Effects of an Increase in Manufacturing Costs of General Motors
Automobiles

(A) General Motors

(B) Other auto manufacturers

Once a price is set and a production decision has been made, the firm will receive information from the market and from its own cost and profit figures. If the product is not selling and inventories are piling up, it may indicate that the product is overpriced. When introducing a new product, it is usually necessary to offer consumers a bit more for their money than they receive from established items, or else they have little incentive to change. As sales increase (i.e., demand facing the firms increases or shifts to the right), the firm may want to adjust the price slightly upward, especially if production cannot keep up with sales. Of course, in times of inflation, with increased wages and prices of raw materials, product price must be increased or the firm will find its average total costs exceeding product price.

Each firm must watch its major competitors. If the firm is small or new in the business, it might decide to play follow-the-leader. If the large, dominant firm increases price, the small firm follows suit; or, if the large firm lowers price, so does the small one. This behavior, common in oligopolistic markets, is referred to as *price leadership*. In addition to relieving the small firm of periodically deciding on its product price, this practice reduces the likelihood that the small firm will provoke the large one into a price war, possibly wiping out the small firm.

Even with price leadership, at least one firm in an oligopolistic market must bear the responsibility of setting a price. One such procedure is sometimes called *average cost pricing*. Here, the firm determines the average total cost of an item, adds a certain percent of that figure for profit, and uses this figure for its price. Of course, this does not guarantee the firm a profit regardless of its costs. If the firm becomes inefficient, other firms may decide that they can sell at a lower price and still cover their costs, including a normal profit. Thus, even a so-called dominant firm has no guarantee of remaining dominant. In addition to contending with the up-and-coming firms on the home scene, it may have to contend with foreign competition. Competitive forces from foreign firms are especially evident in such industries as autos, steel, shipbuilding, shoes, electronics, petroleum, and textiles.

Also, the potential competition of each firm is not limited to existing firms in its industry. If excessive pure profits are evident in an industry, there is usually nothing to stop established firms in other industries from moving in to get a piece of the action. For example, if bicycle manufacturing becomes very profitable, there is nothing to stop General Motors or Ford from getting into the bicycle business. Many of today's conglomerates are involved in several industries simultaneously.

Mergers and Conglomerates

Many firms are in a situation where they must become larger to become more efficient (that is, attain economies of scale) and remain competitive in their field. Since internal growth is often a relatively slow and difficult process, the merging of two or more firms is a popular vehicle for growth. A better appreciation for its popularity can be gained by looking at the advantages of a merger. Two or more firms that become one can gain some advantages of specialization by devoting entire plants to the production of one or two components of their overall product. For an auto firm, one plant might manufacture engines, another bodies, and so on. One may also gain some scale economies by sharing a common management and administrative structure. Instead of having two or three main offices and staffs, the merged firm can get by with one. A larger firm can take advantage of a more efficient advertising medium, such as nationwide television, or borrow at a lower rate of interest, or to sell stock more easily.

In addition to pure scale economies, some firms have obtained tax savings through merger. For example, if a firm incurring losses merges with one reaping pure profits, their overall tax bill may be reduced by writing off the one's losses against the other's profits. Another advantage is the possibility of easing the competitive pressure faced by each firm. The merger of two intense rivals would make life better for all involved. However, where the merger of two competing firms results in a monopoly, the Justice Department is likely to step in and forbid the merger.

Merger is not limited to firms in the same industry. When two or more firms in separate industries merge, they form a *conglomerate*. A well-known conglomerate is International Telephone and Telegraph (ITT), which has holdings in numerous industries. Large firms such as ITT often have sufficient assets to acquire control of other firms and their management, as opposed to working out a mutual agreement, as in a merger.

Hostile Takeovers

The practice of acquiring control of a firm without the consent of the acquired firm's management is a *hostile takeover*. In this case, a firm or person buys the majority of the voting stock in another firm. The acquiring party can then replace the acquired firm's management and sell off parts of that firm. Actually, the word *hostile* describes the view of the acquired firm's management—who fear losing their jobs. The owners or stockholders of the acquired firms are not forced to sell their stock; they willingly sell when the price of the stock is bid up in the market.

Some states have passed legislation making it more difficult for hostile takeovers to occur. It has been questioned whether such legislation is in the best interest of society. If weak firms are taken over by strong ones, efficiency is improved and society gets more out of its resources. Sometimes it is argued that the acquiring firms reorganize or assimilate the acquired firms so that their products are no longer recognizable. This may be true, but the acquiring firms have no incentive to make the resources of their takeover objects less profitable than before; to do so would reduce profits.

Collusion and Antitrust Legislation

The few firms in an oligopolistic market allow the possibility for two or more rival firms agreeing not to compete. Agreements of this nature can be informal, with rivals agreeing to maintain a certain price or to divide up the market. There is also the possibility that participating firms will enter into formal agreements where each firm agrees to a specified price and quantity of the product each will produce. This arrangement is referred to as a *cartel*. A cartel or even an informal agreement results in a market resembling a monopoly. It is as though there were only one firm in the market. As a consequence, we expect a higher price than if there were many firms competing in the market.

The two main legal tools that the government uses to fight nonsanctioned monopolies or cartels are the Sherman Antitrust Act of 1890 and the Clayton Antitrust Act of 1914. The Sherman Act makes restraint of trade or any attempt to monopolize trade a misdemeanor, that is, a criminal offense against the federal government. The Clayton Act essentially duplicates the Sherman Act and details the various illegal activities that might lead to a monopoly or cartel. The intention of this act was curbing a monopoly before it occurred, rather than punishing it after the fact. The Federal Trade Commission (FTC), also set up in 1914, has the power to investigate unfair business practices and take legal action if required.

In addition to government action against monopolies or cartels, there is a market force that acts as a continual deterrent. This is the temptation by colluding firms to cheat on one another. As shown in Figure 17-3, an industry that becomes a monopoly or cartel must reduce its output to raise price. Thus, each firm that agrees to collude must agree to reduce its output for the scheme to work. But, if each firm is maximizing profits by equating MR with MC before the collusion occurs, then after they agree to reduce quantity and raise price, MR for each firm will be greater than MC, as shown in Figure 17-3. Before collusion, each firm maximizes profits by producing Q_1—the quantity that corresponds to the intersection of the MC and MR curves. During collusion, each firm reduces its output to Q_0. We cannot, however, illustrate the new higher price that results from collusion on the diagrams in Figure 17-3 because these are the demand curves that face each firm—not the market demand. We can only assume that the new higher price results in higher net profits for each firm, or else it would not pay to collude.

During collusion, each firm is in a situation where MR is greater than MC. Thus, it is in the interest of each firm to sell a few extra units of output under the table. By doing so, the firm can increase its profits even more. But when all or most firms participating in the collusion cheat in this manner, the market price falls, otherwise, the additional output cannot be sold. Unless the colluders can impose a penalty on the cheaters, collusive agreements tend to break down. It is also difficult to enforce any kind of penalty against a firm for refraining from an illegal activity.

FIGURE 17–3   Effect on Individual Firms of Colluding to Reduce Quantity and Raise
Price

SOCIAL COST OF POLLUTION

Much of the world's pollution results from production by large manufacturing corporations, although it is not limited to this type of firm. Pollution also comes from perfect competition, pure monopoly, and monopolistic competition.

Economists frequently refer to pollution as a social cost. This means that in the production of goods that cause pollution, the full cost is not borne by the producing firm. Part of the cost is borne by society in environmental degradation. The part of the cost borne by society is called *social cost*.

The effect of social cost on an oligopoly, or any imperfectly competitive firm, is illustrated in Figure 17–4. Let MC represent the conventional explicit and implicit marginal cost of the firm. Suppose the production of this product results in waste materials that are piped into a body of water or into the atmosphere. These waste materials represent an additional cost to society for several reasons: They can cause health problems for humans, plants, and animals; Life spans are shortened and/or resources must be devoted to caring for health problems. There is the cost of suffering because of ill health caused by pollution. Moreover, the unsightliness of a polluted environment reduces the utility of people. Polluted water resources cannot be used for recreational purposes. If water is to be used for human consumption or commercial purposes, additional resources must be used to clean it.

FIGURE 17–4 Effect of Pollution Control on the Firm in Imperfect Competition

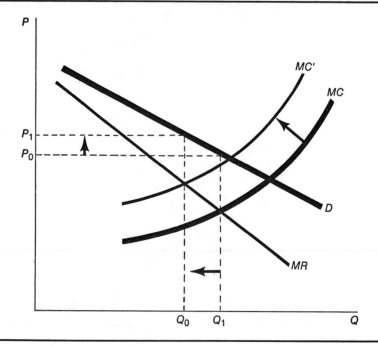

If the individual firm was required to bear the full cost of production, the true or full marginal cost would be higher for any given output level. This is represented by MC′ in Figure 17–4. MC is the firm's marginal cost and MC′ is the full marginal cost to society. The vertical difference between MC and MC′ represents the additional unit cost to the firm of neutralizing or recycling the waste so that it does not damage the environment.

Assuming that the firm tries to maximize profits, it will produce quantity Q_1, corresponding to the intersection of MR and MC. However, at Q_1, society gives up a greater value of alternative goods—including a clean environment—that it obtains from an extra unit of this product. This means that pollution causes an overallocation of resources to production of the product—too much is produced. If the firm incurred the full production cost and made its

FIGURE 17–5   Summary of Demand Curves Facing the Firms in the Four Major Types of Market Situations

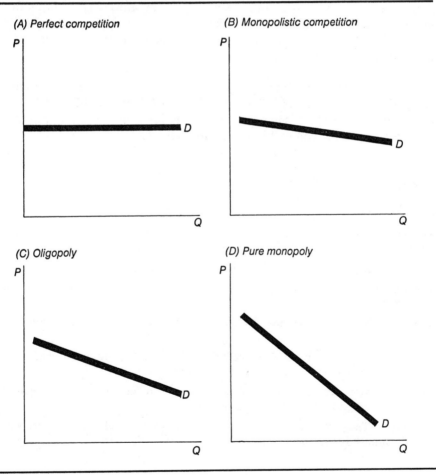

production decision according to MC', Q_0 would be produced. Granted, the price of the product would increase to P_1 from P_0. But, consumers would buy a cleaner environment with the goods. Government regulations that restrict the amount of pollution a firm can emit move MC closer to MC' and improve the allocation of resources.

DEMAND FACING THE FIRM: A SUMMARY

It is useful at this point to summarize and compare the demand curve facing each of the four types of firms we have studied. We began in Chapter 14 with the perfectly competitive firm that faces a perfectly elastic demand. In the following three chapters we looked at three types of imperfectly competitive firms: pure monopoly, monopolistic competition, and oligopoly. Each of these firms faces a downward-sloping demand. In general, the fewer the firms and the more differentiated the product of each firm, the steeper or less elastic the demand facing each firm. The demand curve facing the individual firm in each of the four market situations is illustrated in Figure 17–5.

It is best to think of these four types of firms as a continuous distribution, from perfect competition to pure monopoly, rather than four hard-and-fast categories. These categories are useful in that they identify where in the distribution a given firm is located. Most firms fall somewhere between the two extremes of perfect competition and pure monopoly.

GLOSSARY

oligopoly   A market where a few large firms supply a major share of the market. Oligopolies can sell either homogeneous or heterogeneous products.

price leadership   Market price is set by the dominant firm.

average-cost pricing   Product price is set equal to average total cost plus a markup for profit.

conglomerate   A large firm that owns or controls other firms that may be in different industries.

cartel   When two or more firms collude and act as if they are a single firm—a monopoly. In the United States, this is illegal.

hostile takeover   The acquisition of one firm by another firm or person against the wishes of the acquired firm's management.

social cost   The cost to society of producing a product over and above the cost borne by the firm; it is associated with pollution.

QUESTIONS

1. a. *What is an oligopoly?*
   b. *What characteristics are necessary to have an oligopoly?*

2. *Using the appropriate diagram, illustrate the profit-maximizing price and quantity for an oligopoly.*

3. *Comparable models of GM, Ford, and Chrysler cars sell for about the same price, and when one company changes its price, they all change prices by about the same amount. From these observations can we conclude that the Big Three automakers are colluding to set prices? Explain.*

4. a. *What is a cartel, and why does society consider cartels undesirable?*
   b. *Why do cartels tend to break down?*

5. *In recent years, hostile takeovers have been well-publicized. How can a hostile takeover occur? If one firm doesn't want to sell to another, can it be forced to do so? Explain.*

6. *How does pollution cause a misallocation of a nation's resources?*

7. a. *What factors determine the elasticity of the demand curve facing a firm?*
   b. *Rank the four types of firms from the most to the least elastic demand facing a firm.*

PART SIX

Factor Markets

CHAPTER 18

Labor Markets

OVERVIEW

The next four chapters deal with the markets for the two primary factors of production—labor and capital. The main objective of this chapter is to show how wages are determined and why they differ among occupations.

THE DEMAND FOR LABOR

The labor market, like the product market, consists of demanders and suppliers. The price of labor (wage or salary) is determined by the interaction of demand and supply. Certain groups in society may not like the market-determined wage and may attempt to change the wage. But, let us first see how the market functions before we study attempts to modify it.

The basic concept of demand for labor was presented in Chapter 7—marginal physical product (MPP) of an input. Recall that MPP is units of additional output obtained from one additional unit of an input. To derive the demand for labor we only need to assign values to MPP.

The *value of marginal physical product* (VMP) is defined as the *value* of additional output that is obtained from one more unit of the input. The VMP of an input for a perfectly competitive firm is obtained by multiplying the price of the output (*P*) by MPP:

$$VMP = P \times MPP$$

The VMP label is commonly used in conjunction with perfectly competitive firms—ones that face a perfectly elastic demand.

A parallel concept for imperfectly competitive firms that face a downward-sloping demand is referred to as marginal revenue product (MRP). Its definition is the same as VMP. The difference is that MRP is calculated by multiplying MR times MPP.

$$MRP = MR \times MPP$$

Since product price equals MR for a perfectly competitive firm, MRP can be used for either type of firm.

A graph of VMP or MRP of an input is a demand for that input. The explanation is given in terms of VMP, but the same is true for MRP.

Because of the law of diminishing returns, the MPP of an input declines as

FIGURE 18-1   Relationship between Marginal Physical Product and Value of Marginal Product

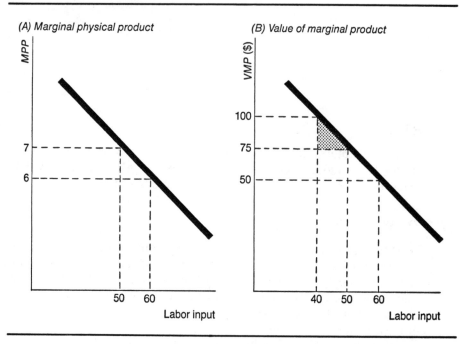

(A) Marginal physical product

(B) Value of marginal product

more of it is used. Therefore, the graph of MPP is a downward-sloping line as in Figure 18–1A. The VMP curve shown in panel B is the same shape; the only difference is that the VMP graph has value or dollars on the vertical axis.

If a firm wishes to maximize profits, it increases the use of an input up to the point where the input price is equal to VMP. If a firm stops short of this point, it gives up profits unnecessarily. This is illustrated in Figure 18–1B. Suppose the price of labor is $75 (per day) and the firm hires 40 labor days. The fortieth day of labor adds $100 to the firm's output. Therefore, if the firm hired one more day of labor beyond 40 it would add roughly $25 to its net profits. Naturally, the firm would do so. By continuing to add labor up to 50 days it adds to its profits a value equal to the shaded triangle in Figure 18–1B. Consequently, if labor received a wage of $75 per day, the firm would hire 50 days, say per week. At $100 per day, 40 days are hired. And at a $50 wage, 60 days are hired. Therefore, the firm's VMP curve of an input also is its demand curve for the input. Remember, though, that it assumes profit maximization for the firm.

Profit–Maximizing Rule for Input Use

In deriving the demand for an input such as labor, we have implicitly derived the profit-maximizing rule for input use: hire an input until the price of the input (P_x) equals the VMP of the input:

$$P_x = \text{VMP}$$

It is proven in the appendix to this chapter that the profit-maximizing rule for input use is equivalent to the profit-maximizing rule for output use, P = MC, presented in Chapter 9.

The market demand for labor is the summation at each wage of the amount demanded by all employers in the market. The procedure is similar to what is used to obtain the market demand for a product.

THE SUPPLY OF LABOR

Labor supply is the other half of the labor market. Similar to the definition of product supply, the supply of labor is a positive relationship between price (wage) and quantity. This implies that people supply more labor when wage is high (other things equal) than when it is low.

It is useful to investigate in a bit more detail the main factors that determine a person's willingness to supply labor. Assume there are two uses of a person's time: work and leisure. The latter includes sleep and any activity that takes up a person's time when he or she is not working for a wage or salary. The money earned by working can be converted into goods and services or saved. If the wage rate increases, the amount of goods that can be purchased also increases. Therefore, if a person takes a day off with a high wage, more goods and services are given up than if the wage was lower. The opportunity cost of leisure is the goods and services given up by not working. When the wage increases, the opportunity cost increases. Another way of saying this is that when wage increases, the cost of leisure increases. Therefore, we can expect people to "buy" less leisure (work more) when its price is high. This is called the *substitution effect*. People substitute goods (work) for leisure when the price of leisure (wage) increases.

There is, however, a second offsetting factor: the income effect. When wage and income increase, people have more money to "purchase" leisure; They may, therefore, work less. It is not possible to predict which of the two effects is stronger. If the substitution effect dominates, the person's labor supply curve will be upward sloping. If the income effect is stronger, the labor supply curve will bend backwards. If the two effects offset each other, the supply of labor will be vertical or perfectly inelastic. The relative magnitude of the two effects can vary from a low wage to a high wage as shown in Figure 18–2.

Over the last half-century, the length of the workweek in the United States has not changed much. This indicates that the two effects offset each other as the wage rate has risen over this time. Of course, supply has continually increased due to population growth.

There may be some question whether people have much choice over the length of the workweek; most jobs entail 40 hours, although if people really wanted to work a shorter week, employers who responded to this wish would be preferred and could have a greater choice in who they hire. Other employers

FIGURE 18–2   Wage Response and Market Supply of Labor

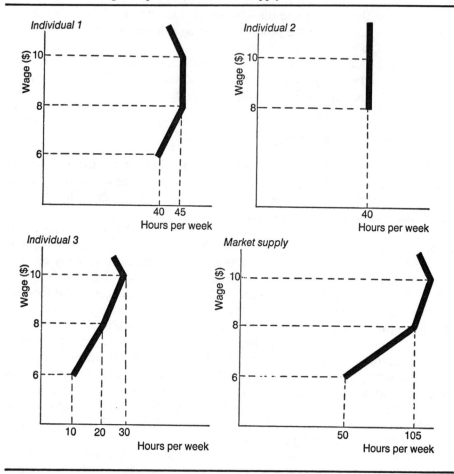

would follow suit, which would cause the nation's workweek to decrease in length.

The differing response to wage increases is illustrated in Figure 18–2. The first three diagrams represent the supply of labor by three individuals. At $6 per hour, individual 1 is willing to supply 40 hours a week of labor. As the wage increases to $8 per hour, she increases her workweek to 45 hours. At $10 per hour, she works the same amount, 45 hours, and at wages exceeding $10, she reduces the length of her workweek. In other words, at the $10 and over wage, the substitution effect does not override the income effect. Individual 2, on the other hand, does not enter the labor force until wages rise to $8 per hour. In the range of wages considered, the workweek remains at 40 hours. Individual 3 increases hours worked from 10 to 30 as wages rise from $6 to $10 per hour. These are examples of what we might expect from different individuals. The first person might be the breadwinner of a family, the second might be semiretired and decide to enter the labor market at an $8 wage, and the third might be a college student holding a part-time job.

If we assume, to keep the example simple, that the three individuals comprise the available supply of labor, the market supply can be derived by adding together the quantity supplied at each price. At $6 per hour, individuals 1 and 3 supply 40 and 10 hours, respectively, making a total of 50 hours. At the $8-per-hour wage level, individual 2 is included in the labor force. Thus, along with the slight increase in labor offered by individuals 1 and 3, raising the wage to $8 obtains a total of 105 hours supplied.

Note that the market supply of labor will be more elastic than the supply of individuals currently working in the market. This is because of the entrance of people into the labor market as wages rise. The result is greater response to wage increases for the market than is true for the average individual in the market.

WAGE DETERMINATION

Wages are determined in the labor market in the same way that prices of ordinary goods and services are determined in their respective markets—by demand and supply. The intersection of the two curves sets the equilibrium wage. If actual wage was above the equilibrium, quantity supplied exceeds quantity demanded and a surplus results. In the labor market, a surplus is called *unemployment*. At a wage below the equilibrium, there is a shortage. If the labor market acted like other markets, a surplus should drive the wage down and a shortage should drive it up. The latter seems to occur, but institutional and psychological factors can keep the wage from declining. The apparent inflexibility of wages on the downside is discussed later.

A. Perfectly Competitive Employer

A perfectly competitive employer of labor hires a small share of the labor market and therefore has no control over the market wage. Such an employer faces a perfectly elastic supply of labor as illustrated in Figure 18–3B. The supply facing the firm corresponds to the wage determined in the market as shown in panel A. To maximize profits, the firm hires Q_1 of labor. Stopping at Q_0 reduces the firm's profits by the area of the shaded triangle in panel A.

Virtually all employers are perfectly competitive buyers of labor because they hire a small share of the market. Even a large firm in a small town can add to its labor force by advertising in out-of-town newspapers. Thus, it can attract workers from the entire country. No single employer hires a large share of the nation's working population.

FIGURE 18–3   Wage Determination: Perfect Competition in the Labor Market

(A) The market

(B) The individual employer

B. Imperfectly Competitive Employer

Although it is not common to find employers that are imperfectly competitive, to round out the discussion the imperfectly competitive case is presented. An *imperfectly competitive employer* faces an upward-sloping supply of labor. This means that the firm must increase wages if it wishes to expand its labor force. Or, it can lower wages if it hires fewer people.

A consequence of an upward-sloping labor supply for a firm is that the additional or marginal cost of adding more labor exceeds the wage of the extra workers. The reason is that the firm must pay a higher wage to attract additional employees, and this higher wage must be paid to all employees.

Economists refer to the cost of adding additional labor as the marginal resource cost (MRC) of labor. At any level of labor hired, the MRC of labor is greater than the wage paid. Thus, if we wish to represent this relationship on a diagram, the MRC curve lies above the supply curve and rises at a faster rate, as shown in Figure 18–4.

Note that marginal resource cost on the buying side of the labor market is analogous to marginal revenue (MR) on the selling side of the product market. Marginal revenue is less than price because to sell more, the price reduction must apply to all units sold; MRC is greater than the wage because to hire more, the higher wage must apply to all labor employed—not just the marginal workers. In other words, the MRC of an additional worker is the wage paid to the worker plus the small increase in total wages that must be paid to each of the firm's other employees.

FIGURE 18–4   Wage Determination: Imperfect Competition in the Labor Market

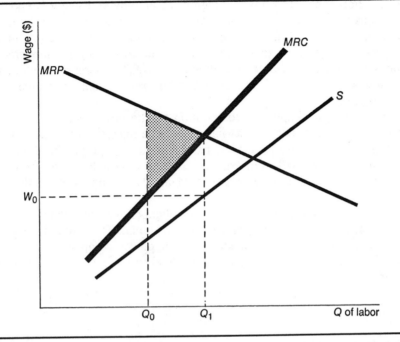

If the firm wishes to maximize profits, it attempts to equate the MRC of its labor with labor's MRP, and it hires Q_1 of labor. If it stopped short of this point, say at Q_0, the contribution of a marginal unit of labor would exceed its cost. As we saw in the preceding section, increasing the labor hired from Q_0 to Q_1 results in an addition to total profits that is equal in value to the shaded triangle in Figure 18–4.

Also note in Figure 18–4 that the wage paid by the imperfectly competitive employer of labor is equal to W_0, the point on the supply curve corresponding to Q_1, the quantity of labor hired. At this quantity of labor, people are willing to work for W_0. Unlike the situation for a perfectly competitive employer, MRP is greater than the wage. This is not to say that the imperfectly competitive firm exploits labor. By attempting to maximize profits, this type of firm behaves exactly the same as a perfectly competitive employer. It is hiring labor up to the point where the additional cost of adding another unit of labor (MRC) is equal to the contribution of that worker to the value of output (MRP).

Also, wages paid by a perfectly competitive buyer of labor should not be any different from wages paid by an imperfectly competitive buyer of comparable labor in the same market. If wages were not equal, employees would quit the low-paying employer and switch to the higher-paying one.

It is not necessary for all employees to be mobile to prevent long-run wage differences between individual employers or markets. When wages paid by an employer differ from wages paid elsewhere, the movement of a small percentage of all employees from low- to high-wage employers usually is enough to force wages up in low-wage markets and bring them down in high-wage jobs. Also, an inequality of wages between areas or regions usually results in some employers moving to the low-wage areas, as illustrated by the movement of northern industry to the South after World War II. This increases labor demand in the low-wage areas and decreases demand in the high-wage areas. As a result, wage differences narrowed.

To differentiate imperfect competition on the buying side of the market from the selling side, economists have labeled a market where there are few buyers as an *oligopsony*. This is comparable to an oligopoly, which characterizes a situation of few sellers in a market. If there were only one buyer of labor, the firm would be called a *monopsony*, comparable to a monopoly on the selling side.

This does not mean, however, that an oligopoly on the selling side results in oligopsony on the buying side, or vice versa. The same is true of a monopsony. For example, a local light and power company might have a monopoly on the sale of electricity, but it is likely a perfectly competitive buyer of labor.

Shifts in Demand for Labor

We have studied how wages are determined in two kinds of labor markets. Now, we will explain changes in the wages and levels of employment. We noted in Chapter 11 that if a product market is in equilibrium, the only way a change in price can occur is by a change or shift in either demand or supply of the product, or both. The same is true for labor. Wages change in response to a change in market demand, supply, or both.

Let us look at changes or shifts in the demand for labor. Most of what we say about shifts in demand for labor can be applied to the demand for any input. Recall from the product market discussion that an increase in demand occurs when it shifts upward and to the right, as shown by D_2 in Figure 18–5A or MRP_1 in Figure 18–5B. Notice that the equilibrium or profit-maximizing wage also increases, and a decrease in labor demand results in a decrease in wages, as illustrated by D_0 or MRP_0 in Figure 18–5.

Because the value of marginal product (VMP) for a perfectly competitive buyer of labor is derived by multiplying marginal physical product (MPP) times product price, we expect either a change in product price or a change in MPP of labor to shift the demand for labor. The same is true for an imperfectly competitive buyer of labor because a change in price also results in a change in marginal revenue. We can conclude, therefore, that the demand for labor will shift in response to a change in product price or a change in the productivity of labor. The same is true for any input. This is a summary of the changes:

FIGURE 18–5   Shifts in the Demand for Labor

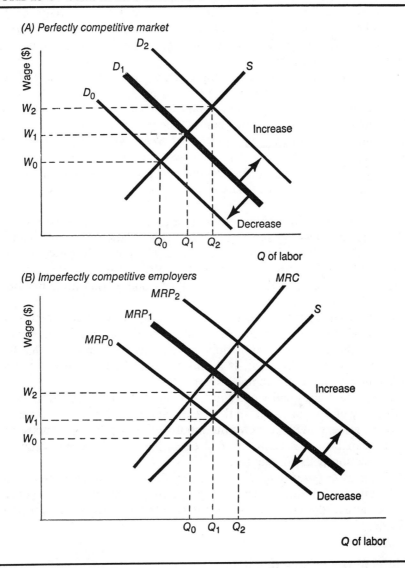

(A) Perfectly competitive market

(B) Imperfectly competitive employers

1. Change in Product Price.   A rise in product price results in a higher VMP or marginal revenue product for a given level of input use. The opposite is true for a decline in product price.

2. Change in Marginal Physical Product.   There are three major factors that can change or shift an input's MPP. These are:

a. Change in Quantity or Quality of Complementary Inputs.   A complementary input increases the MPP of a given input when the use of the complement is increased. Consider, for example, a worker digging a hole with a spade. When given a power shovel, the worker's productivity or MPP increases. Thus, the power shovel is a complement to labor, as are all kinds of raw materials. Without bricks, mortar, or lumber, for example, a construction worker would not be productive.

An increase in the quality of a complementary input has the same effect as an increase in its quantity; that is, it increases or shifts to the right, the MPP curve of the input. For example, a secretary with a new word processor will be more productive than with a slow manual typewriter.

b. Changes in Quantity or Quality of Substitute Inputs. Economists define a substitute input as one that decreases the MPP of a given input when the substitute use is increased. For example, the use of a second worker on one spade reduces the MPP of the first worker—who could use it only part of the time.

It is not obvious in a given production activity whether two inputs are complements or substitutes. Furthermore, this relationship can change at different levels or mixes of input use. For example, giving the power shovel to the two workers with the spade increases the MPP of the worker who operates the machine, but it decreases the MPP of the second worker if the person just stands and watches.

For some labor, therefore, capital or machines are complements; they increase labor's productivity. For other labor, however, usually persons with the lowest skills or seniority on the job, capital may be a substitute that forces them to find other employment. It is this situation that we hear about most regarding automation and unemployment.

An increase in the quality of a substitute input also is similar to an increase in the quantity of such an input. In this case, quality improvement decreases or shifts to the left the MPP curve of the input. For example, an increase in the speed and capacity of a computer decreases the MPP of a bookkeeper if it leaves the person with nothing to do.

c. Changes in Quality of the Input. This factor is especially important for labor. Through education and training, people have become more productive; they have increased their MPP, which has resulted in an increased demand for their labor.

Shifts in the Supply of Labor

The labor supply tends to be more stable than labor demand. The overall supply of labor for the entire economy depends on the population. The more people, the more labor supplied at a given wage. Thus, the aggregate supply of labor in the United States has increased with its population. The proportion of the population participating in the labor force also affects the labor supply. Recently in the United States, increasing numbers of women have joined the labor force—increasing the overall supply of labor. A greater proportion of college students is working part-time, which also adds to the nation's labor force.

The increase in education and skills of the labor force contributes to the supply of labor. If we measure labor in homogeneous efficiency units, a given number of highly skilled people is equivalent to more labor than an equal number of less-skilled people. In the previous section, we mentioned that an increase in people's skills tends to increase their productivity and, hence, their MPP and demand. An increase in the wages from increased skills requires, therefore, that the demand for skills increase more than the supply of skills.

The supply of labor facing a given industry or area also depends on the area's population although in this case, the supply of labor can also shift in response to a change in wages in another industry or area. Suppose, for example, there is a sudden increase in the demand for labor, as with the oil discoveries in northern Alaska. The increase in wages for people to operate oil rigs attracted more labor to this occupation. But, this reduced (shifted to the left) the supply of labor to other nearby industries such as mining, trapping, and the service trades, causing wages in these occupations to increase also.

Wage and Employment Changes

There has been a long-run, upward trend in wages and employment in the United States. Because of our population growth and the increased participation of women in the labor force, the supply of labor has been increasing or shifting to the right. From this information, we conclude that the demand for labor has been shifting to the right more rapidly than the labor supply. Otherwise, there could not have been an increase in wages and employment.

The two main factors that shift labor demand to the right and raise wages are: (1) an increase in the use of complementary inputs, mainly capital, and (2) an increase in the quality of the labor force through education. Recall from the preceding section that these two factors increase the productivity or MPP of labor and thereby increase labor demand.

For individual geographic areas, industries, or firms, however, there are instances of a decrease in the demand for labor. This can occur if there is a decreased demand for the good or service produced. As a result, the firms involved reduce the quantity of inputs used that are complementary to labor, mainly capital and raw materials. There is a corresponding decline in labor's MPP and consequently a decline in labor demand, as shown in D_0 in Figure 18–5A.

The logical expectation in this situation is a decline in wages and employment. If we were dealing with a nonhuman input, this would occur. But with labor, it is unwise for a firm to immediately reduce the wages of its employees in response to a decrease in its marginal revenue product (MRP) of labor. An across-the-board wage cut affects all employees and, to say the least, leaves them unhappy. Disgruntled employees are not conducive to high labor productivity and profits. Moreover, if labor is represented by a union, the wage contract may forbid any wage decrease.

Rather than reduce wages when there is a decline in demand for labor, most firms choose to lay off some people, at least in the short run. A layoff affects the firm's marginal employees—leaving the remainder virtually untouched. The people who are laid off may be disgruntled, but they are not around to affect the firm's productivity. In the event of a severe and prolonged decline in the demand for labor in an area or by an industry, we would see some downward adjustment in money wages, such as occurred during the Great Depression and again in the early 1980s.

The stickiness of wages on the downside causes a surplus of labor known as unemployment. If wage rates were completely flexible, any decrease in demand for labor would cause a reduction in wage rates. As soon as wages settled to lower equilibrium levels, the surplus labor (i.e., involuntary unemployment) would disappear.

There are occupations in which wages have increased substantially over the years but the productivity of workers has not increased much. Some examples include teachers, barbers, and taxi drivers. One can explain the wage increase by the upward shift in the supply curve of labor facing these occupations. If most other occupations have experienced wage increases, people will not enter occupations in which labor productivity has not increased unless they receive wages comparable to what they could earn in occupations in which labor productivity has increased. The relative prices of goods and services will increase in areas where wages increase without productivity gains. Therefore, certain occupations that do not experience gains in labor productivity still can enjoy wage increases if most other occupations in the economy experience a gain in labor productivity.

Wage Differences

The large differences between the wages or salaries of different people or groups sometimes seem unjustified. The movie star or professional athlete may earn $1 million dollars or more per year, possibly working six months, while the laborer has to toil from dawn to dusk for a meager $10,000 per year. Why?

Wage differences are explained by demand and supply. A person lucky enough to possess scarce talent in high demand, such as throwing a baseball or football exceedingly well, tends to enjoy a high wage. Other talents, such as pushing or pulling a lever on a machine all day, which are in abundant supply relative to their demand, are not as well paid.

Some occupations require lengthy training periods, which reduces the supply. The doctor, lawyer, or college professor who spends 8 to 10 years preparing for a profession must be compensated for the investment, or it would not pay to enter the profession. Substantial wage differences exist within and between professions even though the educational requirement is similar. For example, the internationally known heart surgeon or Nobel Prize winner often enjoys an income that is substantially larger than unknown colleagues. Salary or income differences reflect differences in ability and productivity. One does not enjoy an international reputation without some special accomplishment.

Some professions enjoy a higher average level of income than others with similar educational requirements because of a strong union. Medical doctors, for example, tend to earn more than college professors with a Ph.D. The former are represented by a strong "union," the American Medical Association (AMA), while college professors are not, for the most part, unionized. We will discuss how unions and organizations such as the AMA influence the incomes of members in Chapter 19.

There are certain occupations where, in order to enter, one must pay a substantial entrance fee. Two well-known examples are seats on the stock exchange and taxicab medallions in New York City; each sells for thousands of dollars. The existence of an entrance fee indicates that employment in these occupations is not open to all who are qualified and, as a result, the hourly earnings of persons who buy their way in are larger than what could be earned in alternative occupations. For new entrants, the opportunity cost of the money invested in the entrance fee equalizes the net earnings of occupations with other alternatives.

Wages or salaries also reflect differences in working conditions. An occupation that requires exposure to the elements or special hazards tends to pay a higher salary than jobs that provide comfortable, safe working conditions. Construction workers, for example, earn substantially more per year than bank clerks or shoe salespersons. Similarly, steel workers who assemble the superstructure of today's skyscrapers are well paid for their physically demanding work and the risks they take. In general, jobs that present special risks or disadvantages, such as working in remote areas, must offer higher salaries to attract people. The supply of people for these jobs is small relative to the demand, so their wages are high. The relatively high wages of construction workers are also attributed in part to a strong union, and to the seasonality of their work. The wages lost during days when work is impossible because of bad weather are made up during the days when they can work.

On the other hand, occupations that allow one to work in air-conditioned comfort tend to offer somewhat lower salaries, given the educational requirements that accompany such jobs. People who work in these jobs take part of their salaries in attractive working conditions. For these jobs, the supply of people is large relative to the demand, so wages are lower than in less-attractive jobs.

The impact of working conditions and skills on wages is shown in Table 18–1. The highest hourly wage rates are in mining and construction— occupations requiring workers to bear considerable risk of injury or death, or to work in extreme heat or cold. The skill premium shows up in the wages of construction workers in the special trades—electricians, plumbers, bricklayers, and so forth. Not only do these occupations require considerable skill, they also involve harsh working conditions.

The pleasant working conditions of office or store work are reflected in the lower wages of workers in retail trade, finance, and services. In the latter category, skill differences appear by comparing hotel workers with persons offering repair services. The low hourly pay of hotel workers and restaurant

TABLE 18–1 Hourly Earnings of Nonsupervisory Workers, Private Nonagricultural
Payrolls, May 1987, Dollars per Hour

| | Hourly wage rate | |
Occupation	Average	Specific
Mining	$12.42	
Metal		$13.00
Coal		15.58
Oil and gas		11.47
Nonmetal minerals		10.57
Construction	$12.61	
General building		$11.64
Heavy construction		12.04
Special trades		13.19
Manufacturing	$ 9.86	
Durable goods		$ 10.39
Nondurable goods		9.12
Wholesale trade	$ 9.57	
Durable goods		9.68
Nondurable goods		9.42
Retail trade	$ 6.09	
Lumber and hardware stores		$ 7.26
General merchandise stores		6.45
Food stores		6.95
Auto dealers		7.78
Apparel stores		5.57
Furniture		7.48
Restaurants		4.39
Finance, insurance, and real estate	$ 8.71	
Banking		$ 7.50
Credit agencies		7.88
Insurance agencies		9.55
Services	$ 8.38	
Hotels		$ 6.08
Personal services		6.11
Business services		8.62
Auto repair		7.78
Misc. repair		9.04
Health services		8.60
Legal		11.68
Total private	$ 8.93	

SOURCE: "Employment and Earnings," U.S. Dept. of Labor, Bureau of Labor Statistics 34, no. 7 (July, 1987), pp. 117–31.

employees is offset by tips. People will work for lower hourly wages if they receive tips from customers.

The figures in Table 18–1 do not include the highest-skilled professionals such as scientists, medical doctors, lawyers, and corporate executives whose salaries are likely to be in the $50 to $60 per hour range and beyond. Successful business entrepreneurs enjoy similar earnings. Their special skills enable them to do interesting work in pleasant surroundings and be highly paid at the same time.

GLOSSARY

value of the marginal product (VMP)   The value of the additional output obtained by adding one more unit of an input. It corresponds to the demand for labor for a perfectly competitive seller of products.

marginal revenue product (MRP)   The same as VMP; a label designating the demand for labor by an imperfectly competitive seller of products.

substitution effect   When wage increases, the opportunity cost of leisure increases. Thus, workers have an incentive to substitute work for leisure, that is, to work more.

income effect   When wage increases, workers have more income to buy leisure and, therefore, may work less.

oligopsony   Few buyers of an input.

monopsony   One buyer of an input.

complementary input   It increases the MPP of another input when more of the complement is used.

substitute input   It decreases the MPP of another input when more of the substitute is used.

QUESTIONS

1. Why is the VMP or MRP of an input also a firm's demand for the input? What assumption is required?

2. a. Suppose you apply for a job that pays $20,000 per year. What must be true of your VMP or MRP to obtain this job and keep it?

b. *Several of the top entertainers in the United States earn over $50 million per year, while factory, office, service workers, and teachers toil for a fraction of this wage. Are entertainers overpaid? Are low-wage people underpaid for their labor? Explain.*

3. *Suppose you own a small business and employ 10 people. One of your main problems is absenteeism. To ease this problem, you consider raising your employees' wages from $9 to $10 per hour. Do you think this raise would reduce the number of days missed? Explain.*

4. *How do most employers decide on what wage to pay? Illustrate with diagrams.*

5. a. *What happens to the demand for labor when there is a decrease in demand for consumer or investment goods?*
   b. *Why does this phenomenon cause an increase in unemployment?*

6. *Barbers, taxicab drivers, and teachers probably are not much more productive nowadays than they were 30 to 40 years ago. Yet, their real wages have increased substantially. Why?*

7. *Explain how each of the following circumstances will affect the demand for labor:*
   a. *A decrease in demand for the product produced by labor.*
   b. *An increase in the use of capital that is complementary to labor.*
   c. *An increase in the use of capital that is a substitute for labor.*
   d. *An increase in the skills of labor.*

8. *Show that the profit-maximizing rule from the standpoint of output is equivalent to the profit-maximizing rule for input use.*

APPENDIX: PROOF OF THE EQUIVALENCE OF THE PROFIT–MAXIMIZING RULES FOR OUTPUT AND INPUTS

Recall from Chapter 9 that profits are maximized when a firm's output corresponds to the point where product price (P) equals MC.

$$P = MC$$

Also recall that MC is the cost of producing one more unit of output. As pointed out in Chapter 7, the cost of producing one more unit of output using more of an input (x) is P_x/MPP_x.

$$\text{Therefore MC} = P_x/\text{MPP}_x$$

$$\text{Consequently P} = P_x/\text{MPP}_x,$$

$$\text{or } P_x = P \cdot \text{MPP}_x.$$

$$\text{Since VMP}_x = P \cdot \text{MPP}_x,$$

$$\text{then } P_x = \text{VMP}_x$$

This proves that the last expression, $P_x = \text{VMP}_x$, the profit-maximizing rule for inputs, is equivalent to the first, $P = \text{MC}$, the profit-maximizing rule for output.

CHAPTER 19

Labor Unions

OVERVIEW

A discussion of labor is incomplete without considering labor unions. Unions have attempted to improve the welfare of their members in three areas: (1) better working conditions, (2) job security, and (3) higher wages. Most of this chapter centers on the third area, although the other two areas are important and are discussed briefly.

BETTER WORKING CONDITIONS

Competition in the business world requires each firm to produce at the least possible cost to survive and to earn profits. Improving the work conditions of employees costs money; employers have not been in the forefront in this area. Employers especially sensitive to working conditions incur higher costs and can be driven out of business by competitors who are not as sensitive. Granted, their workers would be happier and more productive, but if the increased productivity did not compensate for the added cost, the firm would have to bear the net cost. There is also the uncertainty of whether and how much improved conditions increase worker productivity. In health and safety, the benefits may be a long time in coming. If all employers were required to play by the same rules, that is, if all are required to provide better working conditions, no single employer is penalized. This is like reducing pollution. Individual firms cannot do much to change conditions alone. But, when everyone must meet the same standards, no single firm is penalized and forced out of business.

Labor unions have been active in promoting better working conditions on two fronts: (1) in negotiating union contracts, and (2) in promoting legislation in Congress. If a union represents the majority of workers in an industry, it can persuade the unionized firms to improve conditions under threat of a strike. The union has less power at this level than if legislation is passed—nonunion firms can still undercut unionized firms in the product market. By promoting legislation which specifies workplace standards, even nonunion firms must abide by the rules.

The recent increase in imports from low-income countries threatens working conditions for U.S. workers. It is the same as being undercut by nonunion firms that do not have to follow stringent rules. The problem requires international cooperation and agreement.

JOB SECURITY

Anyone who has been an employee knows the uncertainty and anxiety that results from not knowing whether one's job will exist in the months and years ahead. Employees who have been laid off know this feeling well, and persons who have not found a job after being laid off know it even better. This is not to say that employers are free of such anxiety; their businesses also can disappear in this uncertain world.

Unions have attempted to promote members' job security by union contracts, and legislation. For example, a railroad contract may specify that each train locomotive must have two people in the cab even though the company might argue that one can do the job with the newest technology.

Attempts to promote job security by work rules have been unsuccessful. If new technology makes a job obsolete, eventually it disappears. Unions have been more successful in promoting legislation that helped maintain full employment in the economy. The Full Employment Act of 1946 was a milestone in this area. In times of increased unemployment, unions have advocated increased government spending to reduce unemployment. Everyone's job security is increased when unemployment is low.

HIGHER WAGES

Labor unions have attempted to increase members' wages in three ways: (1) increase the demand for labor, (2) decrease the supply of labor, and (3) bargain for a union wage.

1. Increase the Demand for Labor

This method is probably the most desirable but the most difficult. It is desirable because it results in both a higher wage and greater employment, as illustrated in Figure 18–5 in Chapter 18. It is difficult because unions do not have much influence over the demand for labor.

One way to increase labor demand is to increase demand for the final product. In years past unions utilized advertising urging consumers to buy union-made products; such advertising is uncommon nowadays.

Recently, unions have been active in discouraging imports of foreign-made products by lobbying for protective tariffs or quotas on imports. The success of this effort is difficult to gauge because limiting imports limits our exports. If we do not buy from other nations, they cannot obtain dollars to purchase goods from the United States. As a result, there is a decrease in the export demand of union-made products.

Increasing the productivity of labor (or the MPP) also increases the demand for labor. As a result, unions have attempted to improve working conditions and shorten the workweek to maximize each employee's potential. Unions also have encouraged education and have been active in apprenticeship programs, although apprenticeship programs have been a more effective device for limiting the supply of labor.

2. Decrease the Supply of Labor

Unions have been more successful in raising wages by limiting the supply of labor than by increasing demand. This is particularly true among the so-called craft unions representing skilled workers. The prime vehicle for limiting entry into the profession or trade is by controlling entry into the training or apprenticeship program.

Shifting the supply of labor back and to the left from what it would be with free entry into the profession increases wages and reduces the number of people employed. Trade unions and professional associations such as the AMA have utilized this technique successfully because the outcome (higher wages and less employment) does not, at least in the short run, harm established members of the trade or profession. Their wages are high, and they generally do not have to fear unemployment.

The people harmed by this technique are people who could have obtained higher incomes if they had been allowed to enter the profession; and consumers, who pay more for services rendered. If wages and the cost of services become excessively high, however, public opinion may result in government pressure to allow more freedom of entry. Also, substitute products will appear, as evidenced by mobile homes or factory-built housing which results in a decreased demand for the services of skilled tradespeople.

3. Bargain for a Union Wage

Collective bargaining is the most common means of increasing wages. Here, the union negotiates with the employer and under threat of strike attempts to set a wage higher than in a free-market equilibrium. This technique is used mainly by industrial unions—those that represent the workers of entire industries. Examples include the autoworkers, steelworkers, garment workers, and the teamsters (truck drivers).

Unlike the craft unions, which limit membership, the industrial union's goal is to bring all workers in the industry into union membership. The wisdom of this policy is clear when we remember that because the jobs represented by industrial unions require little or no training, there is always a large pool of substitute labor that can easily step in if union labor becomes more costly than nonunion labor. In addition, the success of industrial unions hinges on the condition that all firms in the industry employ union members. When unionized firms pay a higher wage and hence incur higher costs, the lower-priced products of nonunionized firms soon take over the market.

In bargaining for a union wage, unions attempt to obtain a higher wage for their members than what is determined in a free market. As explained in Chapter 18, this wage corresponds to the intersection of labor's demand and supply in a perfectly competitive market, as illustrated in Figure 19–1A by W_0. The free-market wage in an imperfectly competitive labor market is also denoted in Figure 19–1B by W_0. The union wage is denoted by W_u in both diagrams.

In perfect competition, note that the imposition of the union wage reduces the quantity of labor employed in the market from Q_0 to Q_u^d. For employers to

FIGURE 19–1 Union Wages in the Labor Market

(A) Perfectly competitive employers

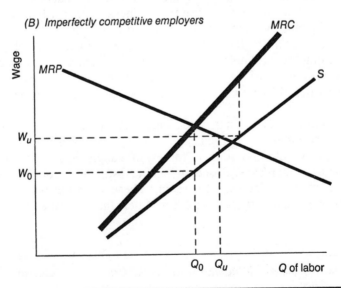

(B) Imperfectly competitive employers

pay the higher wage, they must reduce employment until labor's MRP rises to the wage level. If they did not reduce personnel, the wage of the marginal workers would exceed the value of what they produce. The resulting decline in employment is a check on the union's bargaining power, however. Unions like to minimize unemployment, along with achieving higher wages. Moreover, unions traditionally have not enjoyed a large, loyal membership during high unemployment periods.

Notice also in Figure 19–1A that the quantity of labor seeking employment in the union wage industry increases from Q_0 to Q_u^s, resulting in an unemployed fringe equal to the distance between Q_u^d and Q_u^s. This represents the waiting list of hopeful employees.

The outcome of a union wage in an imperfectly competitive labor market, illustrated in Figure 19–1B is surprising. Note that in a free market the imperfectly competitive buyer of labor pays W_0 and hires Q_0. But when the union bargains for a wage, say W_u, the employer increases employment up to Q_u. This occurs because the union wage nullifies the firm's original MRC curve. At wage W_u, the firm can hire any quantity of labor without paying more for additional workers. The firm's MRC curve under a union wage, therefore, consists of the dashed line that begins at W_u on the vertical axis, runs out to the supply curve, and then extends up to join the original MRC curve of the firm.

At first, the outcome depicted in Figure 19–1B appears highly beneficial to union members: Their wages are higher and their total employment has increased—provided the union wage is set somewhere between the original free-market wage, W_0, and the point where the firm's original MRC curve intersects its MRP curve. We should point out, however, that this outcome is not likely to persist over the long run. As wages are increased, the firm's cost curves are shifted upward and to the left and profits are reduced. Firms making only normal profits will tend to leave the business, output will decline, and the total demand facing the union for its labor also will decline. So, labor still ends up with fewer jobs in the long run. Furthermore, the existence of imperfectly competitive employers should not be taken for granted. Virtually all employers hire a small proportion of the total labor force in their respective labor markets, which means that they face a highly elastic supply of labor, especially in the long run.

Have unions actually increased wages? At first, the answer may seem obvious: We continually observe negotiated wage increases in unionized trades or industries. Would the normal forces of supply and demand result in comparable wage increases? Based on empirical studies, unions have increased the wages of members by 7 to 11 percent.[1] These studies also show, however, that wages of nonunion workers are 3 to 4 percent *lower* than they would be

---

[1] Gregg Lewis, *Unionism and Relative Wages in the United States* (Chicago: University of Chicago Press, 1963).

in the absence of unionism. Since union membership accounts for about 20 percent of the U.S. labor force, it appears that although unions have altered the structure of wages, they have not increased the overall average level of wages in the country.

It is easy to see why unions have been able to raise wages by collective bargaining and by restricting entry. But why should unions cause other workers to receive lower wages? First, an increase in wages in unionized industries results in fewer jobs in these industries or occupations than would otherwise be the case; that is, there is a movement up along the labor demand curve. The people who would have worked in these jobs are forced to find employment in other, nonunion occupations. This increases (shifting to the right) the supply of workers for these occupations. When supply increases from what it otherwise would be, price, or in this case, the wage, is lower.

This phenomenon is illustrated in Figure 19–2. The increase in wages because of union pressure from W_e to W_u and the resulting reduction in the quantity of labor demanded from Q_1 to Q_0 are shown in Figure 19–2A. (In this case, we assume the wage increase results from collective bargaining by an industrial union, but the same overall result would occur because of restricting entry into a unionized trade.) The reduction in people working in the unionized industry increases the supply of people in nonunion occupations, as illustrated in Figure 19–2B. And, as a result, the wage level in a nonunion occupation is decreased.

Minimum Wage Laws

Although minimum-wage laws are not strictly union-inspired, they have similar effects to union wages set by collective bargaining. Also, unions have actively promoted enactment of minimum-wage legislation.

Society has attempted to protect itself against employers who pay excessively low wages through minimum-wage laws. A minimum-wage law requires employers to pay employees covered under the law an hourly wage at least as high as the stipulated minimum. There is a federal minimum wage law that covers workers in manufacturing and industries engaged in interstate commerce. Many states, particularly northern industrial states, have their own minimum-wage laws, especially for employees not covered under federal law. The stipulated minimum wage has steadily increased in this country. The federal law, stemming from the Fair Labor Standards Act of 1938, began with a minimum wage of 25 cents an hour in 1940; it increased to $3.35 an hour in 1981. In the post–World War II years, the minimum wage has been adjusted upward to keep pace with inflation.

The persons most affected by such legislation are at the low end of the wage scale, mainly teenagers working on their first jobs and people with relatively few skills. It may appear that a minimum wage is a boon to low-wage earners. After all, if the minimum wage is $3.35 an hour, take-home pay is larger than if you had to work for a market-determined wage of $2.75 an hour.

FIGURE 19–2   Effect of Union Wage Increase on Union and Nonunion Occupations

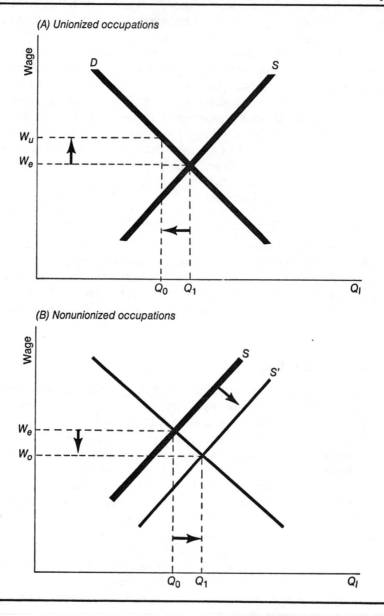

(A) Unionized occupations

(B) Nonunionized occupations

Although a minimum wage law can guarantee that a worker receives a base wage, it cannot guarantee that a job will be available at that wage. In fact, if the minimum wage is substantially above the equilibrium wage for occupations with low hourly pay, a decline in the jobs available to low-wage earners will occur.

If the market demand for labor affected by minimum wage legislation is

FIGURE 19–3   Effect of a Minimum Wage Law on Low-Income People

elastic, which is likely since there are ample substitutes for such labor, then raising the wage rate through minimum wage laws reduces the total earnings of people at the low end of the wage scale. In this case, the percentage reduction in employment is greater than the percent increase in wage rates. Thus, minimum wage laws can make the income distribution more unequal.

This problem is best illustrated with a simple market demand and supply diagram for labor in Figure 19–3. Assume that the minimum wage W_m, is above the market equilibrium wage, W_e. At the minimum wage, the quantity of labor demanded, Q_d, is less than the amount demanded at the equilibrium wage, Q_e. In other words, by imposing a minimum wage law, people at the low end of the wage scale face a decrease in available jobs. Generally, employers substitute capital or machines for higher-priced labor. At the same time, the higher minimum wage draws more people into the market, as illustrated by the increase in the quantity of labor supplied from Q_e to Q_s. The gap between Q_d and Q_s, therefore, represents the number of people who would like to work at this wage but cannot find a job—the unemployed.

The results of minimum wage laws predicted by our theoretical framework also are substantiated by recent empirical studies.[2] The impact of minimum-

[2] See, for example, Douglas K. Adie, "Teen-Age Unemployment and Real Federal Minimum Wages," *Journal of Political Economy*, March–April 1973, pp. 435–41; and M. Kosters and F. Welch, "The Effects of Minimum Wages on the Distribution of Changes in Aggregate Unemployment," *American Economic Review*, June 1972, pp. 323–32.

wage laws is felt most by teenagers, particularly teens from minority groups. It is doubtful, however, that many full-time semiskilled or unskilled workers in manufacturing are affected by such laws. Part-time jobs, particularly in service trades, are most affected.

GLOSSARY

craft union　A union representing workers in a specific craft such as plumbers, electricians, and bricklayers; usually skilled workers.

industrial union　A union representing all workers in an industry such as the steelworkers or the autoworkers.

collective bargaining　Contractual negotiations between a union and an employer specifying wages and working conditions. The objective is to set wages higher than what exists in a free-market equilibrium.

minimum wage laws　State and federal laws stipulating the minimum wage that an employer must pay.

QUESTIONS

1. Businesses have not been active in promoting day care for the children of working parents. Why? If these services are to become commonplace, where will the push come from?

2. By what means have labor unions attempted to improve working conditions?

3. By what means have labor unions attempted to increase job security?

4. a. How have craft unions attempted to increase wages?
  b. What are the limitations of this method?

5. a. How have industrial unions attempted to increase wages?
  b. What are the limitations of this method?

6. How is it possible for unions to have decreased the wages paid in nonunion occupations?

7. a. What effect do minimum-wage laws have on unemployment if wages are set above the market equilibrium? Explain.
  b. Who is most affected by these laws?

CHAPTER 20

Capital and Interest

OVERVIEW

In all production, labor is combined with capital to yield an output. Since most capital lasts for more than one year, the question of how to measure its annual cost is considered in this chapter. Then, the discussion turns to measuring the profitability of capital—mainly its rate of return. The chapter ends with consideration of the market for loan funds, how loan interest rates are determined, and why they differ among borrowers.

CAPITAL DEFINED

In business or economics, the word *capital* has two different meanings. Businesspeople may think of capital as cash or money to operate a business, as in working capital. Economists, however, define *capital* as durable or long-lasting inputs such as land, buildings, machines, and tools that yield a flow of services over time. The quantity of capital is measured in monetary terms, however. Actually, this definition of capital also could apply to consumer durables such as housing, automobiles, and appliances. They are long-lasting and yield a flow of services over time. In view of the discussion of household production in Chapter 7, consumer durables are inputs in the production of utility. Consumer durables generally are not thought of as capital, however, so this chapter will focus on the narrower definition of the word.

The study of capital is separated from the study of labor because there are differences between these two inputs. The first and most obvious difference is that capital is an inanimate, nonliving input devoid of feelings or preferences. Although the owners of capital are concerned about the wage or return it receives, they do not care about its working conditions—such as the length of its workweek or whether it is employed in a prestigious occupation. Thus, many of the factors important for labor are not of concern in our discussion of capital.

A second difference is that capital is generally purchased for use over a long period. For example, you may purchase an asset this year that will produce for the remainder of your lifetime. Labor, or other inputs such as raw materials, are purchased only for immediate or current use. Granted, there may be an understanding between employer and employee about the length of time they will associate, but the employer of labor, unlike the employer of capital, does not usually pay the employee a lump sum for all future services; this difference is important.

A third difference between capital and labor is that the purchase of capital may involve an expenditure in advance of the date it begins to contribute to output. Economists refer to the time interval between the expenditure and the beginning of the output flow as the *gestation period*. This interval is especially important for investment in education, as explained in Chapter 22.

ANNUAL COST OF CAPITAL

What does capital cost? At first, the answer appears obvious. Surely the cost of capital is what buyers pay people who produce it. But the answer is not this simple. Consider the purchase of a $10,000 machine. It is unreasonable to charge the entire $10,000 against this year's sales. The machine likely will be available for service next year. But, it is also reasonable to charge a part of the $10,000 purchase price against the current year's production. Thus, this year's cost will be somewhere between $10,000 and zero; $10,000 is too high and zero is too low.

It is reasonable to charge the current year's production with at least the amount the machine depreciated during the year. Let's say that the market value of the machine decreased to $7,000—resulting in $3,000 depreciation.

The second component of the annual cost of owning a capital item is interest. If the $10,000 came from borrowed funds, the interest charge will be explicit and noticeable. However, even if the money came from the firm's own funds, an interest charge still should be made because of the money's opportunity cost. If the funds were not used to buy the machine, they either could be earning interest or invested in some other capital that yields a return.

Thus, there are two components of the annual cost of owning a capital item: depreciation and interest. If 10 percent could be earned on the money, the first year's interest charge would be $1,000, which makes a total cost of $4,000 for the first year.

In the second year the interest charge should be figured on $7,000 invested because $3,000 of the original $10,000 was written off at the end of the first year. At 10 percent, the interest charge would be $700 the second year. If the machine depreciated another 30 percent the second year, the depreciation charge would be .30 × $7,000 = $2,100. Thus, the total cost of ownership the second year would be $700 + $1,200 = $2,800.

Depreciation

Because depreciation accounts for a large share of the annual cost of owning a capital item, it is useful to examine it in more detail. There are two reasons a capital item depreciates: (1) the wearing out or "using up" of the item, and (2) obsolescence. In regard to the first reason, remember that the current market value of a capital item reflects the present value of its expected future contribution to output. Thus, the older an item, the fewer the years of productive life that remain. For example, a new machine may have 10 years of service ahead of it, while a five-year-old machine may have only five years of life remaining. Even if the used machine could do about the same amount of work per day as the new machine, no one would pay as much for the used item because of the smaller number of work days left in it. Also, there is more uncertainty involved in buying a used machine. For example, the buyer may not know whether the previous owner had taken good care of it. The possibility of high future repair bills will lower the price that buyers are willing to pay.

In an age of change and technological improvement, capital also becomes obsolete. If something new comes on the market that reduces production costs or increases efficiency, the demand for the old capital will decline, hence its price will fall. Thus, the depreciation of capital depends on its own productivity and the productivity of the new capital produced. Because of this, it is difficult, if not impossible, to predict in advance how fast an item will become obsolete. Nor is it easy to separate how much of an item's depreciation is due to wearing out and how much is due to obsolescence; both reduce its market value.

Two widely used methods of estimating depreciation are (1) the straight-line method, and (2) the constant-percentage method. The resulting decline in value of the depreciated item for each of these methods is illustrated in Figure 20–1. The straight-line method amounts to decreasing the value of the capital

FIGURE 20–1   Straight-Line and Constant-Percentage Patterns of Depreciation for a $1,000 Asset

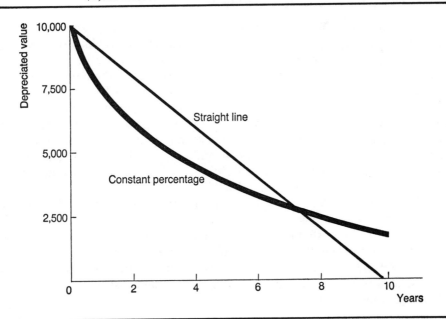

by a constant number of dollars each year. For example, if you were depreciating the $10,000 machine by the straight-line method over a period of ten years, you would assess $1,000 per year as depreciation.

If you use the constant-percentage method, you multiply each year's market value by a constant percentage. For example, if you depreciate the machine 30 percent per year, the first year's depreciation would be $3,000, the second year's $2,100, ($7,000 × 0.30), the third year's $1,470, and so on. With the second method, the annual depreciation is higher when the item is new, which results in a lower depreciated value during its early years of use. With this method, also, the item does not depreciate to zero, although it comes close.

The method of depreciation chosen and the length of time involved depend on the item to be depreciated. The constant-percentage method is more realistic for most items, since depreciation usually is higher during the first few years of ownership. An automobile, for example, tends to depreciate between 20 and 25 percent per year, depending on the make, model, amount of use, and the care it has received. If you purchase an $8,000 automobile, it depreciates $2,000 the first year if the 25 percent rate applies. In calculating the total cost of ownership the first year, include the interest charge, $1,200 if taken at 15 percent, together with gasoline, insurance, license fees, and so forth. With normal use, the total annual cost of an $8,000 automobile is about $4,000 in the first year of ownership. Is it worth it?

THE MARGINAL PRODUCT OF CAPITAL

In deciding whether or not to purchase or keep a machine or other capital item, it is necessary to consider its cost and returns. In previous sections we looked at cost; let us now consider the returns of a capital item. Capital is similar to labor or any other input in that it contributes to the output of goods and services. This contribution to output can be measured either in physical units of output by its marginal physical product (MPP), or in monetary units in terms of its value of the marginal product (VMP)—or marginal revenue product (MRP). Recall that MPP is the additional output obtained from an additional unit of the input—capital in this case—and VMP or MRP is the value of the additional output obtained from an additional unit of capital. To simplify the notation, we will refer only to the MRP of capital.

The MRP of capital is the value of the additional output made possible by utilizing a machine compared with what would be produced if it were not used. Because we are interested in comparing capital's annual MRP with its annual interest plus depreciation charge, we ought to refer to the machine's annual "net" MRP. This is the value of additional annual output less the added expense incurred by owning and operating the machine—such as fuel, repairs, additional labor, and insurance.

THE RATE OF RETURN ON CAPITAL

Because a capital item generally is purchased for use over a number of years, it is common to express its contribution to output during a given year as a fraction of its value at the beginning of the year. The resulting figure is commonly referred to as a *rate of return*. The rate of return on capital is the amount each dollar earns each year after all expenses, including depreciation in this case, have been subtracted. It is commonly expressed as a percentage. For example, suppose after subtracting depreciation and other expenses from the gross MRP of the $10,000 machines that the first year's earnings are $1,200. During this year, its rate of return is equal to 0.12 or 12 percent (1,200/10,000). In other words, each dollar earns 12 cents during the year.

The rate of return on capital is the same idea as the rate of return on a savings account in the bank. However, unlike a savings deposit in a bank, which earns its stipulated rate of return year after year as long as the money is left in the account, the earnings of a machine or building can vary from year to year and eventually end as the item wears out.

There is one kind of capital, however, that does not tend to wear out or depreciate with normal care—land. Suppose you purchase a plot of land for $10,000 and expect it to remain at this price. Also, suppose you collect $1,000 per year return from the land for as long as you want to by renting it out. Assume that there are no other expenses, so the $1,000 is a net return.

For an asset that will yield a stream of returns for all time to come, its annual rate of return can be computed as follows:

$$r = \frac{\text{Annual net returns}}{\text{Capital value}}$$

In the land example above, the rate of return is:

$$r = \frac{\$1,000}{\$10,000} = 0.10 = 10 \text{ percent}$$

Capitalized Value

By manipulating this formula, we can derive another formula that is useful for deciding the maximum price you can afford for a piece of property. In the formula, r represents the interest rate of return, R represents the annual net return, and K represents the capital value. Now we have:

$$r = \frac{R}{K} \text{ or } K \times r = R \text{ or } K = \frac{R}{r}$$

The resulting formula, $K = R/r$, tells how much a piece of property is worth if we know its annual return and the interest charge. To purchase this plot of land, suppose you took out a $1,000 loan at 15 percent. Utilizing this formula, we find:

$$K = \frac{\$1,000}{0.15} = \$6,667$$

If you were assured an annual $1,000 net return on this land and the money to buy it cost 15 percent per year, you could have paid as much as $6,667 for the land. Economists refer to the K in this formula, or the $6,667, as the *capitalized value* of the property. In a competitive market, prospective buyers tend to bid the price of the property up to this amount. And sellers, knowing this, will set the selling price at the capitalized value. If you buy a piece of property for $10,000 that has a capitalized value of $6,667, it is not a good deal unless the price of land appreciates in the future due to inflation. In fact, land in the 1970s sold for three to four times its capitalized value; most likely this was due to the expectation of future inflation.

Also, for a given annual return R, the capitalized value K will vary inversely with the size of the interest rate r. If the interest rate paid on your loan was 20 percent, K would have been $5,000. A lower interest rate, such as 10 percent, would result in a higher capitalized value of $10,000.

Although the relationship between the interest rate and the capitalized value is an algebraic phenomenon—the larger the denominator, the smaller the quotient, and vice versa—it has an underlying economic rationale. At a high interest rate, say 20 percent, the income forthcoming in the future is more expensive to obtain than if the interest rate was lower. At high interest rates, borrowers must pay more for the distant income in terms of either an interest charge on borrowed funds or forgone interest from their own funds; hence, they cannot pay as high an initial price for the capital.

In times of inflation, the value of land and other real assets increases faster than the general price level, particularly in the early stages of inflation. This occurs because of expected future inflation. As inflation persists, both buyers and sellers expect an increase in the future net returns and in the selling price when the land is sold. The increased values are capitalized into the current price of land.

Interest Rate Determination

In the discussion thus far we have taken the interest rate as given. How is the interest rate on borrowed funds determined? The interest rate is the price of loan funds, and prices are determined in markets by demand and supply.

Looking at the demand for loan funds, we can identify two sources of this demand. First, there is the demand from businesses for financing new investment spending. Second, households demand loan funds to make large-scale purchases such as houses, cars, and appliances and for other purposes

FIGURE 20-2   Interest Rate Determination in the Loan Market

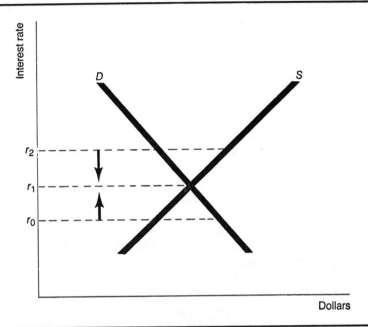

including education, medical bills, and travel. The demand curve for loan funds is a downward-sloping line, as shown by Figure 20–2. The fact that some investments are less profitable than others (lower rate of return) means that a decrease in the interest rate will bring an increase in acceptable investments, which means that more loan money will be demanded to finance this added investment spending.

Turning to the supply side of the loan market, one might ask: Where do loan funds come from? In general, the supply of loan funds is the amount of money people are willing to divert from current consumption to saving. Businesses also save by retaining part of their earnings and returning it into the firm for investment. All firms are owned by people, so the definition holds. The supply curve of loan funds is an upward-sloping line, as illustrated by Figure 20–2. This implies that people will supply a greater number of dollars at relatively high interest rates than at relatively low rates, other things equal. The degree of savers' responsiveness to interest rate changes is an unsettled question in economics. However, if people buy less of an item when its price increases and more when it becomes less expensive, we can expect some increase in the rate of saving (out of a given income) when the interest rate increases. As pointed out in Chapter 4, an interest rate increase raises the price of current consumption relative to future consumption.

As in any other market, there is one equilibrium price (interest rate) and quantity that prevails at any one time, given the demand and supply curves. This interest rate is illustrated by r_1 in Figure 20–2. At a higher rate, say r_2, a greater number of dollars are supplied than are demanded; that is, there will be a surplus of money in the loan market. Borrowers seeing this surplus of funds will press for a rate that is more favorable while lenders will have to agree to the lower rate if they wish to loan out these funds. Similarly, if the interest rate was below the equilibrium, say r_0, there would be a shortage of funds, since a greater number of dollars would be demanded than supplied at this interest rate. As a result, lenders will press for a more favorable rate (to them), and borrowers will have to pay the higher rate or go without funds.

As in the product market and the labor market, the demand and supply curves of loan funds also will shift from one position to another. The demand for loan funds will be closely tied to investment opportunities. If prospects for future profits increase, we can expect some increase in the demand for funds to finance new investment. Or, if totally new and profitable investment opportunities arise, perhaps as the result of new technology, the demand for funds also will increase, or shift to the right.

Changes in the supply of loan funds also will affect the equilibrium rate of interest on these funds. Inflation is an important shifter of the supply of loan funds. An increase in the actual or expected inflation rate causes a decrease in the market supply of loan funds. People who lend money, or place it in a bank or savings institution, are aware that when the money is repaid it has less purchasing power than when it was lent. To compensate them for this loss, lenders (savers) require a higher rate of interest to make funds available. Unless they can obtain higher rates, they might just as well purchase consumer durables or other assets that rise with the price level—such as precious metals or real estate.

INTEREST RATE DIFFERENCES

For simplicity, we have discussed the interest rate as if there was a single rate of interest prevailing in the economy at a point in time. There are, in fact, a number of rates of interest—depending on the loan market under consideration. Banks charge a *prime rate* for their most favored customers and other, higher rates for small business, home, or auto loans. Banks and finance companies charge still higher rates for so-called personal loans, and loan sharks extract rates from their customers that are even higher.

What accounts for these differences? Basically, interest rate differences reflect different demand and supply conditions in the particular loan market under consideration. If the supply of funds is large relative to the demand, then the interest rate will be low, and vice versa.

The differences in interest rates between various borrowers and types of loans are largely the result of differences on the supply side of the market. The major consideration is the expected cost of making the loan. Two cost components are important. Perhaps most important is the risk of making the loan. Although lenders can never be 100 percent certain of being repaid, past experience tells them that certain loans are much less risky than others. For example, large, reputable companies that have been in business for many years and have built up good credit ratings will likely face a supply curve of funds that lies to the right of small, relatively unknown borrowers. As the risk of default increases, lenders are forced to charge a higher rate to pay for the money lost through nonpayment of that type of loan. Lenders attempt to segregate potential borrowers by degree of risk to give lower rates to low-risk borrowers (mainly to get their business), while making high-risk borrowers pay a larger share of the cost of defaults.

In addition to risk, a second cost component that accounts for differences in the rate of interest charged is the administrative cost of making and collecting the loan. On a per dollar basis, this is higher for small loans. For example, the total cost of the paperwork necessary to process a $100,000 loan is not much different from the total administrative cost of making a loan of $1,000. Thus, the cost per dollar is higher for the smaller loan. To recoup these costs, the lender has to charge a higher rate on small loans. The cost of collecting also varies. At the extreme are lenders who employ a staff of "300-pound field men" to search out and persuade borrowers to pay up, or else! Since these lenders (the crime syndicate) must pay for these "services," they have to charge a high interest rate. If their rates are above the legal maximum, as usual, they also have to be compensated for the risk of getting caught and serving a prison term. If loan sharks charge such high rates and use such violent methods of collection, why do people borrow from them? The answer is that not everyone can obtain loans from reputable lenders at the legal interest rates. Ceilings on interest rates, or *usury laws,* force people desperate for loans without adequate collateral or credit ratings into the clutches of unscrupulous lenders.

THE NOMINAL VERSUS THE REAL RATE OF INTEREST

The interest rate we have been discussing is the money or *nominal rate.* The *real rate* is the nominal rate adjusted by the rate of change of the general price level, that is, the rate of inflation. A simple example illustrates the effect of inflation on the interest cost and returns of a loan. Suppose you lend someone $100 at 15 percent interest, to be paid back with interest one year from now, and the inflation rate during this year is 10 percent. At the end of the year, you receive $115. But, the 10 percent inflation rate means that it now takes $110 to buy the same amount of goods and services that the $100 purchased at the beginning of the year. Thus, you have gained only $5 in real purchasing power by making the loan. In other words, you received 5 percent real rate of interest on the loan. Assuming that the borrower spent the $100 on something that increased in value with the price level, the $10 increase in value of the asset over what it would have been partially offsets the interest paid. In this case, the $15 interest is offset by the $10 increase in value of the asset, so the real rate paid by the borrower is 5 percent. The formula for finding the real rate is:

Real rate = Nominal rate − Annual percent change in price level

In the preceding example, the real rate is:

$$5 = 15 - 10$$

If there were no restriction on the level of the nominal rate of interest, the loan market would establish an equilibrium nominal rate of interest high enough to compensate for the expected inflation. In reality, upper limits on nominal interest rates as set by usury laws may restrict the nominal rate of interest from rising to its free market equilibrium. In years of high inflation, the real rate is often negative; that is, the nominal rate is smaller than the rate of inflation. Why do savers offer any funds under such circumstances? Lending, even at a negative real rate, is better than not lending at all and having inflation diminish one's cash even more rapidly. Also, if negative real rates prevail, loans will be selectively rationed to good friends of the lending agency or institution— usually large, low-risk borrowers.

RATIONING AND ALLOCATING FUNCTIONS OF THE INTEREST RATE

Market price is a rationing device whereby people voluntarily limit the use of goods and services that are not free, as noted in Chapter 11. Price also allocates scarce resources to production of goods and services most valued by society. The interest rate, being the price of investment funds, serves to ration and allocate these funds.

The potential amount of investment that could be undertaken during a given year exceeds the resources available to undertake it. As a result, the available funds have to be rationed and allocated to their most valuable uses. Since, in the private sector, investment will not be undertaken unless the expected rate of return is at least as large as the interest rate, the available investment funds are rationed or made unavailable to low-payoff, unprofitable investments.

Moreover, the interest rate allocates the available investment funds to areas where the expected rate of return is highest. The greater the expected rate of return in relation to the interest rate, the more incentive investors have to allocate funds to these areas because of expected profits. Thus, the interest rate keeps funds from being invested in low-return areas and pulls the funds toward more productive investments.

Much investment also takes place with public funds in which profit is not a major consideration. Yet, public planners also need to consider the interest rate. For a public investment to be socially profitable, its contribution to the output of society should be large enough to yield a rate of return at least equal to the before-tax marginal rate of return on alternative private investment.[1]

THE STOCK MARKET

The sale of stock also represents an important source of funds to finance private investment. Although the loan market and the stock market are similar in economic terms and closely related, there is a legal difference in that the people who provide funds in the stock market become part owners of the business they invest in. Although few stockholders actively participate in managing the companies in which they invest, they are the owners. Thus, money raised by sale of stock is sometimes called *equity capital*, while money raised by borrowing is known as *debt capital*.

The price of existing stock is determined by the forces of demand and supply. If the demand for stocks increases relative to the supply, their prices will increase, and vice versa. Many short-run fluctuations in the stock market stem from changing expectations of future business conditions and/or changing expectations of the future value of the stock. For example, if many people who own stock believe stock prices will fall in the near future, they may attempt to sell, thereby increasing supply and lowering stock prices. Thus, the psychology of the market is important in the short run. Over the long run, however, the value of each firm's stock tends to reflect the dividends paid and the growth in value of the firm's assets.

In assessing the value of a firm's stock, a helpful guide is the firm's price-earnings (*P/E*) ratio. This ratio is obtained by dividing the firm's current stock price by the past year's earnings on equity capital. These earnings are obtained by subtracting all expenses, including interest on borrowed funds and depreciation of capital from the firm's sales. If a firm has a *P/E* ratio of 5, it means that the firm's stock is selling for five times its earnings. This means that each $100 of stock earned $20. Another way of stating this is that the firm earned a 20 percent rate of return on equity capital. Of course, this does not mean that the firm's stockholders received a $20 dividend for each $100 of stock they own in the company. Most corporations pay out less than total earnings on equity capital—instead choosing to return some earnings into the company. Such a practice should increase the value of the firm's stock because of the increase in value of assets and net worth of the firm.

---

[1] A figure of 15 percent is frequently used as the before-tax return to investment in the economy.

GLOSSARY

capital   Durable or long-lasting inputs such as buildings or machines that yield a stream of services over time.

gestation period   The time interval between the expenditure on an asset and when it begins to pay off.

annual cost of capital   Interest plus depreciation.

depreciation   A decrease in the value of an asset over time.

rate of return   The number of cents each dollar earns per year.

capitalized value   The amount a piece of property is worth based on its annual net returns which are assumed to continue indefinitely.

prime rate   Interest rate paid by large, low-risk borrowers.

nominal rate of interest   The interest rate quoted on loans or savings accounts.

real rate of interest   The nominal rate of interest minus the rate of inflation.

equity capital   Capital provided by the owners of the firm.

debt capital   Capital obtained from borrowing.

QUESTIONS

1. a. *What is capital?*
   b. *What do capital and consumer durables have in common?*

2. a. *What is the annual cost of owning a $10,000 automobile the first year of ownership if the rate of interest is 15 percent and the auto depreciates 25 percent per year? Assume insurance, license, and maintenance cost $600 per year and that the car is driven 15,000 miles per year at 25 miles per gallon of gasoline. Assume gasoline is $1 per gallon.*
   b. *What is the cost of the second year of ownership?*

3. a. *Why does capital depreciate?*
   b. *What are the common methods of calculating depreciation?*

4. a. *What is capitalized value?*
   b. *What is the capitalized value of a parcel of land that yields $100 annual net returns if the interest rate is 15 percent?*
   c. *What is the capitalized value of the above parcel if the interest rate is 10 percent?*
   d. *During the 1970s, farmland in the United States sold for three to four times its capitalized value. Why?*

5. *Why do interest rates rise during inflation?*

6. *a. What type of borrower pays the highest rate of interest?*
   b. How do usury laws affect such borrowers?

7. *How does the interest rate ration and allocate investment funds?*

8. *a. What determines stock prices?*
   b. How is the price/earnings ratio related to the rate of return on money invested in the stock market?
   c. Why do stock prices change?

CHAPTER 21

Project Evaluation

OVERVIEW

This chapter focuses on how to evaluate an investment project. It applies the technique of cash-flow analysis to an example of investing in an apartment house. Also, three measures of the expected profitability of an investment are presented.

CASH–FLOW ANALYSIS

An important decision made by managers of firms and government agencies is whether to invest in a capital item. Since these decisions run into the millions of dollars, it is important to have a way to determine if the investment will be profitable, i.e., the rate of return on the investment is at least as great as the interest paid on borrowed funds or the opportunity cost of the firm's funds.

A technique in widespread use for evaluating the profitability of an investment is *cash-flow analysis*. It compares the outflow of funds (cost) with the inflow of funds (returns). The information bearing on these figures is contained in a cash-flow table.

CASH–FLOW TABLE

A cash-flow table contains four pieces of information:

1. Gross cash outflow—this is the cost of the capital item. The sum includes the money from both equity and debt financing.

2. Gross cash inflow—the additional gross income received by owning the asset. The figure is approximated by the difference between the estimated income with the asset and the estimated income without the asset.

3. Added expense—these are the additional expenses such as repairs, fuel, taxes, and labor incurred by owning the asset. It *does not* include an interest or depreciation charge. This information is implicitly taken into account in calculating the rate of return.

4. Net cash flow—gross cash inflow minus added expense—the bottom line.

Use of this information in evaluating an investment is best explained in a specific example. Suppose you have an opportunity to purchase an apartment house for $200,000. The necessary information for constructing the cash-flow table follows:

Purchase price:	$200,000
Rental income:	$32,400 per year
Added expenses:	$12,400 per year
Expected selling price in four years:	$200,000

To simplify the example, assume the money used to purchase the house is laid out at the beginning of the first year of ownership, but the rental income and expenses are not forthcoming until the end of each year. The cash-flow table contains this information:

	Year 0	Year 1	Year 2	Year 3	Year 4
Cash outflow	−$200,000				
Gross cash inflow		32,400	32,400	32,400	232,400
Added expense		−12,400	−12,400	−12,400	−12,400
Net cash inflow	−$200,000	+20,000	+20,000	+20,000	+220,000

The reason for large cash inflow figures in the last year of ownership is that this year's figures include the expected selling price of the house; it is a cash inflow when sold.

The four positive net cash inflow figures total $280,000. This looks like a profitable investment; $200,000 is spent and $280,000 is taken in. The problem is that money forthcoming in the future is not worth as much as money in hand at the present; it is necessary to compute discounted present value.

DISCOUNTED PRESENT VALUE

One dollar forthcoming in the future is worth less than one dollar in hand today. If one wished to have the dollar now, a loan could be taken out that requires the payment of interest. This interest would reduce the net value of the dollar once it was obtained. The net value of the dollar obtained in the future after paying the interest on the dollar loan to obtain use of the dollar is called *discounted present value*.

The formula for computing the discounted present value (DPV) is:

$$DPV = 1/(1 + r)^n$$

In this formula r is the rate of interest and n is the number of years $1 is forthcoming in the future. To compute DPV of a sum different than $1, this formula is multiplied by that sum.

We can now calculate the DPV of future returns from the apartment house compared to when the house is purchased.

$$DPV = \frac{20,000}{(1 + r)^1} + \frac{20,000}{(1 + r)^2} + \frac{20,000}{(1 + r)^3} + \frac{220,000}{(1 + r)^4}$$

Choosing an interest rate of 12 percent yields a $188,168 DPV of the apartment house return at the point where the $200,000 was spent. Notice that the future DPV returns' is less than the purchase price; the house doesn't look like a good investment now.

The use of DPV to evaluate the profitability of an investment is an acceptable technique. If the DPV of the return is greater than the cost, buy it. The interest rate used in the formula is the interest paid on borrowed money or the opportunity cost of one's funds.

INTERNAL RATE OF RETURN

Because investments are usually evaluated by their *rate of return*, the information in the cash-flow is frequently summarized by this measure. The *internal rate of return* (IRR) is the rate of interest that makes the DPV of future returns equal to the investment cost.

IRR is obtained by trial and error. If the DPV computed from a given interest rate is less than the investment cost, the IRR is less than the interest rate. Conversely, if the DPV is greater than the investment cost, IRR is greater than interest rate used for the discounting procedure. In the apartment house example, the IRR is about 10 percent. Using a 10 percent rate of interest in the discount formula yields a $200,434 DPV. Thus, the IRR of this investment is slightly larger than 10 percent. Although IRR is a commonly used term, it is acceptable to call the figure "rate of return."

BENEFIT–COST RATIO

Two methods have been presented for evaluating the profitability of an investment: (1) comparing DPV with the asset's purchase price, and (2) comparing IRR with the interest rate. A third method closely related to the first method is the benefit cost (B/C) ratio. The B/C ratio is calculated by dividing the discounted present value of the return (benefits) by the investment cost. If the B/C ratio is greater than one, the investment is profitable. This means that the DPV exceeds the cost of the investment.

THE EFFECT OF INFLATION

In the apartment house example, it was assumed that the price level remained constant over the course of the returns. In reality, one might expect some inflation, although no one knows what future inflation will be. Inflation increases the gross cash inflow, added expense, and net cash inflow figures over time. Even though gross cash inflow and added expense grow at the same percentage rate, in absolute terms the former grows more than the latter because they are larger figures. Hence, net cash inflow becomes larger. The apartment house example showing a 6 percent inflation rate is:

	Year 0	Year 1	Year 2	Year 3	Year 4
Cash outflow	−$200,000				
Gross cash inflow		+34,344	+36,288	+38,556	+292,824
Added expense		−13,144	−13,888	−14,756	−15,624
Net cash inflow	− 200,000	+21,200	+22,400	+23,800	+277,200

Since the net cash inflow figures in this example exceed those figures when no inflation was assumed, the internal rate of return for a given investment increases with inflation. This result does not imply that investments will always be more profitable during a period of inflation. As explained in the preceding chapter, the nominal rate of interest also increases during inflation. This also requires that the IRR is higher for the investment to be profitable.

RANKING OF INVESTMENT OPPORTUNITIES

Most businesses and public agencies have a variety of investment opportunities that they might undertake in a given period. Which ones? A convenient way to answer this question is to list all investment opportunities that exist, perform a cash-flow analysis on each, and then rank them by IRR. A cumulative ranking, illustrated by Figure 21–1, shows the IRR of the marginal dollar invested. If $11,000 is invested, it yields a 21 percent IRR. As more money is invested, lower return projects are done. Investing a total of $24,000 drives the IRR of the marginal dollar down to 15 percent and so on.

With this information, the firm can decide how much to invest. If the interest rate is 15 percent, $24,000 should be invested to maximize profits. Stopping short of this point causes the firm to unnecessarily forego profits equal to the value of the shaded triangle in Figure 21–1.

FIGURE 21–1   Cumulative Ranking of Investments

Although the procedure for evaluating an investment is straightforward, the hard part is finding accurate figures, especially the future costs and returns. The technique does not help much if erroneous figures are used. Although no one has a crystal ball to foresee the future, the accuracy of expected future costs and returns depends on the competence and sound judgment of the evaluator.

GLOSSARY

cash-flow table   Contains expected costs and returns of an investment.

discounted present value (DPV)   The present value of a sum of money forthcoming in the future, calculated by $1/(1+r)^n$ where r is the rate of interest and n is the number of years in the future the money will be obtained.

internal rate of return (IRR)   The rate of interest that makes the DPV of future returns equal to the investment cost.

benefit/cost ratio   The ratio of DPV over the investment cost.

QUESTIONS

1. *In the context of a cash-flow table define these terms:*
   a. *Cash outflow*
   b. *Gross cash inflow.*
   c. *Added expense.*
   d. *Net cash inflow.*

2. a. *Why is a dollar forthcoming some time in the future worth less than a dollar in hand today?*
   b. *What is the discounted present value of $100 forthcoming in two years if the interest rate is 10 percent?*

3. *How would you use the following to evaluate the profitability of an investment:*
   a. *The discounted present value?*
   b. *The benefit-cost ratio?*
   c. *The internal rate of return?*

4. *Compute the internal rate of return of the apartment house example where a 6 percent inflation note is assumed.*

5. *Consider the opportunity of investing in land that you expect will double in value in five years. What is its internal rate of return? Assume the land costs $100,000 now and that there is no added expense of ownership.*

6. a. *How do changes in the rate of interest affect investment spending?*
   b. *How do changes in expectations of future economic conditions affect investment spending?*

7. *If a firm wishes to maximize profits, how much should it invest in new capital each year?*

PART SEVEN

Human Capital

CHAPTER 22

Cost and Returns of a
College Education

OVERVIEW

A college education is an investment with a cost and returns. Estimates of these figures for a typical student are presented along with expected rates of return for various students.

HUMAN CAPITAL DEFINED

We defined capital as durable or long-lasting inputs, such as buildings and equipment, that contribute to the production of goods and services. We noted that capital inputs are expensive and that the present value of their stream of returns must be greater than their purchase price for them to yield a net positive contribution to total output. In recent years, there has been growing awareness that the acquisition of knowledge and skills by human beings also results in the creation of capital—human capital. While the special characteristics of human beings are recognized, there are similarities between human capital, the skills and knowledge acquired through education or training, and nonhuman capital.

First, both kinds of capital, human and nonhuman, enhance the productive capacity of society. Human beings without tools and without knowledge are unproductive creatures. Moreover, even a cursory study of history reveals that human capital must exist before nonhuman capital can be produced. For example, the wheel was invented when humans learned that a round object rolling along the ground encountered less friction and took less power to move than a flat object being dragged. There are innumerable examples of new applications of knowledge that have led to the production of new nonhuman capital.

A second similarity between the two kinds of capital is that they both pay off over a long time. The stream of returns to education for most people covers 30 or more years. Be aware of the consequences of this long payoff period. First, it precipitates great uncertainty. Students are faced with the nagging question of whether the job they prepare for will be available when they graduate, to say nothing of 10 to 20 years in the future. At the high school and undergraduate level of training, it is impossible to predict what kind of employment will be forthcoming. Since a person's job can be expected to

269

change several times during a lifetime, it is important that training, particularly at the college level, facilitates learning new jobs and adjusting to new environments. Another consequence to the long payoff is the need to discount future returns. For instance, $1 forthcoming 40 years from now discounted back at a 10 percent interest rate is worth less than 2 cents today. With the present demand on a young person's resources, such as car, clothes, and travel, the decision to invest now for a payoff far into the future is difficult.

Third, human capital, like some nonhuman capital, requires a lengthy building period. With human capital, the period is longer. Ten years is the least amount of time that can be devoted to the process, and it may run up to 18 or 20 years for people who obtain a Ph.D. or professional degree. This long gestation or building period, coupled with the long payoff period, makes the discounting factor especially important in the case of human capital.

A fourth similarity between the two kinds of capital is that both tend to depreciate. The ultimate depreciation for human capital is growing old and passing from the scene. But there is a more immediate depreciation that begins the minute we learn something new—forgetting. Educators tell us that a large part of what we learn is forgotten in a short time. How much do you recall of a book you read or a course you took last year, or even last term? Depreciation of human capital also occurs because of obsolescence. Each year, new knowledge is produced that reduces the value of existing knowledge. Skills such as the ability to repair a steam locomotive or fly a propeller-driven aircraft are no longer in demand because of new knowledge and technology. Because of obsolescence, most people must continue learning throughout life. This is particularly true for persons in the professions or skilled trades. College professors who want to keep abreast of new knowledge in their field, for example, probably should spend about 20 to 25 percent of their time learning.

The major part of all human capital is the result of formal schooling provided by elementary schools, high schools, trade and vocational schools, and colleges and universities. Not all learning, of course, needs to be of this type. Much learning takes place on the job, either through apprenticeship programs or through learning by doing.

In addition, some learning occurs through individual study, although the truly self-made person, such as Abraham Lincoln, always has been rare. Most of us require someone who can tell us what is important or what to study.

PERSONAL COST OF EDUCATION

Education is not a free good. Indeed, it is more expensive each year, as every student and parent knows. It is useful to itemize the major costs that students or parents bear for education. These include: (1) forgone earnings, (2) tuition, and (3) books and supplies.

It is tempting to exclude forgone earnings (the money you could earn if you were not in school) as part of the cost of an education because this cost is not paid by check or cash. However, a person who decides to go to work after high school gives up a college or technical school education. It is logical to argue that a person who decides to go to school gives up full-time employment earnings during the college years.

In the more developed countries of the world, forgone earnings are negligible for the elementary and junior high school student but are a factor as the student finishes high school and enters college or other advanced training. In developing countries, where educational attainment is low and children enter the labor force at a young age, forgone earnings are important even in the lower grades.

Although the average student may not feel the pinch of forgone earnings as much as the out-of-pocket costs of tuition, books, and so forth, it is necessary to account for this money when deciding how far to go in school. Considering the modest salary that a high school graduate can obtain the first few years out of school, say $10,000 to $12,000 per year, it is clear that even a modest amount of income forgone is large when viewed as a cost.

The other two components—tuition, and books and supplies—are obvious, although tuition generally does not cover the full educational costs of colleges and universities. We will consider this part of the cost in the next section.

One cost item that is conspicuous by its absence is board and room. Surely, a student who pays $3,000 during the school year for a room and meals at the college residence hall should include this amount as a logical part of college costs. But remember that everyone has to be somewhere, so if the student did not pay the $3,000 for living on or near campus, as much or more would have to be paid to live wherever the individual worked. Thus, the cost items listed above include only the *extra* costs involved in attending college as opposed to doing something else. Costs are measured in this manner so they can be compared with the *extra* income obtained by furthering an education.

PUBLIC COST

From the viewpoint of society, all private costs considered in the previous section are a part of the total educational cost that society must bear. The operation of schools and colleges financed in part by tuition, the production of books and supplies, and the loss of earnings during school years, all involve using real resources that could have been used to produce something else—had they not been used to produce education.

In most educational institutions, however, tuition does not come close to covering the cost of operating the schools. In the public elementary and high schools, tuition is zero, so the entire cost is borne by taxpayers. In colleges and universities, tuition varies; some city or community colleges set tuition close to zero, while the more exclusive private schools try to cover a larger share of operating costs by tuition. Most of the high-tuition private schools, however, must rely on endowments to make ends meet. The total cost of education for most students is greater than the cost borne by the individual student.

PERSONAL RETURNS TO EDUCATION

What does an individual obtain from education? There are two components: monetary and nonmonetary. The monetary component is the increased earning power that can be obtained with additional years of schooling. This increased earning power comes from two factors: (1) an increase in the productive capacity of the individual, and (2) the ability to conceive of and produce new goods or services that are more valued by society.

The contribution of education to increased productivity appears to stem, in part, from an increased ability to organize and use resources efficiently, including the scarce resource of time. No one appreciates the importance of time more than the student. With two or three exams coming up and a term paper to finish, the student is forced to make each minute count. The experience gained in allocating time efficiently is one of the most important advantages of a college education, at least from the standpoint of individual productivity. Education also enhances productivity by enabling the individual to accept new technology more readily and use it effectively. Education is particularly important with regard to technology that requires new or different skills. The more educated person seems to possess a greater capacity for self-teaching and adapting to new situations.

The effect of education on the kinds of goods and services produced is demonstrated clearly by comparing the output of a modern industrialized society that has a high proportion of educated people with a traditional society. The traditional society's choice of goods and services is limited to a narrow array of low-quality items, most of which are necessities. The output of the more educated society is of a higher quality and more diverse. The world would be dull for the educated person if education resulted in only greater output of the traditional necessities such as food, clothing, and shelter. Thus, the monetary rewards of additional education stem at least in part from an increased ability to conceive of and produce new and different goods and services that are demanded by a more affluent society.

When considering the monetary rewards of increased education, it is always possible to find exceptions: self-made people with eighth-grade educations who have built up fortunes in the business world, or high school dropouts who made it big in show business. But, if we look at large numbers of people, we find that high school graduates, on the average, earn more than people with an eighth-grade education, and people with college training earn more than high school graduates. Thus, an individual who does not achieve a high school or college education is not necessarily doomed to a life of poverty, but the chances that the person will remain poor are substantially higher than if he or she had received the schooling.

For most people, the returns to additional education exceed the monetary value of increased earnings over a lifetime. The *nonmonetary* returns to education include: (1) the immediate utility or satisfaction that a person receives during the time of schooling, and (2) the long-run stream of increased satisfaction that accrues during his or her lifetime because of the educational experience.

Although few students think fondly of exams or assignments, most derive some satisfaction from being in an educational environment. The friends that are made, the dances and parties, the dates, the sporting events, the good books that are read, even the pleasure of learning, all provide immediate satisfaction that is not measured in monetary terms.

But the nonmonetary rewards to schooling are not limited to the immediate time spent in school. Many friendships that begin in school endure over a lifetime. Many people meet their spouses during school. Also, education enhances the quality of life by facilitating an awareness and greater understanding of the world around us. The lives of educated people are ruled less by superstition and fear and more by rational thought and deliberate choice. Although we do not have adequate quantitative measures of happiness, psychological studies indicate that people with more education are happier and find greater fulfillment in life than persons with less education. Perhaps education is even more important than money in finding that elusive and nebulous good called happiness.

SOCIAL RETURNS

The returns to education are not limited to the individual. Society also gains. Economists call these gains *social returns* or *externalities,* that is, the benefits that are external to the individual receiving the education.

At the family level, the education of the parents should benefit the children. For one thing, it broadens the children's cultural background and opportunities. Children of college-educated parents are more likely to attend college than the children of parents who stopped at the high-school level, although this is less important now because of the accessibility of community colleges. There is also a tendency for at least part of the knowledge gained by parents during their school years to be transmitted to their children. Children who gain an appreciation for the importance of knowledge have gained a great deal.

At the community level, the education of individuals makes the community a better place to live for all. For example, one's chances of getting mugged are greater in neighborhoods where people are poorly educated and have low incomes than in places where the majority is highly educated and affluent. Granted, the income level may be the important factor in this difference, but education has an important bearing on income. An increase in the educational level of people also reduces the amount of fear and suspicion that people have of one another. Because education usually acquaints us with people of different backgrounds and ideas, it helps us become more tolerant of persons who are different than ourselves.

Different kinds of education provide different degrees of social returns.

Education that imparts purely technical skills, such as programming a computer, repairing an automobile, or setting a broken bone, primarily benefits the person receiving the education because of the larger income that can be earned by selling these skills.[1] Social returns may be greatest from an education that provides a better understanding of people and society, such as the liberal arts and social sciences.

The amount of social return derived from the education of individuals is important because it bears on the financing of education. If social returns are important, then society ought to pay part of the cost of educating the individual. If society receives some benefit from education above what is received by the individual, it should pay part of the individual's educational expense for the person to be willing to invest an optimum amount in education. On the other hand, if the individual receives all the benefits of the education, should the individual be willing to buy the amount that provides a return equal to other investments the person could make?

FINANCING EDUCATION

The relative increase in the cost of providing educational services in recent years has prompted considerable discussion on the optimum methods of paying for these services. In the United States and most other countries, a substantial share of the cost of operating educational institutions has been provided by public funds. The popularity of this method stems from a special characteristic of education. People who buy this service, students, have had little or no opportunity to earn and save enough to pay for it. Many other goods and services, such as baby food and the services of pediatricians, also exhibit this characteristic, although their benefits are more certain and immediate than the returns to education. By using public tax funds to finance a part of the cost of education, we spread its current cost over several generations, as opposed to concentrating it on one or two generations, that is, the students or their parents.

One alternative to public tuition payment is for families to pay for the education of their children. Among upper-middle- and high-income people, this is frequently done. However, for a large segment of our population the cost of purchasing 12 to 16 years of quality schooling for their children is prohibitive. Children of poor parents would continue to be doomed to poverty because of an inability to buy a means of escape through education.

A second alternative to public support of education is for students to borrow to pay for it. This alternative has not enjoyed much popularity, even among students in professional and graduate schools, to say nothing of elementary and high school students. Indeed, students are more willing to go

---

[1] The people who purchase the goods and services made possible by education also benefit.

into debt for an automobile than for schooling. It is not clear why, but one explanation is the uncertain future. The automobile provides immediate and certain utility, whereas the payoff to education is both uncertain and far off. Also, lending agencies have not been especially eager to promote educational loans compared with auto loans, for example. No doubt, risk or uncertainty is also a prime consideration for the lender. If a person who borrows for an automobile defaults on the payments, the lender always can repossess the car. But, if a person who borrows for an education defaults, it is not possible to repossess the person—or the education. Granted, there are devices such as wage garnishment, but they have not been popular and they involve added legal expense and effort.

If society desires its young people to continue to achieve 12 to 16 years of quality schooling, then it will have to continue to use public funds to finance part of the education cost. Whether such funding leads to a so-called optimum amount of education is a debatable question. Such funding provides an incentive to overinvest in education because the full cost is not borne by the individual. That is, when the cost of something is subsidized, the individual has an incentive to buy more of it than if the person had to bear the full cost.

On the other hand, the uncertainty faced by the individual who must pay the entire educational cost leads to the purchase of less education than desirable from the standpoint of society. The argument is that the individual faces more uncertainty regarding the payoff to education than a large group of individuals, that is, society. Thus, each individual is inclined to invest less in education than if the person faced the same uncertainty as the whole society. Therefore, society will have to bear a part of the individual's education cost to make the individual willing to purchase as much education as he or she would if faced with the same uncertainty as society. The existence of any so-called social returns, as mentioned previously, also implies the use of public tax funds for education. However, this argument has lost some appeal in recent years because of the inability to quantify the magnitude of such returns or even demonstrate their existence.

An argument for using public funds to support education also can be made on the basis of achieving a more equal distribution of income. If only the rich could afford to buy education for their children, the children of poor parents would remain poor. The use of public funds to finance part of the cost of education has become a widely accepted means of achieving a somewhat more equal distribution of income. Education provides a means of giving people more equality of opportunity to make something out of their lives. Other income redistributive devices such as welfare programs or a negative income tax scheme are less accepted. In these cases, some taxpayers feel that low-income people do not pull their weight in society and live off of persons who work. Education provides a means of escaping poverty, but it requires considerable work. It is a way for society to help persons who are willing to help themselves. Remember, though, that students at the high school and college level will continue to bear a substantial share of the cost of schooling, regardless of how tuition is financed, because of their forgone earnings. Forgone earnings probably loom larger in the minds of poor students than students from high-income families.

The common method of using public funds to finance education is by allocating the funds directly to the educational institutions. An alternative to this procedure is to provide grants in the form of vouchers directly to the students or parents, allowing them to spend the vouchers at the school of their choice. The school then turns in the vouchers and receives money from the government. Major advantages of this approach are that it gives people more freedom of choice and promotes competition among schools. Public schools now enjoy substantial freedom from competitive forces and have little incentive to innovate and improve the quality of their services or strive for greater efficiency.[2]

Although the returns to education are reflected in more than just monetary rewards, it is helpful to obtain measures of both the costs and returns to investment in human capital or education. If education is an acceptable investment from a strictly monetary point of view, then it is an even better investment when nonmonetary returns are considered.

Monetary Costs

Recall that the three major cost components of a college education are: (1) forgone earnings, (2) tuition, and (3) books and supplies. To match the cost of college training with the returns, we estimate in this section the costs that were borne by the student who either graduated or left school in 1984. Forgone earnings are the full-time earnings net of federal income taxes of year-round workers in the 15–19 and 20–24 age categories, depending on the year in school. The earnings are adjusted down to a 40-week work year, which assumes that the student obtains a comparably paying summer job. Tuition and fees are figures from large, public universities. Added expenses for books, supplies, and miscellaneous items are assumed equal to 10 percent of forgone earnings. The figures are summarized in Table 22–1.

The fact that costs are incurred over time rather than at a point in time, as in the apartment house example, makes it necessary to "accumulate" the costs. Costs should be accumulated because the cost today of one dollar spent a number of years ago is greater than one dollar. This is because of the interest that the dollar could have earned had it not been spent on the investment in question. The formula for determing the accumulated cost of one dollar spent n years ago is $(1 + i)^n$, where i is the rate of interest. For example, the accumulated cost of $1,000 spent four years ago is $1,000 (1 + 0.10)^4 = \$1,460$

---

[2] For further discussion of the problems of financing education, see the report, "Investment in Education: The Equity Efficiency Quandary," workshop at the University of Chicago, June 7–10, 1971, sponsored by the Committee on Basic Research in Education of the National Research Council, in T. W. Schultz, ed., *Journal of Political Economy* 80, 2 (May–June 1972).

TABLE 22–1   Summary of Costs for a Four-Year College Education. 1984 Graduates, Current Year Prices

	Freshman	Sophomore	Junior	Senior
Male:				
Forgone earnings	$6,406	$6,458	$10,063	$10,231
Tuition	963	1,018	1,059	1,106
Books, supplies, and miscellaneous	641	646	1,006	1,023
Totals	$8,010	$8,122	$12,128	$12,360
Female:				
Forgone earnings	$5,937	$5,904	$ 8,433	$ 8,879
Tuition	963	1,018	1,059	1,106
Books, supplies, and miscellaneous	594	590	843	888
Totals	$7,494	$7,512	$10,335	$10,873

using a 10 percent interest rate. In assessing the costs of education, it is common to accumulate all costs up to the end of the senior year. The procedure for accumulating the costs incurred by male and female college graduates are shown below; the cost figures are from Table 22–1 using an interest rate of 10 percent. Note that the accumulated cost of a college education was about $50,000 in 1984.

Males:
$$\$8{,}010\,(1.10)^4 + \$8{,}122\,(1.10)^3 + \$12{,}128\,(1.10)^2 + \$12{,}360\,(1.10) = \$50{,}768$$

Females:
$$\$7{,}494\,(1.10)^4 + \$7{,}512\,(1.10)^3 + \$10{,}335\,(1.10)^2 + \$10{,}873\,(1.10) = \$45{,}398$$

Monetary Returns

The figures in Table 22–2 indicate the monetary value of various levels of education for 1984. The main thing to note in Table 22–2 is the increase in income level as years of schooling increase. This relationship is true for all age levels for both men and women. To use these figures to calculate the monetary returns to education, we must compute the *difference* in earnings between the various levels of schooling completed. For example, the monetary value of four years of college over a high school education for males in the 25–34 age group is $27,244–$21,087 or $6,157 per year.

TABLE 22–2   Mean Annual Income Levels by Education, Age, and Sex as of 1984

Age	Four years high school	One to three years college	Four years college
Males:			
25–34	$21,097	$23,299	$27,244
35–44	25,856	28,352	36,673
45–54	27,407	31,454	44,840
55–64	27,366	33,949	45,768
Females:			
25–34	14,827	16,892	19,928
35–44	15,834	19,632	23,428
45–54	15,737	17,891	23,664
55–64	16,394	19,150	24,407

SOURCE: U.S. Department of Commerce, "Consumer Income," *Current Population Reports*, series P–60, 151, (April 1986), pp. 126–33.

However, because of the progressive income tax whereby larger incomes are taxed as higher rates than lower incomes, the net after-federal-income-tax differential is not this large. For example, when these figures are adjusted for federal income tax paid, the income differential is reduced to $5,241 from $6,157. The income differences as of 1984 net of federal income taxes are presented in Table 22–3. (No adjustment has been made for state income taxes or social security taxes.)

TABLE 22–3   Annual Income Differences between Levels of School Completed by Age and Sex as of 1984, Net of Federal Income Taxes

	One to three years of college over high school	Four years of college over high school
Males		
Age 25–34	$1,866	$ 5,241
Age 35–44	2,218	9,013
Age 45–54	3,330	14,043
Age 55–64	5,554	14,867
Females		
Age 25–34	1,795	4,281
Age 35–44	3,185	6,426
Age 45–54	1,820	6,725
Age 55–64	2,243	6,787

SOURCE: Federal Income Tax Rates Were Taken from the *Statistical Abstract*, 1987, p. 305.

The figures in Table 22–3 are the earnings differentials for different age groups as of 1984. While these numbers provide some indication of the future, we should also inquire if there is any reason why they might change in future years. There is one important reason—inflation. In view of the inflationary tendency over the past 40 to 50 years, prices and wages will not remain constant throughout the working lives of present-day college graduates. No one knows what the inflation rate will be next year, much less 40 to 50 years hence.

In projecting future earnings, let us assume a modest inflation rate of 3 percent per year in the working lifetimes of people graduating from or leaving college in 1984. Recall from the preceding chapter that inflation increases the absolute difference between the gross cash inflow and added expenses, therefore increasing the net cash inflow and the internal rate of return. A similar thing happens with education. If earnings of both high school and college-trained people increase at 3 percent per year, the absolute size of the difference between the two series of numbers increases. This occurs because the 3 percent annual change of the larger number (earnings of college-trained people) represents a larger dollar growth than the 3 percent annual change in the smaller number (earnings of high school graduates). Hence the absolute size of the difference between the two numbers increases. For example, the annual earnings differential for female college graduates age 55 increases from $6,787 with stable prices to $17,985 with a 3 percent inflation after 1984.

Although the extra earnings over a working lifetime add up to a substantial figure, especially with inflation, it is necessary to account for two additional factors in order to evaluate the payoff to investment in a college education: (1) the cost of schooling, and (2) each additional dollar earned in the future is not worth as much as a dollar on hand at the present. Because the cost of education is incurred well in advance of the returns, the extra earnings forthcoming should be converted into present value terms using the discounting formula discussed in Chapter 21. Costs are not all incurred at a given time either. This requires that we accumulate the costs over the years the education is taking place.

INTERNAL RATES OF RETURN

In evaluating the costs and returns to a college education it is necessary to discount the future returns back to the same point in time to which costs are accumulated. In this case we use the end of the senior year as the point of reference. The procedure for discounting the future monetary returns to education is the same as that used in the apartment house example of Chapter 21. Some of the figures for female college graduates taken from Table 22–3 (adjusted for inflation) are presented below, using a 10 percent interest rate. It is assumed here that the person begins working at age 23 and works up to age 65.

TABLE 22–4   Estimated Internal Rates of Return of People Graduating from or Leaving College in 1984, Assuming a 3 Percent Inflation Rate in Their Lifetimes

	Internal rate of return
Four-year males	15 percent
Two-year males	14 percent
Four-year females	13 percent
Two-year females	14 percent

SOURCE: Computed from Data in Table 22–2 and 22–3.

$$\frac{\$4,281}{1.10} + \cdots + \frac{\$5,264}{(1.10)^8} + \cdots + \frac{\$10,653}{(1.10)^{18}} + \cdots + \frac{\$14,969}{(1.10)^{28}}$$

$$+ \cdots + \frac{\$20,851}{(1.10)^{38}} + \cdots \frac{\$23,467}{(1.10)^{42}} = \$70,307$$

Because the discounted present value of these returns, $70,307, is greater than the accumulated costs, $45,398, it is evident that the internal rate of return to investment in a four-year degree by females is greater than 10 percent. Recall from Chapter 21 that the internal rate of return is that rate of interest that makes the costs (accumulated in this case) just equal to the discounted returns.

The internal rates of return for the four investment categories presented in Tables 22–1 to 22–3 are in Table 22–4. College graduates are referred to as four-year individuals while those who obtain one to three years of college are called two-year people. Note that the estimated internal rates of return are quite similar for all four categories, ranging from 13 to 15 percent. While these rates of return are not spectacular, they are competitive with the returns to alternative investment in nonhuman capital. Because the earnings differences for large numbers of people in the census data are stable from year to year, these figures come close to what is expected by people leaving college in the mid to late 1980s. What is expected may not be what is realized; no one knows this figure. If inflation exceeds 3 percent over the next 40 years, the returns will be greater; if inflation falls below 3 percent, the realized rates of return will be lower. Also, if the nation experiences real economic growth, the absolute earnings differentials should also rise—increasing the internal rates of return.

GLOSSARY

human capital   Acquisition of knowledge and skills by human beings.

personal costs of education   It includes foregone earnings, tuition, and books and supplies.

public costs of education   Personal costs plus the tax money that pays for part of students' education.

personal returns to education   Monetary plus nonmonetary returns.

monetary returns   Additional earnings due to added schooling.

nonmonetary returns   Additional utility obtained from schooling above what is obtained by higher earnings.

social returns   Benefits received by people who do not receive the education.

QUESTIONS

1. a. What is human capital?
   b. What are the similarities between human and nonhuman capital?

2. What are the personal and public costs of education?

3. What are personal and social returns to education?

4. In recent years, there has been discussion about the voucher plan for funding part of the educational cost of students. Under this plan, students (or their parents) would receive vouchers that they could use to pay tuition at the school of their choice.
   a. Who would benefit from this plan?
   b. Who would be against it? Why?

5. In contrast to most other things that people buy, such as food, clothing, and shelter, a substantial part of the cost of education is paid for by public tax funds. Why should education be different than other goods?

6. As shown in Table 22–3, the annual income differences for people completing one to three years of college are less than half the figures for college graduates. Yet, the internal rates of return for the two groups are similar in Table 22–4. Why?

7. a. Estimate the cost of your schooling this year. What is the cost of this course for each hour the class meets?
   b. What is the accumulated cost of four years of schooling at this institution with the prevailing rate of interest?

CHAPTER 23

Student Allocation of Time

OVERVIEW

Time is a scarce resource. This chapter provides a framework for allocating time to its most productive uses. Emphasis is given to part-time employment by college students and how it influences time allocation and grades. The experience gained in allocating time is one of the most valuable experiences obtained from a college education.

PART–TIME EMPLOYMENT

In measuring the cost of a college education, it was assumed that students receive no earnings during the school year. Yet, more than half of all college students work part-time during the school year. Part-time earnings reduce the total forgone earnings, which represent the largest cost of a college education for most students. Hence, if we accounted for part-time earnings, the total cost of a college education should decrease, and the estimated rate of return should increase.

On the other hand, students who participate in part-time employment during the school year must give up something. The time spent working must be taken away either from school or leisure activities. Since these activities also have value, it is incorrect to subtract part-time earnings from the cost of education without subtracting the value of the utility lost by devoting less time to other activities. The fact that many students decide to work part-time means that they believe they gain more from the part-time employment earnings than what they give up. It is useful to look at the effect of part-time employment on time allocation.

THE STUDENT AS A SMALL, MULTIPRODUCT FIRM

In the study of time allocation it is helpful to cast the student in the role of a multiproduct firm engaged in producing three categories of output: (1) human capital, (2) intermediate goods via the labor market (for students who work part-time), and (3) final goods for current consumption. Because of the output diversity we will use utility as a measure or common denominator of output. Our main interest is the allocation of time to each of the categories of activities. Hence, the marginal physical product (MPP) of time is the extra utility resulting from the input of one more hour of time to any of the three activities.

Human Capital

In the production of human capital, the student combines time with other purchased inputs such as faculty services, instructional facilities, and books. The marginal product of time in the production of human capital depends on the inherent capability of the student and the quantity and quality of complementary inputs such as the teacher and instructional materials. The marginal productivity of study time (for a given quantity) is greater for more capable and highly motivated students than for unmotivated students. Similarly, the marginal product of time is higher for students who have good teachers and effective instructional materials, or for students enrolled in high-payoff programs.

Remember that the MPP of study time depends on the quality and quantity of other inputs used in the production of human capital. If the prices of these inputs become expensive, say, less will be purchased, which will reduce the MPP of study time.[1] In other words, if it becomes more expensive to attend college, fewer educational services will be purchased by young people, which will reduce the amount of time allocated to study. For persons who decide not to attend college, little time is allocated to study.

The utility (returns) derived from human capital production includes both monetary and nonmonetary components. Also, the utility forthcoming in the future, from either monetary or nonmonetary sources, should be discounted back to the present to be comparable with the utility produced through part-time employment or household production. All activities other than school and part-time employment are household production. No student knows how much income will be increased by education or how much education will enrich life in the future. In spite of the difficulties of assessing the utility forthcoming from education, each student must make allocative decisions about allocating time and other inputs within school activities, and between this category and other activities.

Intermediate Goods

Students who work part-time participate in a second kind of production activity. Although work may not result in utility, the income received yields utility through the goods and services it can buy. In addition, some earnings may be used to purchase inputs for the production of human capital, such as in paying tuition or the purchase of books and supplies. For a given input of time to part-time employment, the higher the real wage, the greater the MPP of this time because the extra hour of work allows for the purchase of more goods and services.

Some jobs are less agreeable than others. Therefore, the utility received by the goods and services purchased through earnings from work should be

---

[1] This assumes that study time and educational services are net complements.

adjusted by differences in the kind of work performed. For example, higher wages earned by cleaning the sewer or collecting garbage do not necessarily increase utility in proportion to the higher earnings from these jobs.

Household Production

The third type of activity is household production. Here, the student combines time with conventional goods, such as food, clothing, housing, transportation, and entertainment services to produce utility. The MPP of time in household production depends on individual tastes. For example, the student who loves to ski will spend more time on the slopes than a person who receives more utility from an automobile purchased from the earnings of part-time employment. The second person will spend more time working on a part-time job.

Similar to the production of human capital, the prices of other inputs, such as the car or skiing activities, determine the MPP of time devoted to each activity. For example, if cars become relatively expensive compared to skiing, the MPP of work time devoted to buying the car will decline because the extra hour of work time will buy less car than if cars were cheaper. Most of the discussion in this section will focus on how differences in the price of time influence the allocation of time, but remember that changes in the prices of other inputs used with time also influence its allocation.

UTILITY MAXIMIZATION

Recall from Chapter 4 that a person maximizes utility from a given level of income by equalizing the MU/P ratios. The same is used to maximize the utility from a given value of time. The MPP of time is measured in utils, so MU and MPP are the same. The price of time in an activity is its value in the next best alternative activity—its opportunity cost.

The rule for maximizing utility for a given value of time is:

$$MPP_1/P_1 = MPP_2/P_2 = MPP_3/P_3$$

This rule says that the marginal utility (MPP) per dollar of time should be the same in all three production activities. If one ratio is higher than another, a person's total utility can be increased by allocating more time to the high-ratio activity and less time to other activities. For example, if the MPP per dollar of time is 10 in household production and 15 in the production of human capital, 5 additional units of satisfaction are obtained by transferring $1 of time from household to human capital production.

Because the value of time differs between different people and different times of day, the price of time varies accordingly. During the normal daytime or early evening working hours, the price of time devoted to study will be wages forgone (net of taxes) from a full-time job. Similarly, the price of time devoted to employment during these hours is the implicit value of time devoted to study or household activities, whichever is higher. During normal rest or sleep hours, the price of time devoted to study is the implicit value placed on sleep. Conversely, the price of time devoted to sleep or rest is the implicit value of either study or employment, whichever is higher. The price of time to employment or household activities also varies according to the proximity of examinations, rising just before examinations, when an extra hour of study may have a high payoff in terms of obtaining better grades.

One unique characteristic of time, as opposed to other purchased inputs, is that the individual must utilize 24 hours per day regardless of price. The allocation of time to various activities will vary as price changes, but as long as a person is alive, time is utilized in one of the three production activities. (Leisure and sleep are included in household production of utility.)

Part–Time Employment and Time Allocation

We can use this rule to predict what happens when a student engages in part-time employment. Let us consider a student who is engaged only in the production of utility through school and household activities, that is, a full-time student. Assume that the student maximizes utility by equalizing the MPP/P ratios of time for these two activities. Suppose an attractive job opportunity occurs so that the MU per dollar of time becomes larger in the production of intermediate goods purchased from earnings than in the other two activities. The opportunity of earning higher wages also increase the price of time devoted to school activities. Recall that the price of time is its value in the next best alternative. This throws the student out of equilibrium further by reducing the MPP/P of time in school activities.

The price of time devoted to household production may initially increase because of the superior job opportunity. If the job is available only during daytime work hours on weekdays, the opportunity cost of time to household production may still be the wages that could be earned on less desirable jobs or the implicit value of study time, whichever is higher. If the job entails night or weekend work, the opportunity cost of time devoted to household production of utility will increase initially. However, it ultimately makes no difference whether the job entails day, night, or weekend work; the price of time to household production will still increase as the student adjusts to the new situation.

Assuming that the job requires daytime work, say 20 hours per week, the initial consequence of the job, taking the adjustment in steps, is to reduce study time. If study time is subject to diminishing returns, the reduction in study time will increase the implicit price of time to household activities (entertainment, sleep, and so forth) because the MU obtained from the last hour of study time will increase. This reduces the MPP/time price ratio of time devoted to household production, and consequently the student will utilize some time originally allocated to household production for study. The adjustment in study and household time will occur simultaneously.

As the student approaches a new equilibrium, the amount of time devoted to study and household production must decrease a total of 20 hours per week in this example. How much each is reduced depends on the slope of the MPP curves of time in the production of human capital and household goods. If the MPP curve of study time is steeply sloped relative to the MPP curve of household time, the largest reduction in time will come from the latter. This depends on the individual. The main point is that the decision to work part-time results in a reduction in time allocated to study and to household activities because their MPP/time price ratios are reduced when a job is accepted.

We might also expect the allocation to change between different terms. If the MPP of study time shifts to the right because of stimulating teachers or courses, for example, a greater proportion of work time will be taken away from household activities. Also, the student may quit the job if the MPP of study time shifts to the right enough so that the MPP/time price ratio for study exceeds what is experienced in part-time employment.

We also would expect different students to react differently to the same job opportunity. If the MPP/time price ratios for study and household activities are high because the student is highly motivated, extremely capable, attending a high-quality school, or enrolled in a high-payoff program such as medical school, the job opportunity may be declined. The production of utility from part-time work may also decline after a period of work if the student has saved enough to pay for goods such as room and board in the immediate future. This can explain why students tend to be in and out of the job market.

As real wages increase, however, the MPP/time price ratio in part-time employment also increases. As a result, we may expect a greater proportion of students to find that the above ratio exceeds the corresponding ratios for study and household production. Thus, an increase in real wages will increase part-time employment unless the returns to education increase enough to offset the increase.

Part–Time Employment and Grades

One should not conclude, however, that a reduction in study time necessarily reduces the time allocated to each course. When working on a part-time job, the student has the option of reducing his or her credit load while maintaining the time devoted to each course. Which option the student chooses depends on the value of grades and knowledge given up by working and maintaining a full-credit load versus the cost of extending the degree program. Students who place a high value on good grades because of personal satisfaction, a belief that good grades will increase future income, or because of an intention to pursue graduate or professional study will reduce their credit loads and extend the length of their programs if they decide to work part-time. Of course, as the hours worked per week approaches the equivalent of a full-time job, both grades and credit hours will be reduced.

Although our theory tells us that student participation in part-time

TABLE 23–1   Reductions in Grade Point Averages and Credits Taken of Students Who Work Compared with Students Who Are Not Employed Part-Time*

	(A) Grade point average reductions		(B) Credit reductions per quarter	
Hours worked per week	Freshman-sophomore	Junior-senior	Freshman-sophomore	Junior-senior
1–12	0.22	NS	NS	NS
13–25	0.31	NS	NS	1.44
More than 25	0.39	NS	1.48	2.50

NS = Not Statistically Significant from Zero.
* From a Sample of 155 Students at the University of Minnesota Covering Fall Quarter 1973 and Winter 1974. A = 4.0.

SOURCE: Willis Peterson, The Effect of Part-Time Employment on Student Allocation of Time and Academic Performance," University of Minnesota Staff Paper P75–11, June 1975, p. 12.

employment should reduce the amount of time devoted to school *and* household activities, it does not reveal the magnitude of these reductions. Nor does it tell us whether part-time employment reduces grades, credit load, or both.

Preliminary evidence from a sample of students at the University of Minnesota suggests that students both reduce grades and credit load, although as shown by the figures in Table 23–1, the relative effects are not the same for all students. As indicated in Table 23–1A, freshmen and sophomores who work part-time experience significant grade reductions, while juniors and seniors do not. The numbers in Table 23–1 indicate the reduction in GPA out of a maximum 4.0 for students who work the respective hours per week compared to students who do not work—holding constant a number of student characteristics.[2]

On the other hand, the numbers in Table 23–1B suggest that juniors and seniors are more likely to reduce their credit load when working part-time. These figures indicate the reduction in credits taken per quarter by students who work the respective hours in comparison with students who do not work, again holding constant the characteristics cited in the footnote. The tendency for juniors and seniors to reduce their credit loads when working probably explains why they do not suffer grade reductions. Why juniors and seniors appear to behave differently in these respects is open to speculation. Perhaps

---

[2] Characteristics held constant include hours spent on extracurricular activities, classes cut per week, high school rank, the effect on GPA of math, chemistry, and biology, and a qualitative measure of the importance of grades to the student. The latter, along with classes cut per week, attempts to account for differences in motivation among students.

students who survive the first two years receive the greatest utility from good grades and therefore do not jeopardize grades by attempting to maintain a full-credit load when working.

By now it is evident that the management of time by college students is a complex endeavor. Students have to assess the MPP (utility) of time not only among various activities but also within activities. For example, should the student allocate slightly more time to economics and less to some other subject, or vice versa? It is like juggling 10 balls at once. In addition, the optimum allocation of time will change from one term to the next depending on teachers, courses, the opportunities for part-time employment, recreational and social activities, and so forth. How well a student manages time largely determines the individual's success in college.[3] In fact, the experience gained in managing time may be one of the most important things gained from college. This may surprise students who think that the knowledge gained from courses taken represents the main value of a college education. Certainly this knowledge is important, but learning how to manage time, a valuable and scarce resource, is equally important.

Although the discussion in this chapter has focused on student allocation of time, the principles apply to any individual or family. For nonstudents, there are two broad categories of production: the production of intermediate goods via the labor market and the production of final goods in the context of the household activities during nonworking hours. In this case, the individual should allocate time such that the MPP/time price ratios are equalized within each broad category and among the categories. Again, the MPP of time is the utility produced by an extra hour of time, while the price of time is the value of this hour in the next-best alternative activity. Whenever there is a change in MPP or in the price of time, the individual should reallocate away from the low MPP/time price ratio activities toward activities with high ratios.

GLOSSARY

human capital production   Activities such as attending classes and studying.

intermediate goods production   Part-time employment.

household production   Production of utility from any activity not included in human capital or intermediate goods production.

utility-maximizing rule $MPP_1/P_1 = MPP_2/P_2 = MPP_3/P_3$

---

[3] You might have heard the story of a college student who brought home a grade report showing three *Fs* and a *D*. The student's parents were concerned and inquired about the problem. After some thought, the student replied, "I spent too much time on one subject."

QUESTIONS

1. A college student can be viewed as a small multiproduct firm. What is produced and what are the inputs?

2. a. How should time be allocated so a given value of time yields the greatest utility?
   b. What is the MPP of time? What is the price of time?
   c. What is the meaning of the MPP/time price ratio?

3. A large proportion of college students hold part-time jobs.
   a. According to the theory of time allocation, will part-time work reduce the time allocated to study? Explain.
   b. Does the theory of time allocation tell us that part-time work reduces grades? Explain.

4. College students study hardest just before examinations. Does this behavior represent an efficient allocation of time? Explain.

5. Would the attainment of a straight-A academic record represent an efficient allocation of time for most students? Explain.

6. State whether each of the following college students should allocate an "above-average" or a "below-average" amount of time to study, and explain why.
   a. A bright and highly motivated student.
   b. A student enrolled in a school where the payoff to the training is high.
   c. A talented basketball player who has a chance of signing a million-dollar contract if he makes All-American.
   d. A student working as a high-paid salesperson.
   e. A student who receives little utility from good grades.

CHAPTER 24

Science and Technology

OVERVIEW

The book concludes with an economic analysis of investment in science and technology. Without advances in science, higher education would not exist in its present form. After exploring the nature of research, the discussion focuses on the main contributions of new knowledge in modern society.

THE PRODUCTION OF NEW KNOWLEDGE

In Chapter 22, we said that the process of education, the transfer of knowledge from books and teachers into the minds of students, is an investment involving a cost and a return. In this chapter, we will probe deeper into this process, seeking an undertanding of the production of knowledge.

At the beginning of history, the knowledge in the minds of people was small as measured by today's standards. Hunting and fishing skills and the ability to transform nature's bounty into food, clothing, and shelter consitituted knowledge. Somewhere along the way, humans acquired the ability to communicate by sound. Although we take this skill for granted, reflection suggests the tremendous advance in knowledge that the introduction of verbal skills represented. Every object, action, or thought became associated with a sound. Moreover, there was a common agreement, at least within an area or tribe, about the meaning of sounds produced by vocal cords. Anyone who has studied a foreign language can appreciate the difficulty of learning correct sounds and the advanced knowledge it represents.

As verbal skills were mastered, it became possible to pass on to the next generation important information that otherwise would have been relearned by each individual through trial and error. Equally important was the introduction of written language, which is more efficient as a permanent means of communication and more efficient for the transfer and acquisition of knowledge.

A common characteristic of knowledge produced during the dawn of history is that it occurred by accident. In sustaining themselves, people learned new things about plants, animals, and the environment. In Greek and Roman civilizations, scholars and philosophers began to pursue knowledge as a full-time occupation. In the Middle Ages, the early church emerged as a center of learning. Mendel, one of the church's best-known monks, discovered the principle of hybridization while experimenting with peas. Although the pursuit of knowledge by gifted individuals had important consequences, the knowledge industry, that is, the employment of people solely for advancing knowledge, was unknown. During the Dark Ages, the overall stock of knowledge appeared to decrease.

RESEARCH AS A PRODUCTION ACTIVITY

In history, it became apparent that if certain people could devote themselves to the full-time pursuit of knowledge, a much greater intellectual output per unit of effort was possible than when knowledge was a by-product of daily activities. People with special talents in developing new knowledge could accomplish more if they were freed from other tasks. Galileo, Newton, Edison, Franklin, and Einstein could not have accomplished their achievements if they had to toil as full-time farmers or shopkeepers.

Thus, the production of new knowledge through research began as a by-product of daily activities and gradually emerged as the domain of a select few. Now, it is a full-fledged industry. In the United States during the post–World War II years, research was one of the nation's most rapidly growing industries. We refer to research as an industry because it has much in common with traditional types of production. Research is a production activity. Inputs consist mainly of scientists and engineers, laboratories and testing facilities, output consists of new knowledge. The same concepts we used in our discussion of producer choice and product supply—such as marginal and average product, marginal and average costs, diminishing returns, and economics of scale—also apply to the production of new knowledge.

At the same time, there are unique characteristics of research. First, there is the difficulty of measuring output. Knowledge does not come in easy-to-measure units like kilograms, or dollars. Economists have found ways of measuring knowledge indirectly, however.

A second unique characteristic of research is that there is a possibility that in the aggregate it may not be subject to the law of diminshing returns. Recall that the law of diminishing returns refers to a situation where the addition of a variable input to one or more fixed inputs results in a diminished marginal physical product to the variable input. Scientists and their supporting personnel and facilities are the variable input and nature's secrets or the potential stock of knowledge are the fixed input in the production of new knowledge (research). Will the addition of more scientists result in a diminishing and eventually zero marginal product of scientific research? If nature's secrets or the potential stock of knowledge was finite, we would expect diminishing returns at some point. But if all knowledge, known and unknown, is infinite, then research need not be subject to the law of diminishing returns.

A third unique characteristic of research is that its outcome is uncertain. In most other production activities, quantity and nature of the outcome are predicted with a high degree of certainty. For example, if the blueprint is followed, the construction of a building will result in the expected outcome.

Most other production is routine in nature—it has been done many times before. But research is something that has not been done before. Thus, it is impossible to predict with any certainty the outcome of an individual research project. If we could predict its outcome, the research would not be worth the effort. The implication of the uncertain outcome of research is that some research will add to the stock of knowledge and other research will not. Research is like drilling for oil. Out of every 10 holes drilled, there may be nine dry holes for every gusher. But, the successful projects more than pay for the failures. The uncertainty of the payoff to research makes it impossible to predict the rate of return to individual projects. When large numbers of projects are grouped together, the proportion of successful ventures will remain relatively constant from year to year, which enables one to predict their overall average payoff with some accuracy.

It is useful to probe more deeply into research. It encompasses a wide array of endeavors ranging from basic research to more applied and developmental activity.

Basic Research

Basic research is activity concerned with unlocking the secrets of nature without solving a particular problem. This does not imply that the output of basic research is of little use. Some of the most important research results have come from basic research.

A small proportion of research and development funds is spent on basic research. In recent years, expenditures for basic research amounted to only 10 to 12 percent of all research and development expenditures. It is easy to understand why basic research has remained small. An industrial firm invests in research to increase profits. If the firm has no guarantee that the research results can be applied to the firm's operation, such as for basic research, it has little incentive to pay for it. Some large firms give their scientists a small amount of free time for basic research, but this is mainly a fringe benefit.

Consequently, most basic research is done by colleges and universities or the federal government. Even here, there is reluctance to turn scientists loose; this might be due to a public fear that the funds would be squandered on scientists' pet projects—with little chance for any payoff to society. Basic research is risky business. Perhaps one or two projects out of 10 add something significant to knowledge.

Applied Research

Applied research is concerned with solving a particular problem or finding out an unknown. For example, the problem might be finding a way to reduce air pollution caused by automobiles or to curb the noise of jet engines.

Both industry and public institutions are more willing to finance applied research than basic research. Understandably, a business is more certain that a return will occur if the research is centered on a problem concerning the firm. The same is true for publicly sponsored research. Society feels more certain that it receives its money's worth from research if scientists work on a recognized problem.

Development

Development is the almost exclusive domain of large industrial firms and the federal government. Development activities include building prototypes of new products and testing them before their market introduction. However, it is difficult to separate development from applied research. Development is a kind of applied research because it seeks the unknown of a product or production technique. Most industrial research is lumped into one category and called *research and development* (R&D).

It is not easy to even distinguish between basic and applied research. An applied research project can bring unexpected knowledge totally unrelated to the problem at hand. In this sense, applied research has the same characteristics as basic research. It is best, therefore, to view these three research categories as a continuum ranging from pure basic research, to applied research, to development activity on the other end of the scale. Also, the success of applied research and development activities depends largely on the knowledge produced by basic research.

RESEARCH BY INDUSTRIAL FIRMS (R&D)

Research by industrial firms is concentrated in applied and development activity. The overall motivation for a firm to do R&D is to improve its profit position. Research and development can increase profits for the firm by: (1) the development of new or improved products, which increases demand for the firm's products, or (2) the development of new cost-reducing techniques of production, which reduces average and marginal costs for the firm. The production of new or improved products resulting from R&D is illustrated in Figure 24–1.

Figure 24–1A illustrates the situation for an imperfectly competitive firm before it undertakes the development of a new or improved product. If the R&D program is successful and a new product is developed, the demand facing the firm shifts to the right, as shown by D_1 in Figure 24–1B. This might depict an auto manufacturer that has developed an engine with better gas mileage. The demand for the company's product will shift to the right as customers switch from companies that do not offer the improved engine.

Remember, however, that R&D is costly. Hence, the R&D program increases the firm's average total cost (ATC) and marginal cost (MC). Thus, ATC_1 and MC_1 in Figure 24–1B are drawn in slightly higher than their original position in Figure 24–1A. In this example, total profits, depicted by the shaded

FIGURE 24–1   The Effect of New and Improved Products Resulting from R&D

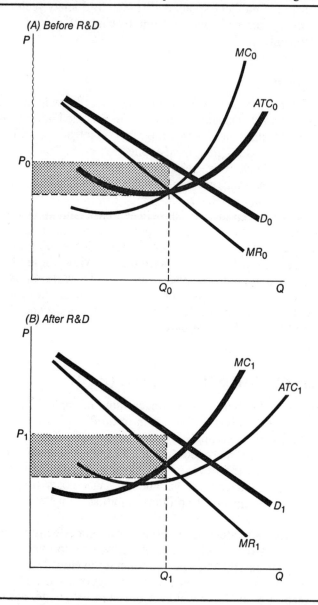

areas, are higher after R&D than before, which indicates that the additional revenue from increased product demand offsets the additional cost of R&D.

The second possibility for increasing profits through R&D is to reduce production costs through the discovery and adoption of new cost-reducing techniques. For example, a firm might develop a new, more efficient method of

FIGURE 24-2   Effect of New Cost-Reducing Techniques Resulting from R&D

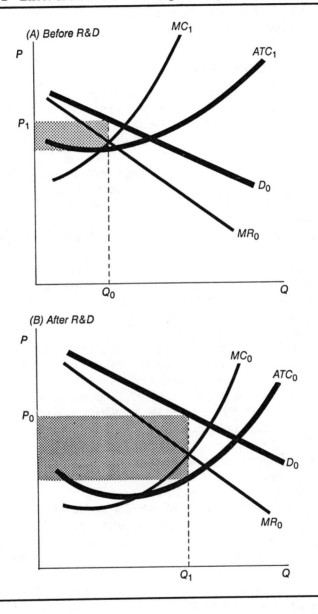

assembling its product with robots. This would shift ATC and MC down and to the right, as illustrated in Figure 24–2. Here, assume that the product remains the same so that the demand and marginal revenue curves are the same in both diagrams.

In this example, we also have assumed that the cost saving obtained through the new technique more than offset the increased costs brought on by R&D. Total profits, denoted by the shaded areas in Figure 24–2, increase as a result of the increased R&D expenditure.[1]

Returns to Industrial R&D

The decision about doing R&D is straightforward; it should be done as long as expected revenue increases more than expected costs. But, in an actual decision-making situation, the main problem is assessing the returns to R&D. The firm has no guarantee that demand will shift to the right or that costs will shift down.

The usual procedure for a firm is to begin with a modest R&D program, perhaps hiring an engineer to think of new ideas. If total revenue increases more than salary and expenses, the firm may add another R&D person, and so on. In other words, decisions about doing R&D are marginal. Because of the substantial increase in R&D recently, we can infer that most firms have found it profitable; hence they are doing it more.

The decision to engage in R&D may also be motivated by the desire to maintain a profit position. If other firms in the industry are investing in R&D to create new or improved products or to lower production costs, the firm that does not keep up will have few customers or excessively high costs and eventually will fail. Even in this context, the effects of R&D are illustrated by Figures 24–1 and 24–2. Profits after R&D are higher than otherwise.

In deciding whether or not to engage in R&D, the overriding consideration by the firm must be whether or not it will be possible to capture a return on its investment. If the knowledge produced by R&D is available to competing firms, the firm that originally produced the knowledge will not gain any special advantage. For example, a pharmaceutical firm that develops a new ingredient that makes a drug more effective will guard its secret closely. If other firms duplicated the ingredient, they could gain all of its advantages without paying the cost. This explains why some firms and governments find it profitable to employ industrial spies.

One alternative for the firm or individual who develops something new is to take out a patent with the government patent office. Patent laws forbid duplication of the patented item or process by other firms or individuals for a period of 17 years. Without these laws or protection, there is little incentive to invest in R&D.

In reality, however, patent laws have not offered perfect protection. Although a patented item cannot be duplicated exactly, in many cases, a close substitute can be developed by making a few minor changes. Patenting certain products or processes actually may hasten their discovery and adoption by

---

[1] For further discussion of the economic aspects of research by industrial firms, see Edwin Mansfield, *The Economics of Technological Change* (New York: W. W. Norton, 1968).

competing firms. For this reason, firms often do not patent something they have developed; they try to keep it a secret. The decision whether to take out a patent depends mainly on the product or process. If it is something easy to keep secret, such as an additive or minute ingredient, it might be best not to patent. But, if it is a machine or a gadget that will be widely used, patenting provides some protection, although rarely complete protection, against copying by other firms.

Another important factor that affects whether or not a firm will invest in R&D is the absolute size of the firm. It will not pay for a small firm to engage in sizable R&D effort. Consider a small farm. Even if no one copied its research results, it would not pay for it to spend several million dollars attempting to increase yields. The expected return would be small compared with the probable cost.

On the other hand, a large firm like General Motors can find it profitable to spend a great deal on something that may improve quality or decrease costs only a small amount per vehicle. Multiplying a small unit gain times a large volume will yield a handsome return to a sizable R&D expenditure. In general, the larger the firm, the more profitable it is to invest in R&D to achieve a given percentage increase in demand or decrease in costs.

Thus far, we have considered only the private returns, that is, extra profits of industrial R&D. But, remember that R&D can still be a good investment for society even if it does not provide higher profits for the firm doing the R&D. Generally, the extra profits from a new product or production technique are eventually eroded away as more firms copy the product or technique.

But, the fact that the individual firm's extra profits from R&D eventually disappear does not mean that society's benefits from R&D also disappear. Society continues to enjoy a return from R&D long after its profits are eroded away because of the resulting new or improved products that continue to be consumed and/or the reduced costs brought about by new technology. In other words, R&D allows society to obtain a greater value of output from its limited resources. Economists refer to this benefit as a *social return*.

PUBLICLY SPONSORED RESEARCH

An industrial firm will not choose to invest in research unless it has reasonable assurance that it will add to profits, and the small firm will not engage in research because the expense is too great to be borne by small output. However, society benefits from research that may not be profitable for an individual firm or that affects the output of industries made up of firms too small to do their own research, such as agriculture. For this reason, federal and state governments either sponsor research or do it in their own laboratories or institutions.

Most publicly sponsored research is done in colleges and universities. Because of the risk involved and the small chance of capturing a profit on the knowledge produced, much of the country's basic research is done in these institutions. With the exception of market research on individual products, most economic research is done in institutions of higher learning. This is also true for the humanities and other social sciences.

The decisions on what kind of and how much public research should be done are more difficult than for industrial research. The decision-making process is slow, cumbersome, and often based on inadequate information. But someone must make these decisions, regardless of the information available. The basic decisions are made by society's elected representatives in state and federal governments. They must decide how much of the taxpayers' money will be devoted to research. Usually the amount allocated to research for a current year is based on what was allocated the year before, plus a little extra for increasing prices and new problems or programs.

Once funds reach research institutions, more decisions are required to further allocate the money. How much goes to physics, chemistry, economics, agriculture, and so forth? Again, the current allocation is made based on past allocation. Marginal changes occur with changes in personnel or with the emergence or recognition of new and pressing problems such as the environment or health.

Ideally, public research allocation should be made based on the highest payoff to research, but the problem is identifying the returns to public research.

Returns to Public Research

The returns to public research, like education, are classified into monetary and nonmonetary components. In the nonmonetary area, society will pay to gain information about itself or about the universe, even though this knowledge may not lead to an increase in the value of real output in society. For example, society has been willing to pay to develop a means of getting to the moon and back. Society also considers it worthwhile to find out more about man's origin. Even though this knowledge may not add to the monetary value of real output, it adds something to the utility of society.

Aside from the space program, most public research is aimed at increasing the value of output for society, that is, a dollar or monetary return. People value good health or the avoidance of the grim reaper before their time; hence, they will pay for medical research. Society places a value on a clean environment, so it supports research on ways of achieving this goal without giving up the goods and services that contribute to pollution. Most basic research, such as the work in physics, chemistry, biology, and mathematics, may not be aimed at a specific problem, but it is anticipated that the knowledge produced will somehow have a monetary value.

Measuring the monetary value of public research is a difficult problem, and much work remains to be done in this area. Unless quantitative measures are available, decisions to allocate public research will have to be made from purely subjective criteria or historical precedence, neither of which guarantees that society gets the most for its money.

AGRICULTURAL RESEARCH

We include a separate discussion of agricultural research for two reasons: (1) it is an area where some progress has been made in estimating social returns, and (2) there is widespread misunderstanding about who benefits from this research.

The nation's agricultural research is done about equally by farm supply firms—including seed, chemical, and machinery companies, and by agricultural experiment stations. The latter are funded by taxes. Private firms tend to conduct research that can be incorporated into a product. A firm must capture a return on its investment, or else it would not pay to invest. Agricultural experiment stations conduct the agricultural research that private firms do not find profitable but, nevertheless, provides a return to society.

The overall objective of agricultural research, whether private or public, is to increase the productive capacity of farmers. The output of such research includes new, higher-yielding crop varieties; breeding and disease-control advances to make livestock and poultry more efficient converters of feed; new inputs such as herbicides and pesticides; new and improved machines; and better management practices for farmers.

As pointed out in Chapter 11, new technology increases, or shifts to the right, the supply curve of individual producers and the industry, as shown in Figure 24–3. For a given price, producers will put more on the market or will sell a given amount for a lower price because their unit costs are lower.

FIGURE 24–3   Effect of Agricultural Research and Resulting New Technology that Shifts Agricultural Supply

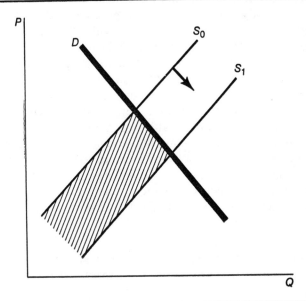

The increase in productive efficiency, and hence the increase in product supply, brought about by agricultural research, increases the total value of agricultural output for a given amount of traditional resources such as land, labor, and capital. In other words, by producing knowledge and new, more productive inputs, society obtains more output from its scarce resources. The annual value of this additional output to society is illustrated in Figure 24–3 by the shaded area lying between S_0 and S_1, bounded on the top by the demand for agricultural products.

Supply curve S_0 in Figure 24–3 represents what the supply of agricultural output would be without new technology. By measuring the increase in the productive efficiency of agriculture, economists have determined the location of S_1 for a given year. The difference between these two curves, therefore, represents the annual value of output attributable to agricultural research.

By comparing the annual expenditure on research with the value of extra output attributable to research, economists have obtained estimates of its internal rate of return. The procedure is the same as computing the rate of return to education. In this case, the cash outflows are expenditures on agricultural research (industrial and public). The cash inflows are the value of additional output obtained from agricultural research—value of the shaded area in Figure 24–3.

Estimates of the *marginal* internal rate of return to *additional* investment in agriculture research in the United States are 40 to 50 percent.[2] It is like the nation places over $2 billion per year (the recent annual investment in agricultural research and extension) in a savings account and reaps a 40 to 50 percent return. This is a high-payoff investment.

This leads to a second major point. The long-run beneficiaries of agricultural research are mainly consumers of farm products rather than farmers. Of course, farmers benefit as consumers along with everyone else. Consumers benefit from agricultural research because the increase in productive efficiency shifts the supply of agricultural products to the right, which increases food output and reduces food prices below what they would otherwise be. The reduction in food prices benefits low-income people more than high-income individuals because the former spend a larger share of their income on food. Also, the major portion of agricultural research conducted in the public sector is paid for by taxes from middle- and high-income people. Thus, agricultural research reduces the inequality of living standards between income levels. It is equivalent to achieving more equality of incomes.

Many people argue, however, that food prices are not cheap judging from current supermarket prices. But, one must look at the real cost of food—the

---

[2] R. E. Evenson, Paul E. Waggonner, and V. W. Ruttan, "Economics Benefits from Research: An Example from Agriculture," *Science,* September 1979, pp. 1101–07.

proportion of a country's resources devoted to food production. Currently, Americans spend about 15 percent of their income on food. Contrast this to most less-developed countries, where food often accounts for 70 to 80 percent of a family's budget.

At the turn of the century, U.S. citizens spent alomst 40 percent of their income on food. A nation with an unproductive agricultural sector must devote many resources to food production. As agricultural productivity increases, more people leave agriculture to produce other things that make life more interesting and enjoyable. If 70 to 80 percent of a nation's population is required to produce food, modern conveniences such as reasonably priced automobiles, adequate medical care, and labor-saving appliances cannot be produced. Life might have been simpler when most people were farmers, but few people today would trade their current standard of living for the past.

The substantial decline in the proportion of incomes devoted to food in the United States understates the decline in the real price of food if we remember the quality improvement that has occurred over the years and the increased amount of services purchased with food nowadays. There are two dimensions to the increase in quality: (1) the increase in the wholesomeness of food, meaning the reduction in disease and insect damage, and (2) the greater share of the nation's food derived from animal sources. Both aspects of quality improvement require more resources and increase the cost of food. Similarly, the purchase of services such as those embodied in bakery bread, cake mixes, and dressed, cut, and frozen meats cost money and add to food bills. If U.S. consumers were willing to buy food of the same quality and with the same amount of services as in years past, or as exists in less-developed countries, they would spend less than 15 percent of their income on food. Of course, there is nothing wrong with people wanting to spend some of their increased purchasing power on higher-quality food and more services.

This is not to say that agricultural research can take sole credit for economic development. Other knowledge also is required to produce the variety of modern goods and services that raise the standard of living. But as developing nations are learning, little progress can be made without techno-logical advances in agriculture.

SOCIAL COSTS OF NEW TECHNOLOGY

There is a growing concern in the United States and other highly developed nations that the true cost of research to produce new knowledge and technology may exceed expenditures for research. One concern is the move-ment of people between occupations and areas. If new technology makes a job obsolete, what is the social cost of having the person who held the job move to another occupation in another location?

It is fairly easy to measure moving costs, but there are other considerations. People who move must leave family, friends, and familiar ways of living for the unknown. Some find moving an exciting experience; others dread it. The largest case is the huge rural-to-urban migration that has occurred in the United States. The increased concentration of population in urban areas has contributed to many problems: air and water pollution and congestion of transportation systems and housing.

Without the new technology would these problems disappear? Perhaps. But, problems have always plagued mankind. Consider the disease, isolation, and long hours of drudgery both in the home and on the job with which our ancestors had to contend. Even pollution existed in those days. Imagine the smell in the cities when vehicles were horse-drawn, or the smoke and soot that spewed out when coal was the main source of heat and power. Some of the worst pollution in the world exists in countries that have experienced little advance in technology. When dealing with present-day problems, we tend to visualize things as we want to see them without regard for their historical background.

GLOSSARY

research   A production activity having inputs and an output.

basic research   Unlocking the secrets of nature without having a specific use in mind.

applied research   Research aimed at solving a specific problem.

development   Experimentation with new knowledge to construct a product or accomplish a task.

social return   The increase in value of output to society because of research.

QUESTIONS

1. *How is research similar to and how is it different from conventional types of investment?*

2. *a. Differentiate between basic and applied research.*
   b. Who does basic research? Who does applied research?

3. *How does research benefit society?*

4. *How does R&D increase profits of private firms?*

5. *It is sometimes agrued that private firms deliberately suppress technological innovations resulting from R&D to maintain the value of assets that utilize older technology. Evalute this argument.*

6. a. Would you expect the social return to private R&D to be equal to private return? Explain.

   b. Would your answer to 6. a. imply anything about whether private firms will invest the optimal amount of funds in R&D each year? Explain.

7. a. How does agricultural research affect the food supply?

   b. If the demand for agricultural products is inelastic, how does agricultural research affect the total revenue received by farmers from the sale of their products?

Index